10th Workshop on Computational Approaches to Subjectivity, Sentiment and Social Media Analysis (WASSA 2019)

Minneapolis, Minnesota, USA
6 June 2019

ISBN: 978-1-5108-8767-1

Printed by Curran Associates, Inc. (2019)

For permission requests, please contact the Association for Computational Linguistics
at the address below.

Association for Computational Linguistics
209 N. Eighth Street
Stroudsburg, Pennsylvania 18360

Phone: 1-570-476-8006
Fax: 1-570-476-0860

acl@aclweb.org

Additional copies of this publication are available from:

Curran Associates, Inc.
57 Morehouse Lane
Red Hook, NY 12571 USA
Phone: 845-758-0400
Fax: 845-758-2633
Email: curran@proceedings.com
Web: www.proceedings.com

10th Workshop on Computational Approaches to Subjectivity, Sentiment and Social Media Analysis (WASSA 2019)

Minneapolis, Minnesota, USA
6 June 2019

NAACL HLT 2019

The Workshop on Computational Approaches to Subjectivity, Sentiment and Social Media Analysis

Proceedings of the Tenth Workshop

June 6, 2019
Minneapolis, USA

Introduction

Two thousand five hundred years ago, Democritus said: "Nothing exists except atoms and empty space. Everything else is opinion." Today, this saying is omnipresent, as the state of our social interpretation of reality has been denominated by the "post-truth society". Research in automatic Subjectivity and Sentiment Analysis (SSA), as subtasks of Affective Computing and Natural Language Processing (NLP), has flourished in the past years. The growth in interest in these tasks was motivated by the birth and rapid expansion of the Social Web that made it possible for people all over the world to share, comment or consult content on any given topic. In this context, opinions, sentiments and emotions expressed in Social Media texts have been shown to have a high influence on social and economic behaviour worldwide.

SSA systems are highly relevant to many real-world applications (e.g. marketing, eGovernance, business intelligence, social analysis) and also to many tasks in Natural Language Processing (NLP), e.g. information extraction, question answering, textual entailment, to name just a few. The importance of this field has been proven by the high number of approaches proposed in research in the past decade, as well as by the interest that it raised from other disciplines (Economics, Sociology, Psychology, Marketing, Crisis Management, Digital Humanities and Behavioral Studies) and the applications that were created using its technology. Next to the growth in the diversity of applications, task definitions changed towards more complex challenges: Subjectivity, polarity recognition and opinion mining has been enriched with fine-grained aspect and target level predictions. Polarity as a concept is complemented by emotion models as defined from psychological research. In spite of the growing body of research in the area in the past years, dealing with affective phenomena in text has proven to be a complex, interdisciplinary problem that remains far from being solved. Its challenges include the need to address the issue from different perspectives and at different levels, depending on the characteristics of the textual genre, the language(s) treated and the final application for which the analysis is done.

The aim of the 10th Workshop on Computational Approaches to Subjectivity, Sentiment and Social Media Analysis (WASSA 2019) was to continue the line of the previous editions, bringing together researchers in Computational Linguistics working on Subjectivity and Sentiment Analysis and researchers working on interdisciplinary aspects of affect computation from text.

For this year's workshop, we accepted 12/19 papers (63 % acceptance rate). The number of submissions has been comparably low in contrast to previous years, given that WASSA 2018 just took place a little more than half a year before WASSA 2019. Nevertheless and given the high quality of submissions, we have an interesting program consisting of 11 oral presentations in 3 sessions. An invited talk by Sven Buechel on "Modeling Empathy and Distress in Reaction to News Stories" complements this year's paper presentations.

Accepted papers deal with a variety of topics, like stance detection, topic and aspect level sentiment analysis, social network analysis, humor detection, and negations and intensifiers in emotion and sentiment analysis, as well as applications of such systems to real-world problems. For the first time, we asked the reviewers for recommendations for a best paper award. Based on these recommendations, the organizers voted secretly on the best paper selection. The result is that the paper "Stance Detection in Code-Mixed Hindi-English Social Media Data using Multi-Task Learning" by Sushmitha Reddy Sane, Suraj Tripathi, Koushik Reddy Sane and Radhika Mamidi wins this year's best paper award.

We would like to thank the NAACL 2019 Organizers and Workshop Chairs for their help and support at the different stages of the workshop organization process. We are also especially grateful to the Program Committee members for the time and effort they spent in assessing the papers.

Alexandra Balahur, Roman Klinger, Véronique Hoste, Carlo Strapparava and Orphée De Clercq
WASSA 2019 Chairs

Keynote talk: Modeling Empathy and Distress in Reaction to News Stories

Sven Buechel

JULIE Lab, Jena University, Germany

Abstract

Computational detection and understanding of empathy is an important factor in advancing human-computer interaction. Yet to date, text-based empathy prediction has the following major limitations: It underestimates the psychological complexity of the phenomenon, adheres to a weak notion of ground truth where empathic states are ascribed by third parties, and lacks a shared corpus. In contrast, this talk describes the first publicly available gold standard for empathy prediction. It is constructed using a novel annotation methodology which reliably captures empathy assessments by the writer of a statement using multi-item scales. This is also the first computational work distinguishing between multiple forms of empathy, empathic concern, and personal distress, as recognized throughout psychology.

Organizers

Organizers:

Alexandra Balahur – European Commission Joint Research Centre
Roman Klinger – University of Stuttgart, Germany
Véronique Hoste – Ghent University, Belgium
Carlo Strapparava – Fundazione Bruno Kessler, Italy
Orphée de Clercq – Ghent University, Belgium

Program Committee:

Jeremy Barnes – University of Oslo
Sabine Bergler – Concordia University
Cristina Bosco – Dipartimento di Informatica - Universita di Torino
Laura Ana Maria Bostan – IMS, University of Stuttgart
Sven Buechel – Friedrich-Schiller-Universität Jena
Erik Cambria – Nanyang Technological University
Luna De Bruyne – LT3, Language and Translation Technology Team, Ghent University
Lingjia Deng – Bloomberg L.P.
Antske Fokkens – VU Amsterdam
Michael Gamon – Microsoft Research
Lorenzo Gatti – Human Media Interaction, University of Twente
Matthias Hartung – Semalytix GmbH
Carlos A. Iglesias – Universidad Politécnica de Madrid
Gilles Jacobs – LT3, Language and Translation Technology Team, Ghent University
Aditya Joshi – CSIRO
Manfred Klenner – Computational Linguistics, University of Zurich
Els Lefever – LT3, Language and Translation Technology Team, Ghent University
Gerard Lynch – University College Dublin
Isa Maks – VU University of Amsterdam
Edison Marrese-Taylor – The University of Tokyo
Saif Mohammad – National Research Council Canada
Karo Moilanen – Dpt of Computer Science, University of Oxford
Malvina Nissim – University of Groningen
Sean Papay – University of Stuttgart
Viviana Patti – Dipartimento di Informatica, University of Turin
Jose Manuel Perea-Ortega – University of Extremadura
Daniel Preoţiuc-Pietro – Bloomberg
Paolo Rosso – Universitat Politècnica de València
Alon Rozental – Amobee inc.
Mohammad Salameh – Diffbot
Josef Steinberger – University of West Bohemia
Mike Thelwall – University of Wolverhampton
Dan Tufiş – Research Institute for Artificial Intelligence, Romanian Academy
Michael Wiegand – Saarland University
Michael Wojatzki – Language Technology Lab, University of Duisburg-Essen
Taras Zagibalov – SmallStep LLC

Table of Contents

Conference Program

Thursday, June 6, 2019

9:00–9:15   ***Opening of the WASSA Workshop by Alexandra Balahur***

9:15–10:15   ***Invited Talk by Sven Buechel: Modeling Empathy and Distress in Reaction to News Stories***

10:15–10:45   ***Morning Coffee Break***

Oral Session 1

10:45–11:10   *Stance Detection in Code-Mixed Hindi-English Social Media Data using Multi-Task Learning*
Sushmitha Reddy Sane, Suraj Tripathi, Koushik Reddy Sane and Radhika Mamidi

11:10–11:35   *A Soft Label Strategy for Target-Level Sentiment Classification*
Da Yin, Xiao Liu, Xiuyu Wu and Baobao Chang

11:35–12:00   *Online abuse detection: the value of preprocessing and neural attention models*
Dhruv Kumar, Robin Cohen and Lukasz Golab

12:00–12:25   *Exploring Fine-Tuned Embeddings that Model Intensifiers for Emotion Analysis*
Laura Ana Maria Bostan and Roman Klinger

12:25–14:00   ***Lunch Break***

Oral Session 2

14:00–14:25 *Enhancing the Measurement of Social Effects by Capturing Morality*
Rezvaneh Rezapour, Saumil H. Shah and Jana Diesner

14:25–14:50 *Using Structured Representation and Data: A Hybrid Model for Negation and Sentiment in Customer Service Conversations*
Amita Misra, Mansurul Bhuiyan, Jalal Mahmud and Saurabh Tripathy

14:50–15:15 *Deep Learning Techniques for Humor Detection in Hindi-English Code-Mixed Tweets*
Sushmitha Reddy Sane, Suraj Tripathi, Koushik Reddy Sane and Radhika Mamidi

15:15–15:40 *How do we feel when a robot dies? Emotions expressed on Twitter before and after hitchBOT's destruction*
Kathleen C. Fraser, Frauke Zeller, David Harris Smith, Saif Mohammad and Frank Rudzicz

15:40–16:10 ***Afternoon Coffee Break***

Oral Session 3

16:10–16:35 *"When Numbers Matter!": Detecting Sarcasm in Numerical Portions of Text*
Abhijeet Dubey, Lakshya Kumar, Arpan Somani, Aditya Joshi and Pushpak Bhattacharyya

16:35–17:00 *Cross-lingual Subjectivity Detection for Resource Lean Languages*
Ida Amini, Samane Karimi and Azadeh Shakery

17:00–17:25 *Analyzing Incorporation of Emotion in Emoji Prediction*
Shirley Anugrah Hayati and Aldrian Obaja Muis

17:25–18:00 ***Closing Remarks***

Stance Detection in Code-Mixed Hindi-English Social Media Data using Multi-Task Learning

Sushmitha Reddy Sane[*1]   **Suraj Tripathi**[*2]   **Koushik Reddy Sane**[1]   **Radhika Mamidi**[1]

[1]International Institute of Information Technology, Hyderabad
[2]Indian Institute of Technology, Delhi
{sushmithareddy.sane, koushikreddy.sane}@research.iiit.ac.in,
surajtripathi93@gmail.com, radhika.mamidi@iiit.ac.in

Abstract

Social media sites like Facebook, Twitter, and other microblogging forums have emerged as a platform for people to express their opinions and views on different issues and events. It is often observed that people tend to take a stance; in favor, against or neutral towards a particular topic. The task of assessing the stance taken by the individual became significantly important with the emergence in the usage of online social platforms. Automatic stance detection system understands the user's stance by analyzing the standalone texts against a target entity. Due to the limited contextual information a single sentence provides, it is challenging to solve this task effectively. In this paper, we introduce a Multi-Task Learning (MTL) based deep neural network architecture for automatically detecting stance present in the code-mixed corpus. We apply our approach on Hindi-English code-mixed corpus against the target entity - "Demonetisation." Our best model achieved the result with a stance prediction accuracy of 63.2% which is a 4.5% overall accuracy improvement compared to the current supervised classification systems developed using the benchmark dataset for code-mixed data stance detection.

1   Introduction

The amount of data that is being generated by Internet users is massive and is multiplying every day. On the social media platform Twitter alone, users send more than 300k tweets per minute[2]. Users express their feelings, views and share their opinions on different topics ranging from politics, sports, government policies, movies, social issues, etc. More often, we observe that users tend to take a stance on a particular topic. Stance is a position on a specific issue, based on consideration of the evidence, often expressed publicly. It is an unpractical task to manually detect the stance represented by the individuals in these texts. The problem of automatic stance detection has caught the attention of researchers to effectively identify the stance taken by the user in numerous texts towards a particular topic.

1.1   Stance Detection

Stance detection addresses the problem of determining whether the author of a text is in FAVOUR of (positive), is AGAINST (negative) or is NEUTRAL (none) towards a particular target topic. The task of detecting stance closely compliments the task of sentiment analysis but is distinctive in nature (Mohammad, 2016). Stance detection considers the authors evaluative outlook towards specific targets rather than merely considering speakers emotions which adds to the problem of sentiment analysis.

1.2   Code-Mixing

The majority of the work in detecting stance has been done in English and other monolingual languages only. Our work focuses on code-mixed Hindi-English texts from users majorly in the Indian Subcontinent. It is improvisation to the task of detecting stance presented (Swami et al., 2018) for the target entity - i.e., Notebandi (Demonetisation), which was implemented in India. The government announced the issuance of new 500 and 2000 banknotes by exchanging with the demonetised notes. This action was taken to curb counterfeit cash used to fund terror groups. Many citizens of India and other nations, voiced their opinions and took a stance on this move by the Government of India.

Example: *"Demonetisation is a step towards the development and betterment of society."*

---

* These authors contributed equally to this work.
[2]http://www.internetlivestats.com/twitter-statistics/

Proceedings of the 10th Workshop on Computational Approaches to Subjectivity, Sentiment and Social Media Analysis, pages 1–5
Minneapolis, June 6, 2019. ©2019 Association for Computational Linguistics

In this tweet, we can observe that the user most likely is in favor of the move. Our model for stance detection determines the stance taken by the tweeter automatically. An example of a tweet in the code-mixed Hindi-English corpus is

Example: *"Notebandi ne foreigners ko bhi pareshan karke rakha hai Demonetisation ."*

Here, the words *demonetisation, foreigners* are English while the others are Hindi. This sentence is transliterated into Hindi and then translated to English for employing English-based word representations.

In this paper, we describe an MTL based framework which makes use of deep learning architecture for automatic stance detection on social media corpus presented by (Swami et al., 2018). One of the major limitations in social media corpus is that users use unstructured text formats, non-grammatical structures and express rather explicitly compared to opinion surveys or formal texts. These informal usages introduce noise in the corpus and make the task very challenging. Also, the code-mixed corpus lacks the presence of word embeddings, commonly used, to train any deep learning model. So, we use machine transliterated and translated English corpus to feed to the network in order to use word2vec (Mikolov et al., 2013) based word embeddings.

The paper is organized as follows. In Section 2, we review related research in the area of stance detection and code mixing. In Section 3, we describe our system architecture to detect stance. In Section 4, we present the results and discuss the evaluation metrics. Finally, we conclude our work in Section 5 followed by future work in Section 6.

2   Related Work

Stance Detection problem is widely discussed and studied for the past few years in opinion mining. One of the initial work on stance classification (Somasundaran and Wiebe, 2010) explores the use of sentiment and arguing features for classifying stances in ideological debates by constructing an arguing lexicon from a manually annotated corpus. The combination of opinion target pair features was employed for the classification task. Later, Anand et al. (2011) identifies that for a particular topic, classification results using lexical and contextual features are far better than the best feature set without any contextual features analyzing the dialogic structure of debates. Walker et al. (2012); Hasan and Ng (2013) studied stance detection in two-side online debate data, and Faulkner (2014) examined document-level argument stance in student essays where the language of the texts are structured, monolingual and grammatically correct. And lately, a shared task for stance detection research focused on Twitter data (Mohammad et al., 2016).

Stance at user-level (Rajadesingan and Liu, 2014) is determined based on the assumption that if several users retweet one pair of tweets about a controversial topic, it is likely that they support the same side of a debate. Djemili et al. (2014) uses a set of rules based on the syntax and discourse structure of the tweet to identify tweets that contain ideological stance. However, none of these works attempts to determine the stance from a single tweet. In the field of social media mining, Guellil and Boukhalfa (2015) described in detail about different works in opinion mining and sentiment analysis and identified a set of open issues. Apart from English language, stance detection is carried out on Czech news commentaries (Krejzl et al., 2017) where maximum entropy classifier approach was used which were initially developed to detect stance in English tweets which uses sentiment and domain-specific features. Also, for the corpus of Spanish tweets (Anta et al., 2013), topic detection, and sentiment analysis approaches are used.

Multi-task learning approach (MTL) jointly trains multiple tasks in parallel, which acts as additional regularization, to improve the underlying network's generalization across all the tasks. It has proven to be a novel and effective learning schema in many NLP problems. Recently, multi-task learning approaches have been used for sentiment and sarcasm detection in (Majumder et al., 2019) , implicit discourse relationship identification (Lan et al., 2017), key-phrase boundary classification (Augenstein and Søgaard, 2017), improving sequence tagging tasks (Changpinyo et al., 2018) and improving named entity recognition tasks (Pham et al., 2019) and target dependent sentiment analysis (Gupta et al., 2019).

3 Method Description

The following subsections explain the preprocessing of the corpus and the deep learning architecture proposed for stance detection.

3.1 Preprocessing

Preprocessing is done on the tweets by removing twitter handles starting with "@" or words that had any special symbol. The word "Notebandi" is replaced by the phrase "noton par prathibandh." Emoticons have been removed, and URLs are replaced with the word "URL." This cleaned corpus is transliterated and translated into English sentences using Google translate API which is later given as input to the model.

3.2 Model Architecture

We propose a multi-channel convolutional neural network (CNN), refer Figure 1, for detecting stance from the given input text. Mutli-channel CNNs are used to expand the network in width without increasing cost of computing as deep networks tend to overfit on the dataset with limited samples per class. The model uses four parallel instances of convolution layer with varying kernel sizes. We experimented with different values for hyperparameters such as kernel number, kernel size, and finalized the following values based on the validation set performance:

- Kernel size:

$$f_1^h = 3, f_2^h = 6, f_3^h = 9, f_4^h = 12$$

- Number of kernels = 200, stride = 1.

3.2.1 Multi-Task Learning

In machine learning, multi-task learning is an old idea studied by Caruana (1997). A widely used technique to apply MTL is to train the main and auxiliary task jointly. In our work, the main task has text utterances which belong to either of the three classes, i.e. in favor, against and neutral whereas the proposed auxiliary task has two classes which comprise of neutral stance tweets and those which show a stance (in favor + against). The MTL framework allows the model parameter to be shared across tasks and enables the incorporation of a combined loss function with a shared underlying representation shown in Figure 1. Shared learning pushes the model to learn the feature representations that generalize well across tasks. The following loss function is comprised of loss of the main task and the auxiliary task. We use a lambda parameter to control the effect of loss of the auxiliary task on the total loss.

- Loss function:

$$L_{total} = L_{task1} + \lambda * L_{task2}$$

Here, λ is a tunable parameter which is optimized as part of the training process. We investigated the effectiveness of multi-task learning in an end-to-end neural network architecture for both the auxiliary task and the main task. We observed that the effect of task selection on model performance where it is validated that using auxiliary tasks improve the performance of the main task (Caruana, 1997).

Given suitable data, this approach is flexible enough to extend to other NLP tasks. It provides synergy between the two tasks, resulting in improved performance in comparison to individual tasks. The combined loss function pushes the model to learn general and complex features across multiple tasks rather than forcing the model to learn the features of a single task independently. This is a particularly interesting technique in NLP since data is scarce for many tasks and shared learning approach reduces the amount of training data needed.

4 Results

Model	Accuracy(%)
RBF Kernel SVM*	58.7
Random Forest*	54.7
Linear SVM*	56.6
CNN	**61.4**
CNN + MTL	**63.2**

Table 1: Detailed accuracies achieved on the benchmark dataset by different models. *RBF Kernel SVM, Random Forest, and Linear SVM accuracies are from (Swami et al., 2018)

The benchmark dataset that is published online by (Swami et al., 2018) is used for evaluating the effectiveness of machine translated input for our proposed architecture. It contains a total of 3545 annotated tweets where 1755 are labeled in favor, 647 as against and 1934 as neutral tweets. For the

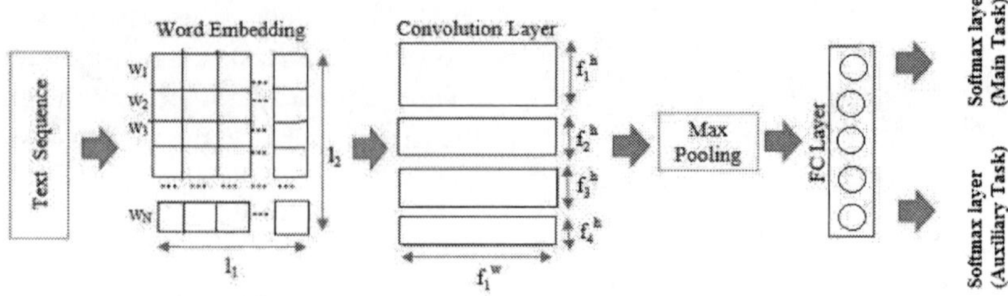

Figure 1: Proposed CNN - MTL architecture

Model	Accuracy(%)
CNN	66.7
CNN + MTL	71.3

Table 2: Comparison of accuracies for the auxiliary task

two tasks, we achieved an accuracy of 63.2%. We carried out 10-fold cross-validation for generating all our experimental results. Using all the features (Swami et al., 2018), the baseline systems: RBF kernel SVM, random forest, linear SVM presented an accuracy of 58.7%. Going forward, to the best of our knowledge, we are the first to experiment with deep learning architecture based on MTL for detecting stance in code-mixed data. The challenges in this task are the linguistic complexity and the lack of clean code-mixed data. And, pre-processing of code-mixed data will increase model performance.

In Table 1, we present the results of both the tasks with the proposed deep learning based architecture with translated data as input. We experimented with both continuous bag of words (CBOW) and skip-gram versions of word embeddings with CNN model and achieved similar results. The substantial accuracy obtained (63.2% for stance) shows more than 4.5% increment from values reported by (Swami et al., 2018). However, these values reflect that there is still a lot of room for improvement, justifying further efforts. We observed more than 4% overall accuracy improvement in the auxiliary task with the introduction of MTL as compared to the performance on the standalone CNN architecture. This indicates that training the main and the auxiliary task jointly can learn robust shared features which leads to improvement on both the main and auxiliary task.

5   Conclusion

We present MTL based deep learning approach for the problem of detecting user stance with respect to a particular topic: "Demonetisation", on Twitter's code-mixed Hindi-English data generated by bilingual users. The machine transliterated and translated corpus is given to the model. We empirically demonstrated the effectiveness of the proposed architecture. The proposed approach of jointly training the main and the auxiliary task proved to be the best-performing model so far for the code-mixed data, indicating that it is a promising new direction in the automated assessment of stance. An accuracy of 63.2% is achieved from our proposed deep learning model based on multi-task learning at detecting stance in code-mixed data which is an improvement of more than 4.5% overall accuracy when compared with current benchmark results.

6   Future Work

Our work provided insights regarding the benefits of training the main and the auxiliary task jointly for code-mixed data. There is a lot of room for improvement, and we hope to get a better understanding of how to improve the techniques for stance classification by primarily improving the corpus quality in our future work. Further, we will compare and contrast with different networks like LSTM, Attention-based architectures, etc. The results of our experiments are encouraging though since they show that it is possible to use classical methods for analyzing code-mixed texts. Furthermore, to address phrasal repetitions, short and simple constructions, non-grammatical words, more corpus without spelling errors need to be constructed as this can help other NLP tasks in multilingual societies.

References

Pranav Anand, Marilyn Walker, Rob Abbott, Jean E Fox Tree, Robeson Bowmani, and Michael Minor. 2011. Cats rule and dogs drool!: Classifying stance in online debate. In *Proceedings of the 2nd workshop on computational approaches to subjectivity and sentiment analysis*, pages 1–9. Association for Computational Linguistics.

Antonio Fernández Anta, Luis Núñez Chiroque, Philippe Morere, and Agustín Santos. 2013. Sentiment analysis and topic detection of spanish tweets: A comparative study of of nlp techniques. *Procesamiento del lenguaje natural*, 50:45–52.

Isabelle Augenstein and Anders Søgaard. 2017. Multitask learning of keyphrase boundary classification. *arXiv preprint arXiv:1704.00514*.

Rich Caruana. 1997. Multitask learning. *Machine learning*, 28(1):41–75.

Soravit Changpinyo, Hexiang Hu, and Fei Sha. 2018. Multi-task learning for sequence tagging: An empirical study. *arXiv preprint arXiv:1808.04151*.

Sarah Djemili, Julien Longhi, Claudia Marinica, Dimitris Kotzinos, and Georges-Elia Sarfati. 2014. What does twitter have to say about ideology? In *NLP 4 CMC: Natural Language Processing for Computer-Mediated Communication/Social Media-Pre-conference workshop at Konvens 2014*, volume 1, pages http–www. Universitätsverlag Hildesheim.

Adam Faulkner. 2014. Automated classification of stance in student essays: An approach using stance target information and the wikipedia link-based measure. In *FLAIRS Conference*.

Imene Guellil and Kamel Boukhalfa. 2015. Social big data mining: A survey focused on opinion mining and sentiments analysis. In *2015 12th International Symposium on Programming and Systems (ISPS)*, pages 1–10. IEEE.

Divam Gupta, Kushagra Singh, Soumen Chakrabarti, and Tanmoy Chakraborty. 2019. Multi-task learning for target-dependent sentiment classification. *arXiv preprint arXiv:1902.02930*.

Kazi Saidul Hasan and Vincent Ng. 2013. Stance classification of ideological debates: Data, models, features, and constraints. In *Proceedings of the Sixth International Joint Conference on Natural Language Processing*, pages 1348–1356.

Peter Krejzl, Barbora Hourová, and Josef Steinberger. 2017. Stance detection in online discussions. *arXiv preprint arXiv:1701.00504*.

Man Lan, Jianxiang Wang, Yuanbin Wu, Zheng-Yu Niu, and Haifeng Wang. 2017. Multi-task attention-based neural networks for implicit discourse relationship representation and identification. In *Proceedings of the 2017 Conference on Empirical Methods in Natural Language Processing*, pages 1299–1308.

Navonil Majumder, Soujanya Poria, Haiyun Peng, Niyati Chhaya, Erik Cambria, and Alexander Gelbukh. 2019. Sentiment and sarcasm classification with multitask learning. *arXiv preprint arXiv:1901.08014*.

Tomas Mikolov, Kai Chen, Greg Corrado, and Jeffrey Dean. 2013. Efficient estimation of word representations in vector space. *arXiv preprint arXiv:1301.3781*.

Saif Mohammad, Svetlana Kiritchenko, Parinaz Sobhani, Xiaodan Zhu, and Colin Cherry. 2016. Semeval-2016 task 6: Detecting stance in tweets. In *Proceedings of the 10th International Workshop on Semantic Evaluation (SemEval-2016)*, pages 31–41.

Saif M Mohammad. 2016. Sentiment analysis: Detecting valence, emotions, and other affectual states from text. In *Emotion measurement*, pages 201–237. Elsevier.

Thai-Hoang Pham, Khai Mai, Nguyen Minh Trung, Nguyen Tuan Duc, Danushka Bolegala, Ryohei Sasano, and Satoshi Sekine. 2019. Multi-task learning with contextualized word representations for extented named entity recognition. *arXiv preprint arXiv:1902.10118*.

Ashwin Rajadesingan and Huan Liu. 2014. Identifying users with opposing opinions in twitter debates. In *International conference on social computing, behavioral-cultural modeling, and prediction*, pages 153–160. Springer.

Swapna Somasundaran and Janyce Wiebe. 2010. Recognizing stances in ideological on-line debates. In *Proceedings of the NAACL HLT 2010 Workshop on Computational Approaches to Analysis and Generation of Emotion in Text*, pages 116–124. Association for Computational Linguistics.

Sahil Swami, Ankush Khandelwal, Vinay Singh, Syed Sarfaraz Akhtar, and Manish Shrivastava. 2018. An english-hindi code-mixed corpus: Stance annotation and baseline system. *arXiv preprint arXiv:1805.11868*.

Marilyn A Walker, Pranav Anand, Robert Abbott, and Ricky Grant. 2012. Stance classification using dialogic properties of persuasion. In *Proceedings of the 2012 Conference of the North American Chapter of the Association for Computational Linguistics: Human Language Technologies*, pages 592–596. Association for Computational Linguistics.

A Soft Label Strategy for Target-Level Sentiment Classification

Da Yin, Xiao Liu, Xiuyu Wu, Baobao Chang
MOE Key Lab of Computational Linguistics, School of EECS, Peking University
{wade_yin9712,lxlisa,xiuyu_wu,chbb}@pku.edu.cn

Abstract

In this paper, we propose a soft label approach to target-level sentiment classification task, in which a history-based soft labeling model is proposed to measure the possibility of a context word as an opinion word. We also apply a convolution layer to extract local active features, and introduce positional weights to take relative distance information into consideration. In addition, we obtain more informative target representation by training with context tokens together to make deeper interaction between target and context tokens. We conduct experiments on SemEval 2014 datasets and the experimental results show that our approach significantly outperforms previous models and gives state-of-the-art results on these datasets.

1 Introduction

Target-level sentiment classification aims to identify the sentiment polarities towards given targets by analyzing sentence context. For example, in the sentence *"The **food** is good but **service** is bad."*, there are two targets *"**food**"* and *"**service**"* mentioned. The sentiment towards *"**food**"* and *"**service**"* are positive and negative respectively.

Neural network models (Tang et al., 2016a; Wang et al., 2016; Tang et al., 2016b; Liu and Zhang, 2017; Ma et al., 2017; Tay et al., 2017; Chen et al., 2017; Huang et al., 2018; Gu et al., 2018) have achieved high accuracy on this task. Most of the neural network models introduce attention mechanism to find the correlation between target and context tokens. However, the combination of word-level features computed by attention weights may introduce noise into model. For instance, in *"The dish tastes bad but its **vegetable** is delicious though it looks ugly."*, these attention-based models tend to highlight some involve some other words such as *"bad"* and *"ugly"*.

Instead of using the attention mechanism, we propose a soft label approach for the target-level sentiment classification task. Intuitively, the task could be treated as a two-step process. Firstly the sentiment words that are related to the given target, called opinion words, are labeled and extracted. Then the final decision on the sentiment polarity would be made by taking all the extracted opinion words into account. However, this kind of hard label strategy, which directly determines whether a token is an opinion word or not, for labeling opinion words is non-differentiable and hinders training through normal back-propagation. Thus we use a soft labeling model to avoid the hard decision and make sure the model works in an end-to-end way.

Specifically, the soft label model is used to measure the likelihood of a context word as an opinion word at each time step. The larger the value of one word's soft label, the greater its effect on target sentiment. In fact, given a target, people are accustomed to going through a sentence from beginning to end, and to judge whether current word is highly related to the target sentiment at each step with comparison of history information till the current word in the reading process. Therefore, we implement an LSTM-based (Hochreiter and Schmidhuber, 1997) soft labeling model by a history-based approach, which utilizes history information (previous soft labels and cell states) together with representation of the current word, to decide how to pay attention to history information or current word representation based on their correlation with target representation.

Moreover, since the convolution layer (LeCun et al., 1989) does better in capturing local active features than other neural networks do and these extracted features are proved to be beneficial to text classification (Kim, 2014; Johnson and Zhang, 2015), we apply a convolution based encoder to extract these features. The distance of the features to target is also essential as texts may be long and contain several targets. The closer tokens

Proceedings of the 10th Workshop on Computational Approaches to Subjectivity, Sentiment and Social Media Analysis, pages 6–15
Minneapolis, June 6, 2019. ©2019 Association for Computational Linguistics

are more likely to affect on the targets. Therefore, we adopt positional weights to scale the features with relative distance information between context tokens and the target.

Target representation is also critical to this task. Previous works, such as Tang et al. (2016a), simply take the average of target embeddings as target representation. In fact, this kind of representation does not incorporate contextual information. Words in a sentence have strong dependencies on each other. Thus it is necessary to train target representation together with context tokens to obtain more informative representation dependent on contextual information.

In summary, our contributions are as follows:

- Our model uses a soft label approach to evaluating the likelihood of a context word as an opinion word based on the history information.

- Our model leverages convolution layer, which is seldom used in the task, to extract features, and these features are accordingly weighed by positional information.

- Our model learns more informative representation of the target, instead of the average of target embeddings, and strengthens the interaction between target and context tokens in soft label computation process.

- We conduct experiments on benchmark datasets and the experimental results show that our approach significantly outperforms previous models and achieves state-of-the-art results on these datasets.

2 Related Work

Early methods mainly apply supervised learning approach with large quantities of handcrafted features (Blair-Goldensohn et al., 2008; Yu et al., 2011; Jiang et al., 2011; Kiritchenko et al., 2014), but ignore context information and deep relations between target and context tokens.

Neural network models have achieved high accuracy on this task. **AE-LSTM** and **ATAE-LSTM** (Wang et al., 2016) simply concatenate target embeddings to context word embeddings to make connection between targets and contexts. However, both models described above do not obtain target representations based on context-aware information. Inspired by the TNet (Li et al., 2018),

which learns deep representations for targets, we propose a model which could strengthen the interaction between target and context tokens.

Recently, most of the previous state-of-the-art models leverage attention mechanism to evaluate the correlation between the tokens in one sentence. **IAN** (Ma et al., 2017) adopts two separate LSTM layers and an interactive attention mechanism. Hazarika et al. (2018) classifies the sentiment polarities of all the targets in one sentence simultaneously with attention mechanism to model inter-target dependencies. **MemNet** (Tang et al., 2016b), **RAM** (Chen et al., 2017), **TRMN** (Wang et al., 2018) and **IARM** (Majumder et al., 2018) introduce deep memory network and multi-hop attention model over sentence-level memories to incorporate target information into sentence representations. Specifically, **TRMN** and **IARM** attach importance to the interaction between targets and contexts, and inter-target relations, which contain the information of relationship between multiple targets in one sentence, respectively. Different from them, our model adopts a novel and effective soft label approach in an intuitive way.

There are few works (Xue and Li, 2018; Huang and Carley, 2018) applying CNN, which is considered to be good at text classification, on target-level sentiment classification. **GCAE** (Xue and Li, 2018) and **PG-CNN** (Huang and Carley, 2018) are both CNN-based models and adopt gate mechanism to make interaction between target and context tokens. To improve the effectiveness of convolution layers, our model further adopts positional weights, which take relative distance information into account.

3 Model

Target-level sentiment classification task is to decide which sentiment is expressed towards a target: positive, neutral or negative.

Our model is illustrated in Figure 1. It is divided into four parts: (1) a Bi-LSTM (Schuster and Paliwal, 1997) layer to get context-aware representations, (2) a convolution based feature extractor, (3) computation of soft labels, and (4) sentiment classification using the soft labels and positional weights.

We introduce the following notations: $s = [w_1, w_2, ..., w_n]$ denotes a sentence which consists of n words. $w_i \in \mathbb{R}^{d_0}$ is the embedding of the i-th word. $t = [t, t+1, ..., t+m-1]$ denotes the posi-

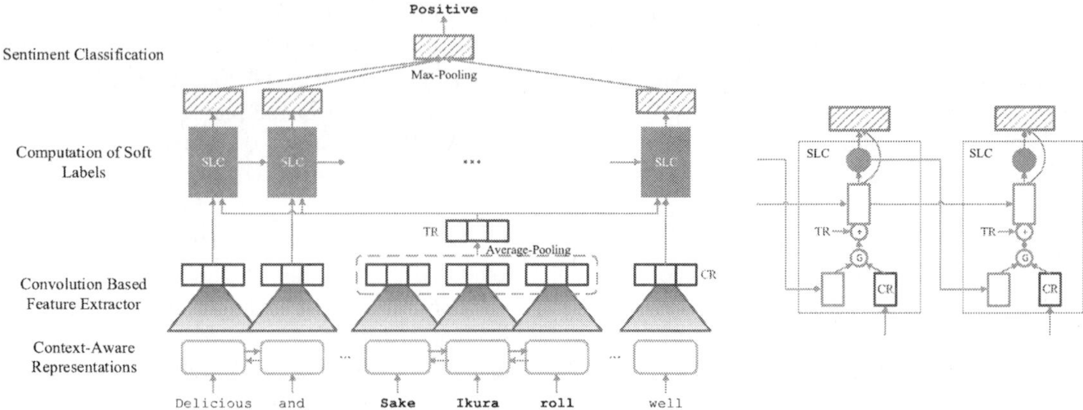

Figure 1: Overall architecture of the proposed method. We use the sentence *"Delicious and good-looking Sake Ikura roll, and sashimi tastes good as well."* as an example. The term "SLC" indicates soft label computation. "TR" indicates target representation and "CR" represents context representation.

tion of the target tokens, where $t \geq 1, t+m-1 \leq n$. The length of the target is m.

3.1 Context-Aware Representations

Since words in a sentence have strong dependencies on each other, it is necessary to fetch context-aware representations to combine context information with words. In order to incorporate the context information into words, we encode them with a Bi-LSTM layer:

$$x_i = [\overrightarrow{\text{LSTM}}(w_i); \overleftarrow{\text{LSTM}}(w_i)] \tag{1}$$

We concatenate the forward and backward hidden outputs of LSTM, of which the dimension size is both d_0', and $[;]$ denotes concatenation. We regard $x_i \in \mathbb{R}^{2d_0'}$ as the context-aware representation of word w_i, and feed it to following layers.

3.2 Convolution Based Feature Extractor

To extract the local active features, we use a convolution layer with three parallel windows, which have different sizes. Each kernel has d_1 filters. For kernel size s_j, let $W^{conv_j} \in \mathbb{R}^{d_1 \times s_j \times 2d_0'}$ be the d_1 filters for the convolution with the same size s_j, and $b^{conv_j} \in \mathbb{R}^{d_1}$ be the bias. x^{conv_j}, the output of the convolution layer is produced by convoluting W^{conv_j} with the word window $x_{i-\lfloor \frac{s_j-1}{2} \rfloor:i+\lfloor \frac{s_j}{2} \rfloor}$ at each $i \in [1, n]$ (positions out of range are padded with zero):

$$x_i^{conv_j} = \text{ReLU}(x_{i-\lfloor \frac{s_j-1}{2} \rfloor:i+\lfloor \frac{s_j}{2} \rfloor} \circ W^{conv_j} + b^{conv_j}) \tag{2}$$

where ReLU indicates a nonlinear activation function, and $\circ$ is element-wise multiplication.

Merging outputs of three kinds of kernels, the word representation is computed as:

$$h_i^E = x_i^{conv_1} \oplus x_i^{conv_2} \oplus x_i^{conv_3} \tag{3}$$

where $\oplus$ is concatenation. The dimension of h_i^E is $d_1' = 3d_1$.

h^{target} is computed by an average-pooling layer to refine the target representation:

$$h^{target} = \frac{1}{m} \sum_{i=1}^{m} h_{t+i-1}^E \tag{4}$$

3.3 Computation of Soft Labels

Instead of using a hard label strategy and labeling explicitly context words as opinion words or not, we adopt a soft labeling model in which soft label is defined as the probability of each context word as an opinion word. An LSTM layer is applied to compute the final word representation h_i^D and the soft label l_i for the i-th word. It takes both the interacted representation produced by the convolution based feature extractor and the soft label of the previous time step as the input, in order to take history contexts into consideration:

$$h_i^D, c_i^D = \text{LSTM}(h_{i-1}^D, c_{i-1}^D, u_i) \tag{5}$$

where $h_i^D \in \mathbb{R}^{d_1'}$ is the output of the i time stamp, $c_i^D \in \mathbb{R}^{d_1'}$ is the LSTM cell state, which could be treated as long-term memory till the i-th word, and u_i is the input which will be described later.

One problem encountered here is that the history information of previous time steps may not be closely related to the target. Consider predicting the sentiment of the target *"service"* in the sentence *"Tasty food but the **service** was dreadful!"*. When the LSTM comes to the word *"dreadful"*, a simple soft label approach might indicate that the sentiment polarity is positive due to the influence of the word *"Tasty"*, which in fact does not modify the target *"service"*. To solve the problem, we apply a gate mechanism to determine the proportion of the history information in the input, according to the ratio of history information and current word information's correlation with the target:

$$g_i = \frac{\exp(c_{i-1}^D W^g h^{target})}{\exp(c_{i-1}^D W^g h^{target}) + \exp(h_i^E W^g h^{target})} \tag{6}$$

where $W^g \in \mathbb{R}^{d_1' \times d_1'}$ is the weight matrix. Also, we intend to strengthen the influence from target representation. Thus we further incorporate target information into the input:

$$u_i = g_i \cdot (W^D l_{i-1}) + (1 - g_i) \cdot h_i^E + h^{target} \tag{7}$$

where $W^D \in \mathbb{R}^{d_1'}$ is the weight parameter and l_{i-1} is the soft label of the $(i-1)$-th word. To reduce the dimensions of LSTM inputs, we fuse the target representation with word representations by a simple addition operation.

With the output of the LSTM layer, the soft label l_i is computed as:

$$\begin{aligned} l_i &= p(e_i = 1 | h_i^D) \\ &= p(e_i = 1 | l_1, l_2, ..., l_{i-1}, h_{i-1}^D, h_i^E) \\ &= \text{sigmoid}(W^l h_i^D + b^l) \end{aligned} \tag{8}$$

where $e_i = 1$ indicates that the word should be considered as bearing sentiment towards the current target, $W^l \in \mathbb{R}^{d_1'}$ and $b^l \in \mathbb{R}$.

3.4 Sentiment Classification

Features that are close to the target often contribute more to the sentiment towards the target. Considering the impact of the distance to the target, we define the positional weights:

$$pos_i = \begin{cases} 1 - \dfrac{t - i}{\beta} & i \in [1, ..., t-1] \\[2ex] 1 - \dfrac{i - t + 1}{\beta} & i \in [t, ..., n - m] \end{cases} \tag{9}$$

where β controls the rate of decaying of the positional weights according to the distances to the target. The value of the rate is $\frac{1}{\beta}$.

Algorithm 1 Training framework of our model.

Input: Sentence w, target t, golden label y.
1: $h^E, h^{target} = ComputeRepresentation(w, t)$
2: **for** word w_i in sentence w **do**
3:     **if** $i == 1$ **then**
4:         $g_i = 0$
5:     **else**
6:         $g_i = ComputeGate(h_i^E, c_{i-1}^D, h^{target})$ (Eq.6)
7:     **end if**
8:     $u_i = ComputeInput(g_i, l_{i-1}, h_i^E, h^{target})$ (Eq.7)
9:     $h_i^D, c_i^D = \text{LSTM}(h_{i-1}^D, c_{i-1}^D, u_i)$
10:     $l_i = ComputeSoftLabel(h_i^D)$ (Eq.8)
11: **end for**
12: $p = Predict(l, h^D, pos)$
13: $L = CrossEntropy(p, y)$
14: Back propagate errors and update parameters θ

Then we combine the soft labels and positional weights together to take both the history contexts and the relative distances into consideration. The integrated weight of the i-th word is:

$$c_i = l_i \cdot pos_i \tag{10}$$

We put the word representations together to predict the sentiment towards the target, according to the integrated weight of each word:

$$p(\tilde{y}|w, t) = \text{softmax}(W^p \max\{c_i \cdot h_i^D\} + b^p) \tag{11}$$

where $\tilde{y}$ is the three categories of sentiment polarity, $max\{\cdot\}$ is the max-pooling operation, $W^p \in \mathbb{R}^{3 \times d_1'}$ and $b^p \in \mathbb{R}^3$ are the prediction matrix and its bias. In summary, the whole algorithm is shown in Algorithm 1.

In training, we utilize the cross entropy loss function as the objective:

$$L = -\frac{1}{T} \sum_{i=1}^{T} \sum_{j=1}^{3} y_{i,j} \log p_{i,j} + \lambda ||\theta||^2 \tag{12}$$

where T is the number of training samples, $y_i \in \mathbb{R}^3$ denotes the ground truth label of sample i, represented by one-hot vector, and $p_{i,j}$ is the predicted probability of sample i with sentiment j. θ is the set of all parameters and λ is the coefficient for L_2 regularization.

Algorithm 1 shows the overall framework of our model.

4 Experiments

4.1 Experimental Setup

We conduct experiments using the benchmark datasets of SemEval 2014 Task 4 (Pontiki et al.,

Dataset		Positive	Negative	Neutral
Restaurant	Train	2159	800	632
	Test	730	195	196
Laptop	Train	980	858	454
	Test	340	128	171

Table 1: Statistics of benchmark datasets.

$2014)^1$, which contain reviews about laptop and restaurant respectively and are used by previous works. The statistics of two benchmark datasets are shown in Table 1. There are three kinds of sentiment polarity: positive, negative and neutral.

In our experiments, we use GloVe.840B.300d embeddings (Pennington et al., 2014)[2] as previous works do. Each word embedding has 300 dimensions. Out-of-vocabulary (OOV) words are randomly sampled from the uniform distribution $\mathcal{U}(-0.02, 0.02)$. Weight matrices are initialized by sampling from uniform distribution $\mathcal{U}(-0.1, 0.1)$. The kernel sizes of convolution based feature extractors s_1, s_2, s_3 are 3, 4, 5. Each kernel consists of 128 filters. The dimension of outputs of LSTM $2d'_0$ and the convolution layer d'_1 are 400 and 384 respectively. We use Adam optimizer (Kingma and Ba, 2014) with learning rate 0.003. The batch size is set to 128. In order to alleviate overfitting, we set the dropout rate to 0.5 and the coefficient of L_2 regularization to 0.00001. The hyperparameter β used to calculate positional weights is set to 40. We choose the model with the minimum loss on testing set among 100 epochs. Besides, since there exists class imbalance in SemEval dataset, we additionally show the Macro-F1 scores of each model together with accuracy metric to further investigate the effectiveness and robustness of our model.

4.2 Comparison Results

In order to evaluate the effectiveness of our model, we compare it with 10 previous state-of-the-art models. The description is below:

• **AE-LSTM** (Wang et al., 2016) encodes the context-aware words to get representation. Then it simply uses the concatenation of context-aware word representations and target embeddings to classify the sentiment. However, the target embeddings do not contain contextual information.

• **ATAE-LSTM** (Wang et al., 2016) additionally leverages attention mechanism on top of **AE-LSTM** to find out relevant words with target.

• **GCAE** (Xue and Li, 2018) is based on CNN and applies Gated Tanh-ReLU Units (GTRU) to control the information flow from the target and build interaction between targets and contexts.

• **MemNet** (Tang et al., 2016b) uses a multi-hop attention mechanism whose query of the first attention layer is target representation. The attention result and the linear transformation of target representation are summed and used as the memory and the query of the next attention layer. Output of the last attention layer is considered as the sentiment representation used for classification.

• **IAN** (Ma et al., 2017) uses two attention mechanisms to select information from contexts and targets according to the average of encoded targets and contexts separately. The concatenation of two attention results is used for sentiment classification.

• **PG-CNN** (Huang and Carley, 2018) is also based on CNN and uses gate mechanism to incorporate target information into CNN architecture.

• The model designed by Hazarika et al. (2018) classifies all the targets in one sentence simultaneously with attention mechanism and inter-target dependencies detected by a complicated two-layer LSTM structure. One LSTM layer is designed to obtain the whole sentence representation based on each target in one sentence, similar to **ATAE-LSTM**. Then the model feeds the sentence representations altogether into the other LSTM to find the inter-target dependencies.

• **RAM** (Chen et al., 2017) uses multi-hop attention mechanism on position-weighted memories and combines the attention results to synthesize important features in difficult sentence structures. The model still constructs the memories by sentence-level information as **MemNet** does.

• **TRMN** (Wang et al., 2018) is a target-sensitive memory network, where various interaction mechanisms between target and context are leveraged. The whole architecture is similar to **MemNet**.

• **IARM** (Majumder et al., 2018) also leverages recurrent memory networks with attention mechanism. The memory is built by the sentence representation based on target information as **ATAE-LSTM** does. In addition, the model con-

---

Models	Restaurant		Laptop	
	ACC	Macro-F1	ACC	Macro-F1
AE-LSTM[*]	76.60	66.45	68.90	62.45
ATAE-LSTM[*]	77.20	65.41	68.70	59.41
GCAE	77.28	-	69.14	-
MemNet[*]	78.16	65.83	70.33	64.09
IAN	78.20	-	72.10	-
PG-CNN	78.93	-	69.12	-
Hazarika et al. (2018)	79.00	-	72.50	-
RAM[*]	79.38	68.86	73.59	70.51
TRMN	-	69.00	-	68.18
IARM	80.00	-	73.80	-
Ours[*]	**80.98**[†]	**71.52**[†]	**74.56**[†]	**71.63**[†]

Table 2: Comparisons with baselines and ablation experiments (%). The best results are in bold. The model with
* means its result is the average value of 5 runs. The result with † means statistical significant at the level of 0.05
with the baselines tagged by *.

centrates on inter-target dependencies by memory networks, instead of vanilla LSTM structure used in the model proposed by Hazarika et al. (2018).

The comparisons with baseline methods are shown in Table 2. Our model significantly outperforms all the baselines. Except for **AE-LSTM**, **GCAE** and **PG-CNN**, the other baseline models adopt attention mechanism to evaluate the correlation between target and context words. However, the attention score for each word is distributed simultaneously according to simple computation by weight matrices. In our model, we intend to estimate the probability of being an opinion word at each time step based on the history information, such as previous soft labels and cell states, to take each word into account individually. Indeed, our model achieves significant improvements over the attention-based baseline models.

Moreover, we find that several baseline methods are based on memory networks, such as **MemNet**, **RAM**, **TRMN** and **IARM**. Note that the memories of these models are all based on the general sentence-level representations which might lose individual consideration and dilute the information of opinion words. Thus, it is better to take advantage of the history contexts and current word representation to consider each token individually instead of the overall sentence-level information.

Also, from the fact that **IAN**, which considers the interaction between target and context tokens, performs better than **AE-LSTM** and **ATAE-LSTM**, we observe the importance of interaction

in this task. Though **GCAE** does not take context-aware representations into account, it still performs better than **AE-LSTM** and **ATAE-LSTM** do. It demonstrates the effectiveness of GTRU and further justifies the necessity of interaction between target and context. In our model, we emphasize the interaction when fusing the target representation with the context word representations and evaluating the correlation with targets to decide which information we should focus on more.

The convolution layer has been proved to be good at extracting local active features. However, the convolution based model **GCAE** and **PG-CNN** behave poorly in this task because vanilla convolution based models tend to find the salient features in the whole sentence rather than figure out the active features which are strongly associated with the target. Intuitively, closer words are more likely to modify the given target, and some of the previous state-of-the-art models also consider the relative position factors. Therefore, inspired by them, we apply a convolution based model combined with position information to achieve better performance.

4.3 Ablation Study

To evaluate the effect of each part in our model, we remove some important components or replace them with widely used alternatives. The comparisons with ablated tests are shown in Table 3. The results of ablation tests are the averages of 5 runs.

The biggest change from previous models is

Models	Restaurant		Laptop	
	ACC	Macro-F1	ACC	Macro-F1
Ours	**80.98**‡	**71.52**‡	**74.56**‡	**71.63**‡
with Hard Labels	78.34	68.17	73.14	69.01
with Attention	79.01	68.61	73.35	69.18
w/o Convolution Layer	79.15	68.45	73.28	69.24
w/o Soft Labels	79.34	68.37	73.62	69.52
w/o History Information	79.53	67.98	73.07	69.17
with AVG	80.29	69.65	73.84	70.31
w/o Positional Weights	80.54	69.95	73.65	70.44

Table 3: The results of ablation tests (%). The best results are in bold. **w/o History Information** indicates the soft label approach without consideration of history information. **with AVG** indicates the target representation is replaced by the averaged target embeddings. The result with ‡ means statistical significant at the level of 0.05.

that we use the soft label approach based on history information, such as previous soft labels and cell states, instead of using attention scores. To further confirm the effectiveness of the soft label strategy, we replace it with attention mechanism, which treats the target representation as a query and uses a weight matrix to compute the correlation between target and context words. The experimental results show that the accuracy drops over 1.97% and 1.21% and Macro-F1 score drops 2.91% and 2.45% respectively. It strongly proves the effectiveness of our soft label strategy and the better performance can be attributed to the careful consideration of each word at each time step. Additionally, we compare our model with **w/o History Information**, which does not feed previous time step's soft label and cell states information into the input of the current time step and simply uses a weight matrix to project the hidden outputs to the values of soft labels. The improvements show that the history information is indispensable for the task. The whole process of determining the soft label value in our model is fairly similar to the process of people reading a sentence and predicting the sentiments for targets discussed in Section 1. Besides, our model outperforms **with Hard Labels**, where the value of the label is either 0 or 1, because the soft approach can alleviate the propagation problem caused by hard decision. Moreover, our model greatly improves the performance compared with **w/o Soft Labels**. Obviously, the history-based soft label approach has great effects.

As mentioned before, the interaction between target and context is important in this task. Compared with the model **with AVG**, our model has

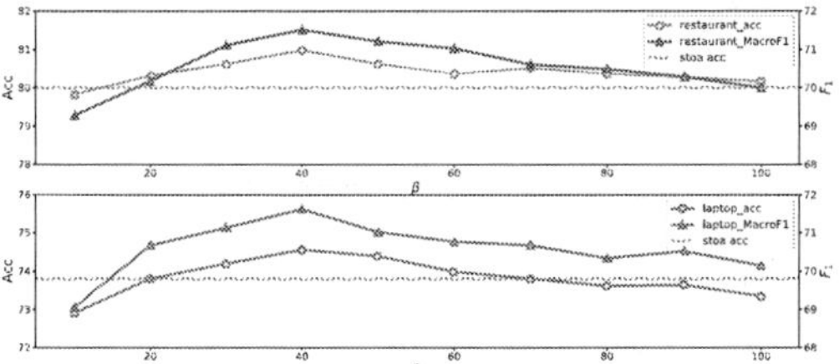

Figure 2: Effect of β on two datasets.

better performance on the two datasets for the target representation of our model contains contextual information and thus is more informative. The results indeed prove the usefulness of strengthening interaction. Lastly, without the convolution layer, the performance drops 1.83%, 1.28% on accuracy and 3.07%, 2.39% on Macro-F1 score respectively, suggesting that the convolution layer is capable of extracting active features for sentiment classification. Using relative distance information, our model greatly improves the performance of **w/o Positional Weights**. It indicates that position-aware information is beneficial to our model.

4.4 Impact of Rate of Decaying on Positional Weights

As our model involves the rate of decaying of positional weights which is controlled by β, we attempt to investigate which value is proper for β. Eq. 9 shows that the bigger β is, the slower the rate is. In our experiments, we keep the other experimental setups the same, and then vary β from 10 to 100, increased by 10. The results on two datasets are shown in Figure 2. Firstly, we notice that our model is better than most of the state-of-the-art

12

models on two datasets even if we do not optimize on β, suggesting that the other components of our model are effective. Besides, we observe that the performance tends to get better before β reaches 40, and there is a downward trend after it. When β equals 10, the rate of decaying is relatively fast. Since there are some long sentences in the datasets, the positional weights would lead to the loss of word information and result in worse performance. When β is large, like 100, the rate is slow and the positional weights may negligibly affect the classification process. Thus, it is necessary to choose a proper value for β.

4.5 Case Study

To further manifest the performance of our proposed model, we choose a case and show it in a heatmap form. In this case, the input sentence is *"The **dish** tastes bad but its **vegetable** is delicious though it looks ugly."* and the given target is *"**vegetable**"*. There are two targets and three important sentiment words (*"bad"*, *"delicious"* and *"ugly"*) in the sentence. The challenge the model faces is to find out which sentiment word contributes more to the sentiment polarity of *"vegetable"*. The upper part of Figure 3 is the visualization result of **with Attention** instead of using our proposed soft label strategy. We can easily find that the model attends on all the three sentiment words listed before, especially on *"bad"* and *"ugly"*, and wrongly predicts the sentiment as a negative one. It partially justifies attention mechanism's ability of extracting the sentiment words, but the wrong prediction could be attributed to the simultaneous weight distribution of attention scores and lack of individual consideration on each word.

Our proposed soft label approach is a good solution that could deal with the difficulty of matching multiple opinion words to the given target. The lower part indicates the visualization result of the value of soft labels and represents the process of soft label computation from the beginning of the sentence to the end. Besides, the proportions of history information g_i are all above 0.4, except for those of *"bad"* and *"delicious"*, which are 0.217 and 0.105 respectively. The relatively small value means that there might be a sentiment change in the place of the word. When the model browses to the word *"bad"*, as words before do not contain strong emotions, the cell states are now combined with the sentiment information of *"bad"*.

When turning to *"delicious"*, the model recognizes that *"delicious"* is more relevant to the target while competing with the previous memory. Thus, its soft label's value becomes higher than that of *"bad"* and the word accounts for relatively great proportion of the cell states. Lastly, the model considers the cell states containing the information of *"delicious"* are more closely connected with the target than the word *"ugly"* is. As a result, the value of the soft label of *"ugly"* is low. Since the value of the soft label of *"delicious"* is the highest among those of all the other tokens in the sentence, the model predicts the sentiment correctly. The complex case strongly demonstrates the effectiveness of finding correct opinion words for target.

5 Error Analysis

Though our model achieves good performance by adopting the soft label strategy, we find that our model fails to predict the sentiment correctly in some cases. For example, when predicting the sentiment of the target *"**staff**"* in the sentence *"The **staff** should be a bit more friendly."*, our model tends to classify the sentiment as a positive one because of the opinion word *"friendly"*. Actually, the modal verb *"should"* represents the implicit meaning that the staff is not friendly and the customer hopes the staff could change the attitude towards customers. Therefore, there is still a room for our model to mine the kind of implicit semantics, not only based on the explicit opinion words. Additionally, we choose to detect the sentiment of *"**startup times**"* in the sentence *"**Startup times** are incredibly long: over two minutes."* and find that our model wrongly predicts the sentiment as a positive one. Though *"long"* is usually used to praise the quality of battery, it represents negative meaning when modifying the *"startup times"*. The fact that the same opinion word represents totally different sentiments in different contexts may lead to the error.

6 Conclusion and Future Work

We propose a soft label approach to target-level sentiment classification task. Our model benefits from the soft label strategy based on history information, positional weights to take relative distance into account, and deeper interaction between target and context tokens. Experimental results on two benchmark datasets show that our model indeed substantially outperforms previous works. In

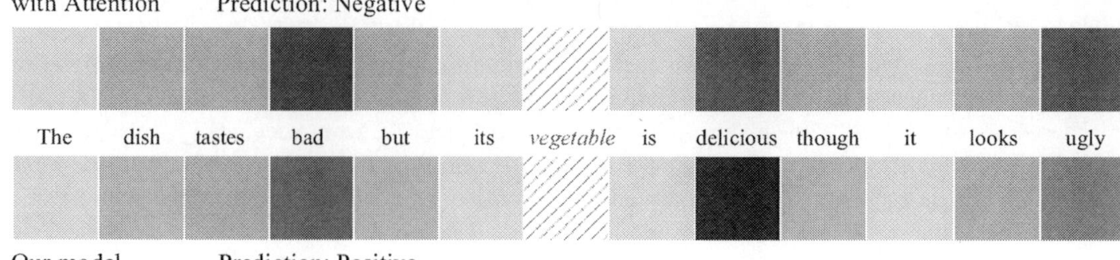

Figure 3: Case study of our proposed model and **with Attention** described in Section 4.3. The given target is *"vegetable"* and the sentiment towards it is positive. The deeper the blue is, the bigger the values of attention scores and soft labels are. Notice that the values of soft labels are normalized and they do not contain any position information.

the future, taking the encountered errors into account, we will do further researches on mining implicit semantics and distinguishing different sentiments expressed by the same opinion word in various kinds of contexts.

Acknowledgement

We would like to thank the anonymous reviewers for the helpful discussions and suggestions. This work is supported by National Natural Science Foundation of China under Grant No.61876004, No.61751201 and M1752013. The corresponding author of this paper is Baobao Chang.

References

Sasha Blair-Goldensohn, Kerry Hannan, Ryan McDonald, Tyler Neylon, George A Reis, and Jeff Reynar. 2008. Building a sentiment summarizer for local service reviews. In *WWW workshop on NLP in the information explosion era*, volume 14, pages 339–348.

Peng Chen, Zhongqian Sun, Lidong Bing, and Wei Yang. 2017. Recurrent attention network on memory for aspect sentiment analysis. In *Proceedings of the 2017 Conference on Empirical Methods in Natural Language Processing*, pages 452–461. Association for Computational Linguistics.

Shuqin Gu, Lipeng Zhang, Yuexian Hou, and Yin Song. 2018. A position-aware bidirectional attention network for aspect-level sentiment analysis. In *Proceedings of the 27th International Conference on Computational Linguistics*, pages 774–784. Association for Computational Linguistics.

Devamanyu Hazarika, Soujanya Poria, Prateek Vij, Gangeshwar Krishnamurthy, Erik Cambria, and Roger Zimmermann. 2018. Modeling inter-aspect dependencies for aspect-based sentiment analysis. In *Proceedings of the 2018 Conference of the North American Chapter of the Association for Computational Linguistics: Human Language Technologies, Volume 2 (Short Papers)*, pages 266–270. Association for Computational Linguistics.

Sepp Hochreiter and Jürgen Schmidhuber. 1997. Long short-term memory. *Neural computation*, 9(8):1735–1780.

Binxuan Huang and Kathleen Carley. 2018. Parameterized convolutional neural networks for aspect level sentiment classification. In *Proceedings of the 2018 Conference on Empirical Methods in Natural Language Processing*, pages 1091–1096. Association for Computational Linguistics.

Binxuan Huang, Yanglan Ou, and Kathleen M. Carley. 2018. Aspect level sentiment classification with attention-over-attention neural networks. In *Social, Cultural, and Behavioral Modeling - 11th International Conference, SBP-BRiMS 2018, Washington, DC, USA, July 10-13, 2018, Proceedings*, pages 197–206.

Long Jiang, Mo Yu, Ming Zhou, Xiaohua Liu, and Tiejun Zhao. 2011. Target-dependent twitter sentiment classification. In *Proceedings of the 49th Annual Meeting of the Association for Computational Linguistics: Human Language Technologies-Volume 1*, pages 151–160. Association for Computational Linguistics.

Rie Johnson and Tong Zhang. 2015. Semi-supervised convolutional neural networks for text categorization via region embedding. In *Advances in neural information processing systems*, pages 919–927.

Yoon Kim. 2014. Convolutional neural networks for sentence classification. In *Proceedings of the 2014 Conference on Empirical Methods in Natural Language Processing (EMNLP)*, pages 1746–1751. Association for Computational Linguistics.

Diederik P Kingma and Jimmy Ba. 2014. Adam: A method for stochastic optimization. *arXiv preprint arXiv:1412.6980*.

Svetlana Kiritchenko, Xiaodan Zhu, Colin Cherry, and Saif Mohammad. 2014. Nrc-canada-2014: Detecting aspects and sentiment in customer reviews. In *Proceedings of the 8th International Workshop on Semantic Evaluation (SemEval 2014)*, pages 437–442.

Yann LeCun, Bernhard Boser, John S Denker, Donnie Henderson, Richard E Howard, Wayne Hubbard, and Lawrence D Jackel. 1989. Backpropagation applied to handwritten zip code recognition. *Neural computation*, 1(4):541–551.

Xin Li, Lidong Bing, Wai Lam, and Bei Shi. 2018. Transformation networks for target-oriented sentiment classification. In *Proceedings of the 56th Annual Meeting of the Association for Computational Linguistics (Volume 1: Long Papers)*, pages 946–956. Association for Computational Linguistics.

Jiangming Liu and Yue Zhang. 2017. Attention modeling for targeted sentiment. In *Proceedings of the 15th Conference of the European Chapter of the Association for Computational Linguistics: Volume 2, Short Papers*, pages 572–577. Association for Computational Linguistics.

Dehong Ma, Sujian Li, Xiaodong Zhang, and Houfeng Wang. 2017. Interactive attention networks for aspect-level sentiment classification. In *Proceedings of the Twenty-Sixth International Joint Conference on Artificial Intelligence, IJCAI 2017, Melbourne, Australia, August 19-25, 2017*, pages 4068–4074.

Navonil Majumder, Soujanya Poria, Alexander Gelbukh, Md Shad Akhtar, Erik Cambria, and Asif Ekbal. 2018. Iarm: Inter-aspect relation modeling with memory networks in aspect-based sentiment analysis. In *Proceedings of the 2018 Conference on Empirical Methods in Natural Language Processing*, pages 3402–3411.

Jeffrey Pennington, Richard Socher, and Christopher Manning. 2014. Glove: Global vectors for word representation. In *Proceedings of the 2014 Conference on Empirical Methods in Natural Language Processing (EMNLP)*, pages 1532–1543. Association for Computational Linguistics.

Maria Pontiki, Dimitris Galanis, John Pavlopoulos, Harris Papageorgiou, Ion Androutsopoulos, and Suresh Manandhar. 2014. Semeval-2014 task 4: Aspect based sentiment analysis. In *Proceedings of the 8th International Workshop on Semantic Evaluation (SemEval 2014)*, pages 27–35, Dublin, Ireland. Association for Computational Linguistics and Dublin City University.

Mike Schuster and Kuldip K Paliwal. 1997. Bidirectional recurrent neural networks. *IEEE Transactions on Signal Processing*, 45(11):2673–2681.

Duyu Tang, Bing Qin, Xiaocheng Feng, and Ting Liu. 2016a. Effective lstms for target-dependent sentiment classification. In *Proceedings of COLING 2016, the 26th International Conference on Computational Linguistics: Technical Papers*, pages 3298–3307. The COLING 2016 Organizing Committee.

Duyu Tang, Bing Qin, and Ting Liu. 2016b. Aspect level sentiment classification with deep memory network. In *Proceedings of the 2016 Conference on Empirical Methods in Natural Language Processing*, pages 214–224. Association for Computational Linguistics.

Yi Tay, Luu Anh Tuan, and Siu Cheung Hui. 2017. Dyadic memory networks for aspect-based sentiment analysis. In *Proceedings of the 2017 ACM on Conference on Information and Knowledge Management, CIKM 2017, Singapore, November 06 - 10, 2017*, pages 107–116.

Shuai Wang, Sahisnu Mazumder, Bing Liu, Mianwei Zhou, and Yi Chang. 2018. Target-sensitive memory networks for aspect sentiment classification. In *Proceedings of the 56th Annual Meeting of the Association for Computational Linguistics (Volume 1: Long Papers)*, volume 1, pages 957–967.

Yequan Wang, Minlie Huang, Xiaoyan Zhu, and Li Zhao. 2016. Attention-based lstm for aspect-level sentiment classification. In *Proceedings of the 2016 Conference on Empirical Methods in Natural Language Processing*, pages 606–615. Association for Computational Linguistics.

Wei Xue and Tao Li. 2018. Aspect based sentiment analysis with gated convolutional networks. In *Proceedings of the 56th Annual Meeting of the Association for Computational Linguistics (Volume 1: Long Papers)*, pages 2514–2523. Association for Computational Linguistics.

Jianxing Yu, Zheng-Jun Zha, Meng Wang, and Tat-Seng Chua. 2011. Aspect ranking: identifying important product aspects from online consumer reviews. In *Proceedings of the 49th Annual Meeting of the Association for Computational Linguistics: Human Language Technologies-Volume 1*, pages 1496–1505. Association for Computational Linguistics.

Online abuse detection: the value of preprocessing and neural attention models

Dhruv Kumar
University of Waterloo
d35kumar@uwaterloo.ca

Robin Cohen
University of Waterloo
rcohen@uwaterloo.ca

Lukasz Golab
University of Waterloo
lgolab@uwaterloo.ca

Abstract

We propose an attention-based neural network approach to detect abusive speech in online social networks. Our approach enables more effective modeling of context and the semantic relationships between words. We also empirically evaluate the value of text pre-processing techniques in addressing the challenge of out-of-vocabulary words in toxic content. Finally, we conduct extensive experiments on the Wikipedia Talk page datasets, showing improved predictive power over the previous state-of-the-art.

1 Introduction

Over the past few years, there has been increasing attention devoted to the problems of abusive language and hate-based activity in online social networks, with big social media platforms feeling the pressure from governments to perform some moderation of their activities. The AI research community has begun to design automated methods to detect instances of hate speech in these networks, with a primary approach proposing the use of Natural Language Processing (NLP) to perform document classification (Schmidt and Wiegand, 2017).

A major challenge to performing this task is the intentional word and phrase obfuscation done by users to avoid detection (Nobata et al., 2016). Examples such as 'sh*t', '1d10t' and 'banmuslim' are human-readable but difficult to detect using algorithms that rely on keyword spotting. Obfuscation makes context modeling, a challenging problem in NLP, even harder. For example, in the sentences "You feminist cnt" and "I cnt understand this", 'cnt' is used as a shorthand. However, without considering the context, it is difficult to tell whether 'cnt' represents 'cannot' or a derogatory remark.

Early work in hate speech detection used classifiers such as Support Vector Machines and Logistic Regression, with features such as word n-gram counts and the number of insult words (Greevy and Smeaton, 2004; Kwok and Wang, 2013; Mehdad and Tetreault, 2016). With the recent success of deep learning models in solving a variety of classification problems, they have also become the state-of-the-art in detecting abusive speech.

In this paper, we make the following contributions towards detecting hate speech in social networks.

1. We propose the use of attention based deep learning models, the first being the usual word attention layer and the second being a self-targeted co-attention layer that considers the semantic relationships between word pairs.

2. We examine the value of text pre-processing techniques to reduce the number of out-of-vocabulary (OOV) words. We find that pre-processing not only helps to improve the accuracy of existing models, but also improves the proposed attention models.

Our solution addresses the main challenges in detecting abusive content: capturing context to identify important words when making classification decisions, which we achieve through the attention models, and out-of-vocabulary words, which we deal with through preprocessing. Altogether, we improve classification accuracy over the previous state of the art on the Wikipedia Toxicity, Personal Attack, and Aggression datasets (Wulczyn et al., 2017).

In the remainder of this paper, Section 2 discusses related work, Section 3 presents our pre-processing method, Section 4 discusses our deep learning models and the baseline, Section 5

Proceedings of the 10th Workshop on Computational Approaches to Subjectivity, Sentiment and Social Media Analysis, pages 16–24
Minneapolis, June 6, 2019. ©2019 Association for Computational Linguistics

presents experimental results, and Section 6 concludes the paper with directions for future work.

2 Related Work

Among the first to study the problem of online abuse detection were Yin et al. (2009) who focused on harassment on the Web. They used a linear Support Vector Machine (SVM) with character and word n-grams, sentiment, and contextual features of the document (cosine similarity of neighbouring text). One of the first to study hate speech were Djuric et al. (2015) who used comments from the Yahoo Finance website. They learned text embeddings using the neural language model from Le and Mikolov (2014) and used them to train a binary classifier. Nobata et al. (2016) trained a regression model on multiple features such as word and character n-grams, as well as linguistic (e.g., number of hate blacklist words), syntactic (part-of-speech tags) and distributional semantic features (e.g., embeddings). They showed that although best performance was achieved when all features were used together, character n-grams were the most important.

Waseem and Hovy (2016) released a dataset containing 16,000 tweets that were manually labeled as either racist, sexist or clean. They used a Logistic Regression classifier and showed that character n-grams were important features. Working with the same dataset, Badjatiya et al. (2017) were one of the first to apply deep learning. They used a Gradient-Boosted Decision Tree (GDBT) on word embeddings learned using a Recurrent Neural Network (RNN). Also, Gambäck and Sikdar (2017) used Convolutional Neural Networks (CNN) on the same dataset. Furthermore, Park and Fung (2017) used the following two-step process. They first detected whether a tweet was abusive or not, and then, using another classifier, further classified the tweet as racist or sexist. They used a HybridCNN model, which is a variant of CNN that uses both words and characters to make classification decisions.

Wulczyn et al. (2017) created three datasets from the English Wikipedia Talk Page: one annotated for personal attacks, one for toxicity, and one for aggression. Their best model was a multilayer perceptron trained on character n-gram features. Pavlopoulos et al. (2017) then improved the accuracy on the toxicity and personal attack datasets using RNNs. In addition, they released another dataset, with 1.6 million manually annotated user comments from the Greek Sports Portal (Gazzetta), and embeddings trained on this dataset. Mishra et al. (2018) generated embeddings for OOV words and used them with RNNs and character n-gram features on the Twitter and the Wikipedia datasets. Lee et al. (2018) analyzed another dataset released by Founta et al. (2018), which also consists of tweets manually annotated into various categories of abusive speech.

Recently, attention models have been shown to be effective in various areas of NLP such as machine translation (Luong et al., 2015), question answering (Seo et al., 2016), entailment classification (Rocktäschel et al., 2015), and document classification (Yang et al., 2016). The idea is that different words in a sentence can have different relative importance. Attention models help identify this by assigning importance scores to words. However, there has been limited effort on exploring the utility of these models for detecting online abusive speech. One study on moderating user comments (Pavlopoulos et al., 2017) experimented with adding an attention module, and showed benefits for the Greek Sports Portal dataset, but found little improvements for the Wikipedia dataset. Another effort focused on Twitter (Lee et al., 2018) was also unable to see improvements, but since attention works better on longer sentences, this result is not surprising.

Co-attention is a specific kind of attention mechanism that was introduced for the task of Question Answering (QA) to measure the relationship between all pairs of context and query words (Seo et al., 2016; Xiong et al., 2016). Since hate speech detection takes single sentences as input, self targeted co-attention may be more appropriate, whose aim is to model a sentence against itself, and thus extract the relative importance of every word pair. We also take inspiration from a recent work by Tay et al. (2018) who applied a co-attention model for sarcasm detection. The modest effort to date with attention models for abuse detection and the limited success of these efforts provides an important opportunity for us to present a novel approach, with more effective results.

3 Preprocessing Methods

Social media content is noisy: it may contain shorthand, typos, emojis, etc. Furthermore, abusive content may be intentionally obfuscated to avoid detection. However, we found previous work to be inconsistent with the use of text preprocessing techniques and with quantifying their effects. Some approaches, such as Mishra et al. (2018); Pitsilis et al. (2018), applied minimal preprocessing, similar to our baseline defined below. Others, such as Zhang et al. (2018), used additional methods including Twitter tokenizers and normalizing Twitter hashtags. In our view, text preprocessing can be an important factor in improving hate speech detection capabilities and therefore we take on the task of measuring its value. Below, we detail the baseline and the preprocessing technique we use in this work.

std-approach serves as our baseline. It comprises of lower casing the text, light text cleaning such as handling elongated text (e.g., coverting 'yaaaay' to 'yaay'), and removing whitespaces and stop words. For tokenization, we use the standard nltk text tokenizer[1].

adv-approach consists of the following steps:

- **AT**: We replaced the nltk tokenizer with an advanced tokenizer[2] (Baziotis et al., 2017), designed for noisy data from social networks. It handles common emoticons, URLs, dates, and hashtags. It also labels common censored words such as sh*t but does not modify their form, e.g., it converts 'sh*t' to 'sh*t (censored)'.

- **SW**: We remove punctuation and words appearing only once. We also limit words to 50 characters (trimming longer words down to 50 characters). However, in contrast to the std-approach, we do not remove stop words since we observed that pronouns play an important role in hate speech detection (details in Section 5).

- **SC**: We employ a state-of-the-art spelling correction tool (Ekphrasis) to remove typos and obfuscation. However, we only use this tool on words whose suggested corrections are present in our pre-trained word embedding vocabulary (details in Section 5).

- **WS**: We then deal with concatenated words such as 'stupidperson' or 'stupid_person'. The first case can be handled by replacing dashes with spaces and then applying a spell

checker on the segmented words to identify typos. For the second case, we use a word segmenter library (Ekphrasis). Again, we only consider the result of the segmenter if each separated word is part of our embedding vocabulary. As a result, adv-approach cannot identify phrases composed of incorrectly spelled words such as 'bnamuslmis'.

4 Deep Learning Methods

In this section, we describe the deep learning methods for hate speech detection, including baselines and attention models.

4.1 BiRNN

Our first baseline is the Hidden State (HS) method adopted from Mishra et al. (2018). We refer to our modified version as BiRNN. Instead of using two layers of RNNs, we use a single-layer Bidirectional RNN (BiRNN) since it gave better results. A BiRNN consists of two RNNs, one operating on the sequence of words in the forward direction like a standard RNN, and the other going backwards. Each cell in a BiRNN is a GRU (Gated Recurrent Unit) (Chung et al., 2014). The model accepts a sentence as input. First, the embedding layer converts each word into a low dimensional embedding vector, producing a sequence of word embeddings $W \in R^{(n \times d)}$, where n and d denote the number of words in the sentence and the embedding dimension size, respectively. Thus, the sentence can be denoted by $(w_1, w_2, ..., w_n)$ where w_i represents the i_{th} word through its embedding vector. This is given as input to the BiRNN, which creates two sets of hidden states, $\overrightarrow{h}$ and $\overleftarrow{h}$. We concatenate these two hidden states to obtain the final hidden state vector $h \in R^{(n \times 2m)}$ represented as $(h_1, h_2, ..., h_n)$, where m is the number of hidden dimensions of each GRU cell. Finally, we perform a max-pooling over time operation (Collobert and Weston, 2008) over the hidden states to obtain the final representation vector.

4.2 Attn

Our second model is a variant of the attention mechanism originally proposed by Yang et al. (2016) and used by Pavlopoulos et al. (2017) on the same Wikipedia Talk datasets that we use in our experimental evaluation[3]. The intuition be-

---

[1] https://www.nltk.org/
[2] https://github.com/cbaziotis/ekphrasis

[3] However, they did not see any improvements in their results. We suspect this was because their attention model was

hind this attention model is that since not all words contribute equally to a sentence, the model should learn to focus on the important words. This mechanism is applied over the hidden states $(h_1, h_2, ..., h_n)$ of the BiRNN as shown below.

$$u_i = (ReLU(W_w h_i + b_w))$$

$$a = Softmax(u_i^T u_w)$$

$$v = \sum_{i=1}^{n} h_i a_i$$

Here, $W_w \in R^{(2m \times p)}$, $b_w \in R^{(p)}$ and $u_w \in R^{(p \times n)}$ is a context length vector, where m is the number of hidden dimensions of each GRU cell, p is a hyperparameter, and $ReLU$ is a rectified linear unit describing the activation function. All of these weights are learned during the training process. Thus, we obtain the attended hidden state vector v, which is given to the dense layer.

4.3 Co-Attn

Finally, we consider a co-attention model inspired by recent work on sarcasm detection (Tay et al., 2018). However, we propose several modifications. As shown in Figure 1, the model is composed of a co-attention module and a BiRNN. The idea behind co-attention is to learn the semantic relationship between each word pair in the sentence whereas the BiRNN learns the long-range dependencies in the sentence.

We apply the co-attention layer directly on the embedding vectors (we also tested it over the outputs of the BiRNN but obtained worse accuracy). We generate a similarity matrix $S \in R^{(n \times n)}$ to learn the relationships between words, where s_{ij} denotes the score between words e_i and e_j. Our similarity matrix is as follows:

$$s_{ij} = WEW^T$$

where $E \in R^{(d \times d)}$ is a learnable weight matrix, and, as mentioned earlier, $W \in R^{(n \times d)}$ is the word embedding matrix, where n and d denote the length of sentence and embedding dimension size, respectively. We also mask the values in S where $i == j$, so the similarity of a word with respect to itself is not considered. Next, we apply a row-wise average pooling operation to S (as

---

deeper than the one we propose and may have led to overfitting.

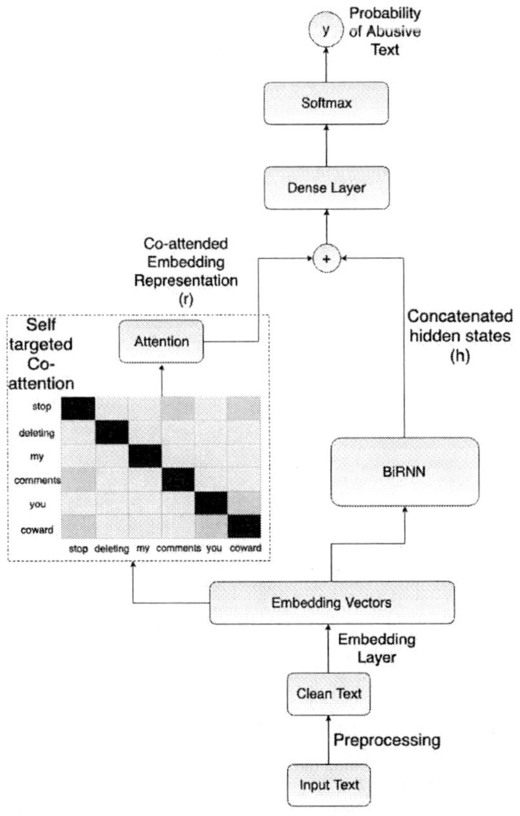

Figure 1: Structure of the Co-Attn model. (Best viewed in color)

compared to max pooling that was originally proposed), which is followed by a Softmax to learn the attention vector a:

$$a = Softmax(avg_{row}(S))$$

where $a \in R^{(n)}$ represents the learned attention weights. Then the attention vector is used to learn the weighted representation $r \in R^{(d)}$ of W, given by the equation below.

$$r = \sum_{i=1}^{n} w_i a_i$$

Now, instead of learning only from the output of the final hidden state of the BiRNN, the classification layer learns from the joint representation of the co-attended embedding representation (r) and the BiRNN last hidden state vector (h_n), as shown below:

$$f = (ReLU(W_f([r; h_n]) + b_f))$$

where $W_f \in R^{((d+2m)\times m)}$ and $b_f \in R^m$. The embedding representation captures relationships between words while the BiRNN captures the sequential information within the sentence.

5 Experiments

For consistency with previous work, our experiments are based on the recently released Wikipedia datasets: Toxicity (W-Tox), Personal Attack (W-At) and Aggression (W-Ag) (Wulczyn et al., 2017). W-Tox contains 159,686 records, while W-At and W-Ag both contain 115,864 records each. These datasets were created by having annotators from the Crowdflower platform label Wikipedia Talk Page comments as toxic or not, personal attack or not, and aggressive or not, respectively. Each comment was judged by multiple annotators, and, in this work, we take the majority vote as the class label. This gives us a binary classification problem. Roughly 10 percent of the comments in each dataset are labelled as toxic, personal attacks or aggressive. For a fair comparison to Mishra et al. (2018), we use a 60:40 training-testing split.

Following Mishra et al. (2018), we use 300-dimensional Glove (Pennington et al., 2014) embedding vectors and we further tune them during training via back-propagation. We create embedding vectors for OOV words with random values in the range ± 0.25. We use 175 as the length of the sequence and we use cross-entropy loss with the Adam optimizer (Kinga and Adam, 2015), with an initial learning rate of 0.001 and L2 regularization of 10^{-6}. Each GRU cell has a hidden dimension size of 150. We experimented with batch sizes of 128, 200 and 256. We implemented all the models in Pytorch (Paszke et al., 2017) and we use the sigmoid output layer in all the models. Our source code is available at `https://github.com/ddhruvkr/Online_Abuse_Detection`

We first evaluate the two methods of pre-processing from Section 3, std-approach and adv-approach. We then evaluate the models from Section 4. To measure the accuracy of the models, we report macro (i.e., average) F1 scores over both classes (labelled "Overall" below) as well as the (micro) F1 scores for just the toxic classes (defined in the standard way, as a harmonic mean of precision and recall). In some experiments, we also report precision (P) and recall (R) individually. For each method, we repeat the experiments five times

Method	W-Tox	W-At / W-Ag
std-approach	13617	10703
adv-approach	3418	2755

Table 1: OOV counts after applying standard and advanced pre-processing techniques.

Method	Overall	Toxic
W-Tox		
std-approach	88.76	79.58
std-approach + AT	89.05	80.19
std-approach + SW	88.95	80.04
std-approach + WS + SC	88.93	79.94
adv-approach	89.47	81.02
W-At		
std-approach	87.08	77.09
std-approach + AT	87.53	77.89
std-approach + SW	87.71	78.27
std-approach + WS + SC	87.41	77.71
adv-approach	88.03	78.89
W-Ag		
std-approach	86.45	76.15
std-approach + AT	86.71	76.63
std-approach + SW	86.86	77.01
std-approach + WS + SC	86.64	76.48
adv-approach	87.22	77.59

Table 2: Overall and toxic F1 score after applying various preprocessing techniques using the BiRNN baseline model.

and report the average.

5.1 Impact of Pre-Processing

We first compare the OOV word count in the data after the simple preprocessing method (std-approach) to after applying additional preprocessing (adv-approach). Table 1 compares the OOV word count after applying the two preprocessing approaches on the three tested datasets. Our advanced preprocessing method reduces the number of OOV words by a factor of 4.

To assess the impact of the different preprocessing steps from Section 3 on classification accuracy, Table 2 shows the Overall average F1 scores and the toxic class F1 scores for the BiRNN model (baseline model). We test the standard approach, the standard approach plus the advanced tokenizer (AT), the standard approach plus punctuation and rare word removal, and stopwords added back (SW), the standard approach plus spellchecking (SC) and segmenting concatenated words (WS),

Method	W-Tox	W-At	W-Ag
Context HS+CNG*	89.35	87.44	-
BiRNN	89.47 ± 0.18	88.03 ± 0.20	87.22 ± 0.23
Attn	89.65 ± 0.15	88.18 ± 0.11	**87.49 ± 0.22**
Co-Attn	**89.76 ± 0.14**	**88.34 ± 0.08**	87.35 ± 0.16

Table 3: Overall Macro F1 scores in the three datasets. * denotes results taken directly from the original papers.

and the advanced approach, which includes all of AT, SW, SC, and WS. In general, the adv-approach outperforms the std-approach on all three tested datasets. In particular, the inclusion of stopwords (SW), specifically pronouns, contributes the most to improving the performance on the W-At and W-Ag datasets. On the other hand, the advanced tokenizer (AT) is the most important preprocessing step for the W-Tox dataset. Word Segmentation (WS) and spelling correction (SC) also improve the scores for all three datasets.

5.2 Impact of Attention Models

The remainder of our experiments examine the value of neural attention models, Attn and Co-Attn, compared to 1) the baseline BiRNN 2) and a variation of the baseline that also uses character n-gram features in addition to a RNN, abbreviated Context-HS+CNG. (Mishra et al., 2018). We include Context-HS+CNG because it is the previous state-of-the-art model on our datasets.

First, to compare overall performance, Table 3 shows the overall macro F1 scores of each tested method on the three datasets. We take the scores of Context HS+CNG directly from the original papers (they did not test it on W-Ag, so we omit this number). Overall, we observe that the baseline model BiRNN with text pre-processing already performs better than the previous state-of-the-art. Applying the attention mechanism (Attn) improves the scores, and the Co-Attn model is even better than Attn on W-Tox and W-At.

In addition to reporting the average macro F1 scores, Table 3 also includes the standard deviation over the five experimental runs. In addition to having the highest scores on W-Tox and W-At, Co-Attn also has the lowest standard deviation.

To obtain further insight into the performance on the minority (toxic, personal attack or aggression) class, we show the micro precision (P), recall (R) and F1 scores for the minority class in Table 4. The attention models outperform the baselines in terms of recall and F1, but not precision. The Co-

Method	P	R	F1
W-Tox			
Context HS+CNG*	**85.42**	76.17	80.53
BiRNN	83.49	78.69	81.02
Attn	83.57	79.04	81.24
Co-Attn	83.67	**79.42**	**81.49**
W-At			
Context HS+CNG*	81.39	74.28	77.67
BiRNN	**83.43**	74.81	78.89
Attn	82.28	76.40	79.23
Co-Attn	81.42	**77.62**	**79.47**
W-Ag			
Context HS+CNG*	-	-	-
BiRNN	**82.32**	73.37	77.59
Attn	81.57	**75.13**	**78.22**
Co-Attn	81.8	74.55	78.01

Table 4: Micro precision, recall and F1 scores for toxic/personal attack/aggression classes.

attn model gives the best F1 score for the W-Tox dataset, improving it by close to one point over the previous state-of-the-art (Context-HS+CNG). For the W-At dataset, Co-Attn also has the highest F1 score, improving the baseline by 1.8 points. For the W-Ag dataset, the Attn model improves the BiRNN baseline by about 0.6 points. Using a paired t-test, we found that the differences between BiRNN and Co-Attn for the W-Tox and W-At datasets and between BiRNN and Attn for the W-Ag dataset are statistically significant using a p value of 0.05.

5.3 Interpretability

A useful feature of attention mechanisms is that they can help interpret the classification decisions made by the models. To do so, we analyze the representations formed by the attention layers. In Table 5, we consider five comments marked as personal attacks in the W-At dataset. We examine examples where both Attn and Co-Attn predicted the correct label and where their prediction

Model	Prediction	Confidence (in%)	Sentence
Attn	Attack	85.13	stop deleting my comments you coward
Co-Attn	Attack	92.42	stop deleting my comments you coward
Attn	Attack	59.04	you queer boy stop messing with my edits
Co-Attn	Attack	82.87	you queer boy stop messing with my edits
Attn	Non-Attack	71.41	hey queer boy stop messing with my edits
Co-Attn	Attack	64.39	hey queer boy stop messing with my edits
Attn	Attack	77.41	thanks for testing my resolution not to refer to anyone as douchebag
Co-Attn	Attack	74.87	thanks for testing my resolution not to refer to anyone as douchebag
Attn	Attack	65.11	thanks for testing my resolution not to refer to anyone as douche bag
Co-Attn	Non-Attack	50.25	thanks for testing my resolution not to refer to anyone as douche bag

Table 5: Visualization of attention maps, predicted class, and the confidence percentage of the two attention models on personal attack (W-At) comments.

was incorrect. We highlight words found to be important (darker shading means the word was more important), and we show the confidence percentage scores, which represent the probability of the class predicted by the models.

For the first sentence, both models give an accurate prediction. The Attn model captures the relationship between "you" and "coward" whereas the Co-Attn model focuses on the word "stop" in addition to "coward". In general, we observed that the Attn model relied heavily on pronouns. We see an example of this in the next two sentences.

For the second sentence, both models correctly predicted the class. The Attn model relies on "you" and "queer". In the third sentence, we replace the word "you" with "hey", and we see that the Attn model incorrectly labels the sentence as not a personal attack. On the other hand, the Co-Attn model is still able to predict the label correctly.

The next two sentences demonstrate where the Co-Attn model breaks. In the fourth sentence, both models are correct in their predictions. However, the Attn model mainly attends to the word "douchebag" whereas Co-attn observes the interaction between the words "anyone" and "douchebag". However, when we modified the sentence by splitting the word "douchebag" into two (last sentence), the Co-Attn model attends to both "anyone" and "bag" along with the word "douche". This results in the model being indecisive and incorrectly predicting that the label is not a personal attack. The confidence score of 50.25% further confirms that the model is uncertain of its prediction. On the other hand, the Attn model still correctly predicts the class as it only focuses on the word "douche". In general, we found that the Co-attn model was able to capture more interactions between words as compared to the Attn model.

6 Conclusions and Future Work

In this paper, we demonstrated the utility of attention models in detecting online abusive speech. We also showed the importance of reducing the number of out-of-vocabulary words through preprocessing techniques. Our experimental results showed that combining text processing with attention mechanisms, both of which aim to filter out as much noise as possible, is more effective than the previous state of the art, especially at predicting the minority (toxic) class.

In future work, we will investigate alternative spell checkers. In the context of hate speech detection, a problem with standard spell checkers is with their handling of profanity. For example, "sh*t" is corrected to "shot" and "b*tch" to "batch". Recent work on context-sensitive spelling correction may be a good starting point for this extension (Gong et al., 2019), although it is not clear if intentional obfuscation should be corrected since it can be a strong indicator of hate speech.

We also plan to investigate the performance of our preprocessing and attention methods on other datasets such as Twitter and Facebook (Waseem and Hovy, 2016; Waseem, 2016; Kumar et al., 2018). As mentioned by Mishra et al. (2018), the Wikipedia datasets that we used in this paper have more standard language and less obfuscation than Twitter datasets. Thus, we expect preprocessing to be important for those datasets as well. We will also study the importance of different preprocessing steps when combined with contextualized character embeddings such as ELMo (Peters et al., 2018).

Another interesting direction for future work is to explore *adversarial training* in hate speech detection. This concept originated in the field of computer vision, and refers to the practice of adding noise to training data so as to make the model resistant to noise in test data (Goodfellow et al., 2015). For example, in computer vision, it was observed that when some calculated noise was added to the training data of an image classification model, the model made an incorrect classification decision even though there was no change to a human eye. It can be argued that intentional obfuscation of hate comments affects hate speech classifiers in a similar way. Recent work found that adversarial training does not completely mitigate these issues in hate speech detection and that character level features are more robust than word level features (Gröndahl et al., 2018). However, more work can be done to explore the potential of this idea.

Finally, Schmidt and Wiegand (2017) point out that little research has been done in the field of hate speech detection in languages other than English. They mention that hate speech could have strong cultural implications and therefore advancing the area of multi-lingual hate speech detection is important. They further state that it remains to be seen that how successful techniques in detecting hate speech in English perform when applied to different languages.

Acknowledgements

We thank Michael Cormier, Mount Allison University, for his input on this paper. We also thank the anonymous reviewers for their valuable comments and suggestions.

References

Pinkesh Badjatiya, Shashank Gupta, Manish Gupta, and Vasudeva Varma. 2017. Deep learning for hate speech detection in tweets. In *Proceedings of the 26th International Conference on World Wide Web Companion*, pages 759–760. International World Wide Web Conferences Steering Committee.

Christos Baziotis, Nikos Pelekis, and Christos Doulkeridis. 2017. Datastories at semeval-2017 task 4: Deep lstm with attention for message-level and topic-based sentiment analysis. In *Proceedings of the 11th International Workshop on Semantic Evaluation (SemEval-2017)*, pages 747–754, Vancouver, Canada. Association for Computational Linguistics.

Junyoung Chung, Caglar Gulcehre, KyungHyun Cho, and Yoshua Bengio. 2014. Empirical evaluation of gated recurrent neural networks on sequence modeling. *arXiv preprint arXiv:1412.3555.*

Ronan Collobert and Jason Weston. 2008. A unified architecture for natural language processing: Deep neural networks with multitask learning. In *Proceedings of the 25th international conference on Machine learning*, pages 160–167. ACM.

Nemanja Djuric, Jing Zhou, Robin Morris, Mihajlo Grbovic, Vladan Radosavljevic, and Narayan Bhamidipati. 2015. Hate speech detection with comment embeddings. In *Proceedings of the 24th international conference on world wide web*, pages 29–30. ACM.

Antigoni Maria Founta, Constantinos Djouvas, Despoina Chatzakou, Ilias Leontiadis, Jeremy Blackburn, Gianluca Stringhini, Athena Vakali, Michael Sirivianos, and Nicolas Kourtellis. 2018. Large scale crowdsourcing and characterization of twitter abusive behavior. In *Twelfth International AAAI Conference on Web and Social Media.*

Björn Gambäck and Utpal Kumar Sikdar. 2017. Using convolutional neural networks to classify hate-speech. In *Proceedings of the First Workshop on Abusive Language Online*, pages 85–90.

Hongyu Gong, Yuchen Li, Suma Bhat, and Pramod Viswanath. 2019. Context-sensitive malicious spelling error correction. *arXiv preprint arXiv:1901.07688.*

Ian J Goodfellow, Jonathon Shlens, and Christian Szegedy. 2015. Explaining and harnessing adversarial examples. corr (2015).

Edel Greevy and Alan F Smeaton. 2004. Classifying racist texts using a support vector machine. In *Proceedings of the 27th annual international ACM SIGIR conference on Research and development in information retrieval*, pages 468–469. ACM.

Tommi Gröndahl, Luca Pajola, Mika Juuti, Mauro Conti, and N Asokan. 2018. All you need is" love": Evading hate-speech detection. *arXiv preprint arXiv:1808.09115.*

D Kinga and J Ba Adam. 2015. A method for stochastic optimization. In *International Conference on Learning Representations (ICLR)*, volume 5.

Ritesh Kumar, Aishwarya N Reganti, Akshit Bhatia, and Tushar Maheshwari. 2018. Aggression-annotated corpus of hindi-english code-mixed data. In *Proceedings of the Eleventh International Conference on Language Resources and Evaluation (LREC-2018).*

Irene Kwok and Yuzhou Wang. 2013. Locate the hate: Detecting tweets against blacks. In *Twenty-seventh AAAI conference on artificial intelligence.*

Quoc Le and Tomas Mikolov. 2014. Distributed representations of sentences and documents. In *International Conference on Machine Learning*, pages 1188–1196.

Younghun Lee, Seunghyun Yoon, and Kyomin Jung. 2018. Comparative studies of detecting abusive language on twitter. *arXiv preprint arXiv:1808.10245*.

Minh-Thang Luong, Hieu Pham, and Christopher D Manning. 2015. Effective approaches to attention-based neural machine translation. *arXiv preprint arXiv:1508.04025*.

Yashar Mehdad and Joel Tetreault. 2016. Do characters abuse more than words? In *Proceedings of the 17th Annual Meeting of the Special Interest Group on Discourse and Dialogue*, pages 299–303.

Pushkar Mishra, Helen Yannakoudakis, and Ekaterina Shutova. 2018. Neural character-based composition models for abuse detection. In *Proceedings of the 2nd Workshop on Abusive Language Online (ALW2)*, pages 1–10.

Chikashi Nobata, Joel Tetreault, Achint Thomas, Yashar Mehdad, and Yi Chang. 2016. Abusive language detection in online user content. In *Proceedings of the 25th international conference on world wide web*, pages 145–153. International World Wide Web Conferences Steering Committee.

Ji Ho Park and Pascale Fung. 2017. One-step and two-step classification for abusive language detection on twitter. In *Proceedings of the First Workshop on Abusive Language Online*, pages 41–45.

Adam Paszke, Sam Gross, Soumith Chintala, Gregory Chanan, Edward Yang, Zachary DeVito, Zeming Lin, Alban Desmaison, Luca Antiga, and Adam Lerer. 2017. Automatic differentiation in pytorch. In *NIPS-W*.

John Pavlopoulos, Prodromos Malakasiotis, and Ion Androutsopoulos. 2017. Deep learning for user comment moderation. In *Proceedings of the First Workshop on Abusive Language Online*, pages 25–35.

Jeffrey Pennington, Richard Socher, and Christopher Manning. 2014. Glove: Global vectors for word representation. In *Proceedings of the 2014 conference on empirical methods in natural language processing (EMNLP)*, pages 1532–1543.

Matthew E Peters, Mark Neumann, Mohit Iyyer, Matt Gardner, Christopher Clark, Kenton Lee, and Luke Zettlemoyer. 2018. Deep contextualized word representations. *arXiv preprint arXiv:1802.05365*.

Georgios K Pitsilis, Heri Ramampiaro, and Helge Langseth. 2018. Detecting offensive language in tweets using deep learning. *arXiv preprint arXiv:1801.04433*.

Tim Rocktäschel, Edward Grefenstette, Karl Moritz Hermann, Tomáš Kočiský, and Phil Blunsom. 2015. Reasoning about entailment with neural attention. *arXiv preprint arXiv:1509.06664*.

Anna Schmidt and Michael Wiegand. 2017. A survey on hate speech detection using natural language processing. In *Proceedings of the Fifth International Workshop on Natural Language Processing for Social Media*, pages 1–10.

Minjoon Seo, Aniruddha Kembhavi, Ali Farhadi, and Hannaneh Hajishirzi. 2016. Bidirectional attention flow for machine comprehension. *arXiv preprint arXiv:1611.01603*.

Yi Tay, Anh Tuan Luu, Siu Cheung Hui, and Jian Su. 2018. Reasoning with sarcasm by reading in-between. In *Proceedings of the 56th Annual Meeting of the Association for Computational Linguistics (Volume 1: Long Papers)*, volume 1, pages 1010–1020.

Zeerak Waseem. 2016. Are you a racist or am i seeing things? annotator influence on hate speech detection on twitter. In *Proceedings of the first workshop on NLP and computational social science*, pages 138–142.

Zeerak Waseem and Dirk Hovy. 2016. Hateful symbols or hateful people? predictive features for hate speech detection on twitter. In *Proceedings of the NAACL student research workshop*, pages 88–93.

Ellery Wulczyn, Nithum Thain, and Lucas Dixon. 2017. Ex machina: Personal attacks seen at scale. In *Proceedings of the 26th International Conference on World Wide Web*, pages 1391–1399. International World Wide Web Conferences Steering Committee.

Caiming Xiong, Victor Zhong, and Richard Socher. 2016. Dynamic coattention networks for question answering. *arXiv preprint arXiv:1611.01604*.

Zichao Yang, Diyi Yang, Chris Dyer, Xiaodong He, Alex Smola, and Eduard Hovy. 2016. Hierarchical attention networks for document classification. In *Proceedings of the 2016 Conference of the North American Chapter of the Association for Computational Linguistics: Human Language Technologies*, pages 1480–1489.

Dawei Yin, Zhenzhen Xue, Liangjie Hong, Brian D Davison, April Kontostathis, and Lynne Edwards. 2009. Detection of harassment on web 2.0. *Proceedings of the Content Analysis in the WEB*, 2:1–7.

Ziqi Zhang, David Robinson, and Jonathan Tepper. 2018. Detecting hate speech on twitter using a convolution-gru based deep neural network. In *European Semantic Web Conference*, pages 745–760. Springer.

Exploring Fine-Tuned Embeddings that Model Intensifiers for Emotion Analysis

Laura Bostan and **Roman Klinger**
Institut für Maschinelle Sprachverarbeitung
University of Stuttgart
Pfaffenwaldring 5b, 70569 Stuttgart, Germany
{laura.bostan, roman.klinger}@ims.uni-stuttgart.de

Abstract

Adjective phrases like "a little bit surprised", "completely shocked", or "not stunned at all" are not handled properly by currently published state-of-the-art emotion classification and intensity prediction systems which use predominantly non-contextualized word embeddings as input. Based on this finding, we analyze differences between embeddings used by these systems in regard to their capability of handling such cases. Furthermore, we argue that intensifiers in context of emotion words need special treatment, as is established for sentiment polarity classification, but not for more fine-grained emotion prediction. To resolve this issue, we analyze different aspects of a post-processing pipeline which enriches the word representations of such phrases. This includes expansion of semantic spaces at the phrase level and sub-word level followed by retrofitting to emotion lexica. We evaluate the impact of these steps with À La Carte and Bag-of-Substrings extensions based on pretrained GloVe, Word2vec, and fastText embeddings against a crowd-sourced corpus of intensity annotations for tweets containing our focus phrases. We show that the fastText-based models do not gain from handling these specific phrases under inspection. For Word2vec embeddings, we show that our post-processing pipeline improves the results by up to 8% on a novel dataset densely populated with intensifiers.

1 Introduction

Emotion detection in text includes tasks of mapping words, sentences, and documents to a discrete set of emotions following a psychological model such as those proposed by Ekman (1992) and Plutchik (1980), or to intensity scores or continuous values of *valence–arousal–dominance* (Posner et al., 2005). The shared task on intensity prediction for discrete classes proposed to combine both (Mohammad et al., 2018; Mohammad and Bravo-Marquez, 2017a). In this task a tweet and an emotion are given and the goal is to determine an intensity score between 0 and 1.

Especially, but not only in social media, users use degree adverbs (also called intensifiers Quirk, 1985), for instance in "I am *kinda happy*" vs. "I am *very happy*." to express different levels of emotion intensity. This is a relevant task: 10% of tweets containing an emotion word are modified with such an adverb in the corpus we describe in Section 3.1. In this paper, we challenge the assumption that models developed for intensity prediction perform well on tweets containing such phrases and analyze which of the established embedding methods Word2vec (Mikolov et al., 2013), GloVe (Pennington et al., 2014), and fastText embeddings (Bojanowski et al., 2017) performs well when predicting intensities for tweets containing such phrases. We will see that the performance of the popular and fast-to-train Word2vec method can be increased with a simple postprocessing pipeline which we present in this paper.

As a motivating example, the DeepMoji model (Felbo et al., 2017) predicts *anger* for both the example sentences "I am not angry." and "I am angry."[1]. Using the model by Wu et al. (2018) (one of the state-of-the-art intensity prediction models from Mohammad et al. (2018), building their model on top of Word2vec embeddings) we also obtain *anger* as having the highest intensity for both examples. We argue that the models should be more sensitive to the difference between *negations*, *downtoners* and *amplifiers*.

With this paper, we contribute to alleviate this situation in three aspects. Firstly, we provide an analysis of the distribution of degree adverbs (in-

---

[1] https://deepmoji.mit.edu

Proceedings of the 10th Workshop on Computational Approaches to Subjectivity, Sentiment and Social Media Analysis, pages 25–34
Minneapolis, June 6, 2019. ©2019 Association for Computational Linguistics

cluding negations) with emotion words and show that not all such combinations are equally common. Secondly, we perform a crowdsourcing experiment in which we collect scores for different combinations of degree adverbs and emotion adjectives. We use these data, which we make publicly available, as an additional challenging test set for the task of intensity prediction for English. Thirdly, we use a state-of-the-art intensity prediction model (Wu et al., 2018) on this test set and evaluate two methods to improve these predictions, namely the inclusion (Zhao et al., 2018) and n-gram embeddings via À La Carte of additional subword information with Bag-of-Substrings (Khodak et al., 2018). We evaluate based on Word2vec, GloVe and fastText embeddings and show that particularly the first two benefit from these changes, but to different extents.

2 Related Work

2.1 Degree Adverbs in Linguistics

Adverbs that express intensity are named *degree adverbs*, *degree modifiers* or *intensifiers*.[2] The entities they intensify are located on an abstract scale of intensity (Quirk, 1985). The intensifiers that scale upward are named amplifiers and are further categorised as maximizers, such as "completely" and "totally" or boosters, such as "really" or "truly". Those that scale downward are called downtoners and are further classified as approximators, such as "almost" or "kind of", compromisers, such as "fairly", "pretty" and "quite", diminishers, such as "slightly" and "a bit", and minimizers (Quirk, 1985; Paradis, 1997; Nevalainen and Rissanen, 2002, *i. a.*). Further distinction of degree modifiers is concerned with the fact that there are intensifiers that imply boundaries, such as "totally", "fully", and "completely" and those that do not, such as "very", "utterly", "pretty" (Paradis, 1997, 2001, 2000). Finally, in the context of discourse, there is the property of expressing focus, which is present in the so-called *focus modifiers*, such as "only" and "just", which are also further classified in additives, such as "also" and "too" and restrictives, such as "only" and "merely" (Quirk, 1985; Athanasiadou, 2007).

English degree modifiers have also long history of research in English studies and more generally in Language Studies. Most English studies focus on the incidence and distribution of these adverbs in different corpora, e.g. Peters (1994) study letters

---

²In this paper, we will use these terms interchangeably.

from Early Modern English and shows the how the distributions of boosters change across time. Nevalainen (2008) study the social variation in intensifier use, with a focus on the suffix *-ly*. More recently, Napoli and Ravetto (2017) collect a volume of papers that explore the process of intensification following a corpus-based, cross-linguistic and contrastive approach. The volume contains various works on the variation in the distribution and incidence of the intensifiers based on sociolinguistic features and in a diachronic fashion. The work brings in attention intensification in ancient languages as well as modern languages.

A more recent work investigates the differences in the use of intensifiers and considers English speech of adults and teenagers as corpus. It explores two maximizers in-depth, namely "absolutely" and "totally" and shows that those prove to be more "flexible" in the language used by teenagers (Pertejo and Martínez, 2014).

2.2 Modifiers in the context of Sentiment and Emotion Analysis

In the context of sentiment analysis the discussion of intensifiers and negations has gained quite some attention, since those are primarily markers of subjectivity (Athanasiadou, 2007).

Negations, and in particular negation cue detection (with the goal of scope recognition) have been the research interest of Councill et al. (2010) and Reitan et al. (2015), who use a lexicon for negation cue detection and a linear-chain conditional random field for scope recognition. In the area of distributional semantics, the investigation of word vectors with a focus on negated adjectives (Aina et al., 2018) is complementary to our work with regards to negation in terms of the methods and data used. Following this approach, one could build a distributional semantic model whose vocabulary includes the modified phrases. In practice, each occurrence of a modified adjective by a degree adverb could be treated as a single token (*e. g.* "not happy" would be represented as "not_happy"). For a general overview of modality and negation in computational linguistics we refer the interested reader to the work by Morante and Sporleder (2012).

Furthermore, Zhu et al. (2014) study the effect of negation words on sentiment and evaluate a neural composition model. Kiritchenko and Mohammad (2016a) create a sentiment lexicon of phrases that include modifiers such as negators, modals, and degree adverbs. The phrases and their constituent words are annotated manually with the same annotation procedure we will discuss in detail. We follow this work closely and apply the same procedures in the context of emotion analysis.

Dragut and Fellbaum (2014) study the effect of intensifiers on the sentiment ratings and shows that the degree adverbs do not carry an inherent sentiment polarity but alter the degree of the polarity of the constituents they modify.

We argue that there is not enough work on transferring the methods used in sentiment analysis to the more fine-grained analysis of emotions, except for Strohm and Klinger (2018), who limit themselves to analysis and do not apply state-of-the-art prediction models for handling degree adverbs, and Carrillo-de Albornoz and Plaza (2013) who consider modified emotions but predict sentiment.

3 Methods

In the following, we explain how we create the data sets for our analysis (Section 3.1) and then how we set up the experiments to measure the impact of À La Carte and Bag-of-Substrings on the modified phrases (Section 3.2).

3.1 Data Collection and Annotation

As a basis of our work, we create a compositional emotion lexicon for English Twitter and retrieve crowdsourced ratings using *Best-Worst Scaling* (Louviere et al., 2015; Kiritchenko and Mohammad, 2016b). We show later that these ratings are by and large independent of context and can therefore be interpreted as a labeled emotion lexicon of compositional phrases.[3]

3.1.1 Data Collection

Each query we use to retrieve tweets consists of a pair of an adjective with one or a combination of several degree adverbs (intensifiers (including amplifiers and downtoners) and negations), for instance "not at all surprised" or "not very happy". We first generate a comprehensive list by mapping each of Ekman's fundamental emotions (Ekman, 1992) to their corresponding adjective *sad, happy, disgusted, afraid, surprised, angry* and augment this list to 333 emotion adjectives and their synonyms from the Oxford Dictionary of English

(Ehrlich, 1980), the New Oxford American Dictionary (Stevenson and Lindberg, 2010) and Macmillan Online English Dictionary[4] and further filter this list to 43 entries which are intersubjectively agreeable. This filter step is performed via crowdsourcing on Prolific[5], in which we asked native speakers of English which emotion is the closest to each synonym. We only keep those synonyms where all annotators agreed. The inter-annotator agreement is $\kappa = 0.63$ (Fleiss' κ over 9 annotators).

The list of degree modifiers is a combination of Quirk (1985); Paradis (1997); Strohm and Klinger (2018). From the cartesian product of degree modifiers with emotion adjectives, we keep those which we find at least 10 times in the general Twitter corpus we discuss below. That leads to 266 phrases.

We base our analysis on a set of 32 million tweets obtained from Twitter with the official API between March 2006 and October 2018, using a combination of diverse search terms corresponding to isolated emotion word synonyms, those in combination with degree adverbs, and frequent hashtags. We filter out retweets and full quotes, tweets with more than 140 characters and those with less than 10 tokens, as well as those consisting of more than 30% hashtags, links, or usernames, which we replace by generic respective tokens otherwise. Tweets with more than 30% of non-ASCII characters are also removed.

3.1.2 Annotation Procedure

For each tweet (t) and emotion (e) we obtain emotion intensity scores $s_{t,e} \in [-1, 1]$ via *Best-Worst Scaling* (BWS, Louviere et al., 2015). In general with BWS, the annotators are shown a subset of a number of items from a list and are asked to select the *best and worst* items (or most and least some given property of interest). Within our study, we show four items at once to the annotators. In a first setting, we show them four tweets that contain the queries we want to have scores assigned for. In a second setting, we show them only the queries without the context (the tweet) in which they were found. In both scenarios, the annotators need to select the tweet or the query with the highest and lowest intensity of each emotion.

These groups of tweets are sampled under following constraints that have been empirically

---

[3]Our data is available at https://www.ims.uni-stuttgart.de/data/modifieremotion.

[4]http://www.macmillandictionaries.com/dictionary-online/
[5]https://prolific.ac

1. I'm really sad there's barely any Little Witch Academia content on Twitter dot com,, it's my favorite anime in years stop sleeping on it

2. Actually really scared about how much my hair is falling out.. 😔

3. <username> She just has very watery eyes but don't worry she's a very happy little doggo just ask <username>

4. happy 2 months to the boy who had made me so happy 🖤 🖤 <link>

Q1. Which of the four tweets expresses JOY the MOST? (required)

1	2	3	4
○	○	○	○

Q2. Which of the four tweets expresses JOY the LEAST? (required)

1	2	3	4
○	○	○	○

Q3. Which of the four tweets expresses SADNESS the MOST? (required)

1	2	3	4
○	○	○	○

Q4. Which of the four tweets expresses SADNESS the LEAST? (required)

1	2	3	4
○	○	○	○

Figure 1: An example of what contributors see on the Figure Eight Platform. The 4 sentences shown are an example of a group of four tweets the contributors have to annotate. The questions Q1 to Q4 that follow below are a subset of the questionnaire.

proven to lead to reliable scores (Kiritchenko and Mohammad, 2016c), resulting in 532 samples (twice the amount of queries): (1) no two samples have the same four queries (in any order), (2) no two queries within a sample are identical, (3) each query occurs in 8 ($\pm$1) different samples, (4) each pair of queries appears in the same number of samples. We perform two annotation experiments on the crowdsourcing platform Figure Eight[6]: In Experiment 1, we present the whole tweet to the annotator, in Experiment 2, we only show the query phrase. This enables us to evaluate the importance of context, shown in Section 4.2. Each sample was annotated by three contributors that confirmed to be English native speakers.

3.2 Adaptations of Embeddings

In the following, we discuss the three methods to improve the embeddings and later to test if these improvements add additional information with respect to intensifiers for emotion analysis. The evaluation will be on the downstream task of emotion intensity prediction.

We focus on subword-level information and phrase-level information, as those, presumably, capture intensity information.

[6] https://www.figure-eight.com

3.2.1 À La Carte

With this method we learn a representation of yet unseen phrases within an embedding space through a linear transformation of the average of the word embeddings in the feature's contexts. The method constructs a representation for a new phrase given a set of contexts where this phrase occurs in.

Given our Twitter corpus $\mathcal{C}_w$ consisting of contexts of words w and the pre-trained word embeddings $\mathbf{v}_w \in \mathbb{R}^d$, of dimension d, our goal is to construct a representation $\mathbf{v}_q \in \mathbb{R}^d$ of a query q given a set $\mathcal{C}_q$ of contexts it occurs in.

We learn the transform $\mathbf{A} \in \mathbb{R}^{d \times d}$ that can recover *existing* word vectors $\mathbf{v}_w$ via *linear regression* by summing their context embeddings

$$\mathbf{v}_w \approx \mathbf{A} \left(\frac{1}{|\mathcal{C}_w|} \sum_{c \in \mathcal{C}_w} \sum_{w' \in c} \mathbf{v}'_w \right). \tag{1}$$

Using the learned transformation matrix $\mathbf{A}$ we can embed any new query $\mathbf{v}_q$ in the same semantic space as the pre-trained word embeddings via

$$\mathbf{v}_q = \mathbf{A} \left(\frac{1}{|\mathcal{C}_q|} \sum_{c \in \mathcal{C}_q} \sum_{w \in c} \mathbf{v}_w \right). \tag{2}$$

3.2.2 Bag-of-Substrings

BoS generalizes pre-trained semantic spaces to unseen words. The established approach to represent word phrases or sentences is to take a bag of words of word embeddings.

BoS achieves its goal by first learning a mapping between the subwords present in each word and its corresponding pre-trained vector. Then, by using this learned subword transformation, the model is able to generate new representations for any new word as a set of its character n-grams. For us this is relevant, since we can consider our focus phrases to be character n-grams instead of word n-grams.

Formally, the representation for a word $\mathbf{v}_w$ from the lookup table V (which stores the embeddings of dimension d for each possible substring of length within a range) is:

$$\mathbf{v}_w = \frac{1}{|\mathcal{S}_w|} \sum_{t \in \mathcal{S}_w} \mathbf{v}_t, \tag{3}$$

where $\mathcal{S}_w$ is the set of each possible character n-grams of length within a given range over w and $\mathbf{v}_t$ is the vector in V indexed by t.

The model views the vector of a phrase as the average vector of all its substrings, which are trained by minimizing the overall mean squared loss between the generated and given vectors for each word:

$$\min_V \frac{1}{|W|} \sum_{w \in W} l\left(\frac{1}{|\mathcal{S}_w|} \sum_{t \in \mathcal{S}_w} \mathbf{v}_t, \mathbf{u}_w \right) \quad (4)$$

where $\mathbf{u}_w \in \mathbb{R}^{d \times |W|}$ are the target vectors of the dimension d over the vocabulary W and $l(\mathbf{v}, \mathbf{u}) = \frac{1}{2}\|\mathbf{v} - \mathbf{u}\|_2^2$.

After training, similarly to the previous method, one can use the learned space to generate a new word vector $\mathbf{v}_q$ as the average of the vectors of all of its substrings through Equation 3.

Since BoS produces vectors for unknown words from vectors of substrings of characters contained in it, this allows to build vectors for misspelled words and concatenation of words. Particularly on Twitter data, we benefit from getting a representation for phrases like "soooexcited:)", "verrry cheerful", "soo unhappy:(". Relevant for our analysis is that BoS uses special characters to mark the start and the end of the word and thus helps the model to distinguish morphemes that occur at different word parts, like prefixes or suffixes. Through that we learn to distinguish morphemes like "un-", "-er" and "-est" that are part of our focus phrases.

Note that this method uses the same idea as in fastText (Bojanowski et al., 2017), but is for our case computationally more efficient, since the BoS model is trained directly on top of pre-trained vectors, instead of predicting over text corpora.

3.2.3 Retrofitting

We use the method of retrofitting existing embeddings (Faruqui et al., 2015) in order to enrich word vectors using synonymity constraints provided by semantic lexicons. The algorithm learns the word embedding matrix $A = \{\mathbf{v}_1, \mathbf{v}_2, \ldots, \mathbf{v}_n\}$ with the objective function:

$$\Psi(A) = \sum_{i \in V} [\alpha_i \|\mathbf{v}_i - \hat{\mathbf{v}}_i\|^2 + \sum_{(i,j) \in E} \beta_{ij} \|\hat{\mathbf{v}}_i - \hat{\mathbf{v}}_j\|^2] \quad (5)$$

where an original word vector is $\mathbf{v}_i$, its synonym vector is $\mathbf{v}_j$, and inferred word vector is $\hat{\mathbf{v}}_i$.

Our lexicon of synonymity constraints was automatically constructed from the data we collected in Section 3.1.1 by adding an entry for each emotion adjective with its synonyms crowdsourced as previously described. We also added entries for

Focus phrase	joy	sadness	anger	fear	surprise	disgust
so happy	+.73	−.43	−.50	−.51	−.10	−.66
not happy	−.52	+.41	+.02	−.16	−.11	+.17
kinda happy	+.53	−.70	−.67	−.55	−.47	−.76
so sad	−.50	+.66	+.04	+.13	−.16	+.03
not sad	+.55	−.60	−.57	−.55	−.45	−.52
kinda sad	−.41	+.62	−.02	+.02	−.18	+.02
so angry	−.39	+.26	+.86	+.21	+.02	+.63
not angry	+.40	−.36	−.82	−.17	−.27	−.45
kinda angry	−.80	+.68	+.84	+.32	+.08	+.64
so scared	−.07	+.15	−.21	+.83	+.15	−.13
not scared	+.35	−.35	−.28	−.66	−.53	−.33
kinda scared	+.03	+.10	−.03	+.71	−.13	−.13
so surprised	+.34	−.27	−.09	+.02	+.81	.00
not surprised	+.60	−.56	−.50	−.60	−.83	−.60
kinda surprised	+.37	−.37	−.17	+.01	+.72	−.20
so disgusted	−.11	−.02	+.30	+.16	+.33	+.88
not disgusted	+.42	−.39	−.42	−.36	−.36	−.84
kinda disgusted	−.16	+.08	+.41	−.01	+.08	+.80

Table 1: Example queries with their BWS crowdsourced scores for the modifiers "so", "kinda" and the negation "not". For every focus phrase we have an intensity score between −1 and +1 for each emotion. The focus phrases are shown in groups made around the emotion adjectives.

the phrases in the lexicon for retrofitting, as follows, for each emotion phrase according to the intensifiers classification described in Section 2.1. For instance, "not happy" had as an entry in the lexicon the phrases "unhappy" and "not happy at all" while "completely cheerful" had in its entry phrases like "totally cheerful", "totally happy", "completely happy", among others (since "completely" and "totally" are in the same class). We apply retrofitting on phrases which origin from the extension of the space with À La Carte.

4 Results

In the following, we explore the Twitter corpus described previously, the results of the BWS annotation of the pairs of degree adverbs and adjectives, and finally we discuss our experimental setting and evaluation on the downstream task of emotion intensity prediction on the different embedding adaptation methods.

4.1 Corpus Analysis

The Twitter corpus described in Section 3.1 contains 34,297,941 tweets out of which 2,948,397 contain emotion phrases. Most dominant are amplifiers (49%) followed by downtoners (24%) and negations (19%). Only 8% contain the emotion adjectives in superlative or comparative.

Figure 2 shows how often the top 30 modifiers are used with adjectives from the basic set of emotions. We see that *disgust* is rarely downtoned and *anger*, *sadness*, and *surprise* are amplified most often. *Joy* and *fear* are relatively equally amplified, with *joy* being more negated and *fear* being more downtoned. The amplifiers "so" and "really", as well as the downtoners "just" and "kind of/kinda" are frequently used. The downtoner "just" is the most frequently used downtoner and acts at times as an amplifier, which could explain its frequent use. We hypothesize that this is due to their use as fillers and their grammaticalization (cf. Tagliamonte, 2006). Most frequently downtoned emotion is *surprise* (which is often used in phrases like "a little surprised", "quite surprised", "a bit surprised").

In Figure 3 and Figure 4 we observe that the use of modifiers with respect to an emotion vary a lot within the same class of modifiers among both more frequent and less frequent modifiers. In Figure 3, we observe that the focus modifier "only" scales downward *surprise* the least, while all the other "true" scaling adverbs are more impactful. *Sadness* is the emotion that is mostly expressed through the focus adverb "only" in this setting. The figure also (implicitly) shows that certain modifiers prefer certain adjectives, e.g. the adjectives that express *disgust*, such as "disgusted" is mostly modified by "absolutely", "truly", "utterly", "pretty" and not by "extremely", "incredibly" or "only". This distinction show the "harmony" between adjectives and degree adverbs (Quirk, 1985).

Looking in more depth into the most frequent used amplifiers and downtoners in Figure 4 we see that among the top used amplifiers "so", "really", "very" we find that *joy*, *anger*, and *disgust* prefer "so" over "really" and "very", the emotions *fear* and *surprise* prefer "very" over "so" and "really" and *sadness* is modified rather equally by the three amplifiers. Between the downtoners "kind of" and "kinda" there is a notable difference in use for *sadness*, *fear* and *anger*, with "kind of" being prefered over "kinda" in the context of *sadness*, with the opposite holding true for *fear*.

4.2 Annotation Analysis

Table 1 shows examples of phrases annotated with real-valued scores following the annotation pro-

	Spearman's rank correlation		
Emotion	*w/ context*	*w/o context*	*between*
anger	.84	.82	.88
fear	.84	.73	.81
joy	.90	.86	.91
sadness	.90	.86	.88
surprise	.71	.71	.81
disgust	.86	.86	.88
average	.84	.80	.86

Table 2: Split-half reliabilities and Spearman's rank correlation between these settings.

cedure described in Section 3.1. We see that we have scores for each phrase in the context of each emotion. For instance, "kinda surprised" has the score $-.37$ for *sadness* and $+.17$. We observe that the negation "not" paired with any emotion adjective, excluding *happy* obtains a positive score for *joy*, and a negative score for every other emotion. The phrase "not happy" obtains a negative score of only $-.52$. In the complete annotation results we include as negations also the phrase "not happy at all", which in this case gets closer to the lower limit of the potential scores.

We measure the reliability by randomly dividing the sets of 4 responses to each question into two halves and comparing the Spearman rank correlation coefficient between the two sets (Kiritchenko and Mohammad, 2016b). Both with and without having access to context, the annotators mostly agree regarding their annotations, as Table 2 shows in the first two columns. Lowest reliability is achieved for *surprise*, with .71 Spearman's rank correlation and the highest for *joy* and *sadness* (.9). The reliability drops most when context is not available for fear (by 11 percentage points).

Figure 5 shows the distribution of the scores assigned through the annotation per emotion. We observe that *disgust* is mostly amplified and rarely negated (only once). The outliers in each boxplot mostly correspond to negated phrases.

4.3 Embedding Adaptations

Figure 6 summarizes our experimental setup. We build on top of pretrained embeddings obtained with Word2vec (Mikolov et al., 2013) (300d, negative sampling, Google News corpus), fastText (Bojanowski et al., 2017) (300d, news corpora), or GloVe (Pennington et al., 2014) (300d, Com-

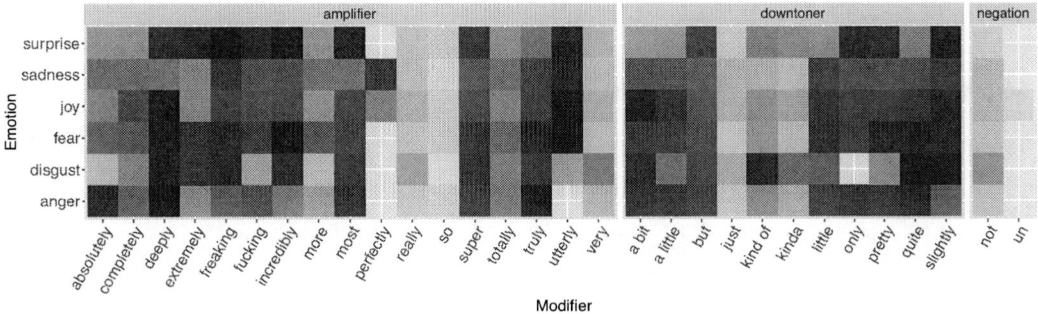

Figure 2: Relative frequencies of the most common 30 modifiers in the Twitter Corpus (from dark (infrequent) to yellow (frequent).

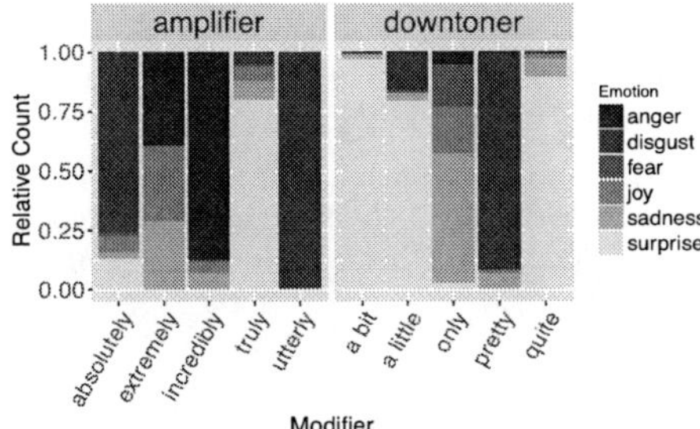

Figure 3: Amplifiers and downtoners that vary the most in use with regards to emotion

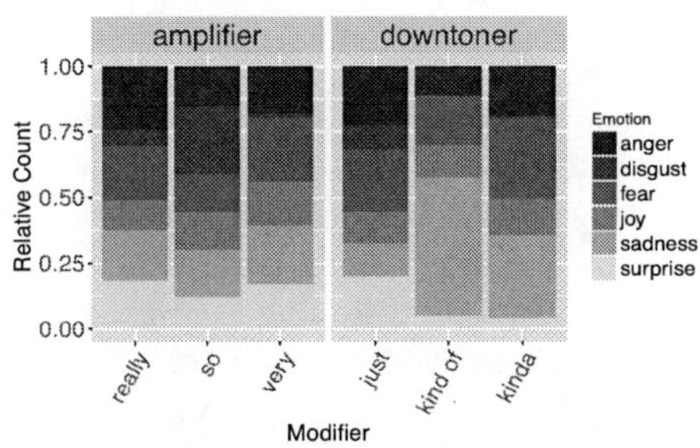

Figure 4: Most frequent three amplifiers and downtoners used across all emotions and their variation with respect to emotion.

mon Crawl). Each embedding is then optionally augmented with phrase and subword embeddings and fed into a CNN-LSTM model as proposed by Wu et al. (2018), trained on the Affect in Tweets Dataset used at Sem Eval 2018 Task 1 (Mohammad et al., 2018). Their system achieved an average Pearson correlation score of 0.722, and ranked 12/48 in the emotion intensity regression task.

Table 3 shows Spearman's rank correlation between the predicted intensity scores and the emotion scores obtained in the annotation of our Twitter

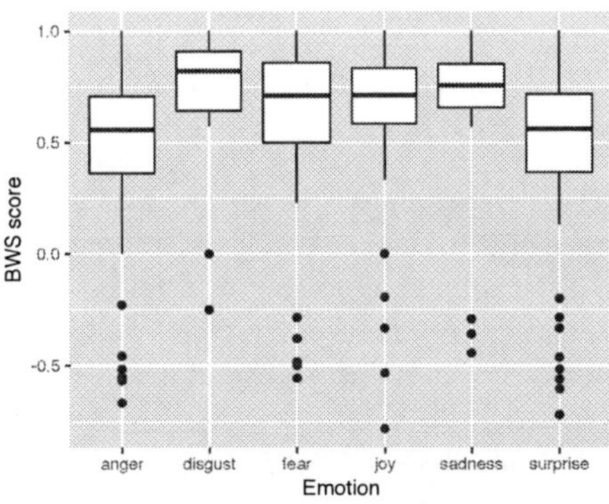

Figure 5: Distribution of the aggregated emotion scores obtained by applying the counting procedure BWS

corpus or the EmoInt data (Mohammad and Bravo-Marquez, 2017b).

The fastText-based models underperform constantly on our Twitter dataset. For GloVe embeddings, À La Carte (ALC) and Bag-of-Substrings (BoS) lead to a substantial improvement, of 7pp (see Table 3, G vs. G+ALC) and 8pp (G vs. G+BoS) over the baseline of using the pretrained embeddings unchanged. On Word2vec embeddings BoS and ALC show the same improvement of 7pp (W2V vs. W2V+ALC/BoS).

While on average, ALC and BoS can only substantially contribute based on GloVe and Word2vec, this is not the case for individual emotions. For Word2vec, sadness figures to be particularly challenging, leading to an overall comparably low performance. Most importantly, we observe that our extensions of the semantic spaces do not negatively affect the results on the EmoInt dataset.

Unexpectedly, retrofitting does not help in all settings in our post-processing pipeline except for

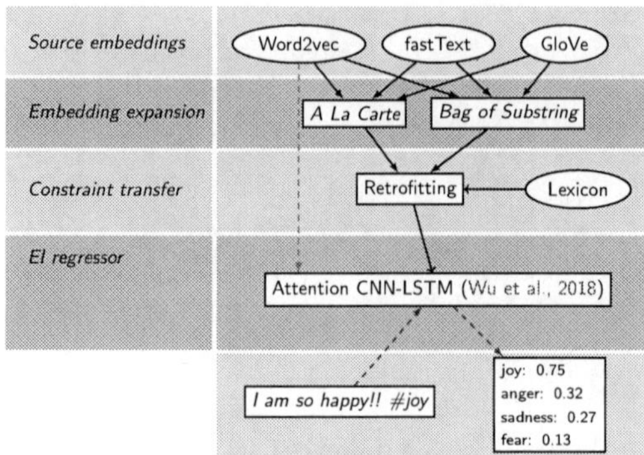

Figure 6: Experimental Setup. The green arrow from Word2vec to the regressor unit shows the information flow in the baseline. The black solid arrows show the different experimental settings. The purple dashed arrows at the bottom show the prediction phase.

	joy		sadness		anger		fear		average	
	T	EI	T	EI	T	EI	T	EI	T	EI
G	.20	.60	.21	.59	.24	.60	.27	.61	.23	.60
G+ALC	.23	.61	.31	.63	.33	.62	.35	.62	.30	.63
G+BoS	.24	.58	.30	.60	.34	.59	.36	.57	.31	.59
G+ALC+RF	.19	.60	.21	.61	.26	.63	.28	.61	.24	.61
G+BoS+RF	.19	.62	.21	.60	.28	.62	.25	.61	.23	.61
W2V	.16	.60	.12	.59	.19	.60	.23	.63	.18	.62
W2V+ALC	.20	.60	.24	.64	.28	.65	.28	.64	.25	.63
W2V+BoS	.20	.61	.23	.64	.28	.66	.29	.60	.25	.64
W2V+ALC+RF	.21	.60	.25	.54	.28	.69	.28	.64	.26	.62
W2V+BoS+RF	.16	.60	.12	.61	.24	.67	.20	.60	.18	.63
FT	.16	.58	.14	.53	.21	.65	.22	.60	.18	.61
FT+ALC	.16	.59	.14	.52	.21	.59	.23	.62	.19	.59
FT+BoS	.16	.60	.14	.59	.22	.63	.23	.61	.18	.62
FT+ALC+RF	.18	.54	.16	.62	.22	.64	.25	.59	.20	.60
FT+ BoS+RF	.16	.60	.14	.57	.22	.62	.21	.57	.18	.63

Table 3: Evaluation: Spearman's rank correlation between predicted emotion intensity scores and annotated scores on our dataset (T) or the EmoInt dataset (EI). We report results only for the 4 emotions annotated in the EmoInt data.

fastText embeddings. We assume that is a consequence of using a too small lexicon for retrofitting, and the method would improve the embeddings if sentiment or emotion lexicons would be used instead. However, this needs further investigation.

5 Conclusion & Future Work

With this paper, we presented the first analysis of the distribution of degree adverbs and negations on Twitter in the context of emotions. In addition, we proposed a pipeline with different modules to expand embeddings particularly for emotion phrases. Our evaluation shows substantial differences based on the combination of input embeddings and the postprocessing method. Our pipeline improves the results obtained while evaluating the downstream task of emotion intensity prediction on our dataset. Finally, we contribute a novel emotion phrase lexicon of high precision.

For future work we propose to analyze other baseline approaches, particularly learning a composition function over pairs of adjectives with degree adverbs. The modifiers could be considered as functions over adjectives and would be represented as matrices.

Another further improvement of this work would be to expand this analysis to verbal and nominal expressions of emotion, which we hypothesize as also being frequent. In order to obtain meaningful representations for the phrases we focus on, another natural next step is expanding the postprocessing pipeline and including a comparison to other adaptation methods such as counterfitting (Mrkšić et al., 2016). Presumably, this will also generate additional insights into the aspect that we were only able to show a limited improvement based on retrofitting.

Given the recent advances in representing contextualized word embeddings as functions computing dynamically the embeddings for words given their context, we hypothesize and intend to further verify that these embeddings would be a better choice for input to systems that predict intensity scores. It would be interesting to compare models such as word embeddings from language models (Elmo) (Peters et al., 2018), bidirectional encoder representations from transformers (BERT) (Devlin et al., 2018), and generative pre-training OpenAI (GPT) (Radford et al., 2019) to the ones we already discussed, since the contextualized embeddings assign a different vector for a word in each given context. These approaches presumably produce a different vector for "happy" in the context of "not" than in the content of "very" or "completely".

Lastly, we plan to also adjust the lexica created such that it covers more domains, sources, and languages.

Acknowledgements

This research has been funded by the German Research Council (DFG), projects SEAT (Structured Multi-Domain Emotion Analysis from Text, KL

2869/1-1). We thank Jeremy Barnes, Evgeny Kim, Sean Papay, Sebastian Padó and Enrica Troiano for fruitful discussions and the reviewers for the helpful comments.

References

Laura Aina, Raffaella Bernardi, and Raquel Fernández. 2018. A distributional study of negated adjectives and antonyms. In *Proceedings of CLiC-it 2018 the 5th Italian Conference on Computational Linguistics*.

Jorge Carrillo-de Albornoz and Laura Plaza. 2013. An emotion-based model of negation, intensifiers, and modality for polarity and intensity classification. *Journal of the American Society for Information Science and Technology*, 64(8):1618–1633.

Angeliki Athanasiadou. 2007. On the subjectivity of intensifiers. *Language sciences*, 29(4):554–565.

Piotr Bojanowski, Edouard Grave, Armand Joulin, and Tomas Mikolov. 2017. Enriching word vectors with subword information. *Transactions of the Association for Computational Linguistics*, 5:135–146.

Isaac Councill, Ryan McDonald, and Leonid Velikovich. 2010. What's great and what's not: learning to classify the scope of negation for improved sentiment analysis. In *Proceedings of the Workshop on Negation and Speculation in Natural Language Processing*, pages 51–59. University of Antwerp.

Jacob Devlin, Ming-Wei Chang, Kenton Lee, and Kristina Toutanova. 2018. Bert: Pre-training of deep bidirectional transformers for language understanding. *arXiv preprint arXiv:1810.04805*.

Eduard Dragut and Christiane Fellbaum. 2014. The role of adverbs in sentiment analysis. In *Proceedings of Frame Semantics in NLP: A Workshop in Honor of Chuck Fillmore (1929-2014)*, pages 38–41. Association for Computational Linguistics.

E. Ehrlich. 1980. *Oxford American Dictionary*. Oxford University Press.

Paul Ekman. 1992. An argument for basic emotions. *Cognition & emotion*, 6(3-4):169–200.

Manaal Faruqui, Jesse Dodge, Sujay Kumar Jauhar, Chris Dyer, Eduard Hovy, and Noah A. Smith. 2015. Retrofitting word vectors to semantic lexicons. In *Proceedings of the 2015 Conference of the North American Chapter of the Association for Computational Linguistics: Human Language Technologies*, pages 1606–1615. Association for Computational Linguistics.

Bjarke Felbo, Alan Mislove, Anders Søgaard, Iyad Rahwan, and Sune Lehmann. 2017. Using millions of emoji occurrences to learn any-domain representations for detecting sentiment, emotion and sarcasm.

In *Proceedings of the 2017 Conference on Empirical Methods in Natural Language Processing*, pages 1615–1625, Copenhagen, Denmark. Association for Computational Linguistics.

Mikhail Khodak, Nikunj Saunshi, Yingyu Liang, Tengyu Ma, Brandon Stewart, and Sanjeev Arora. 2018. A la carte embedding: Cheap but effective induction of semantic feature vectors. In *Proceedings of the 56th Annual Meeting of the Association for Computational Linguistics (Volume 1: Long Papers)*, pages 12–22. Association for Computational Linguistics.

Svetlana Kiritchenko and Saif Mohammad. 2016a. The effect of negators, modals, and degree adverbs on sentiment composition. In *Proceedings of the 7th Workshop on Computational Approaches to Subjectivity, Sentiment and Social Media Analysis*, pages 43–52. Association for Computational Linguistics.

Svetlana Kiritchenko and Saif M. Mohammad. 2016b. Capturing reliable fine-grained sentiment associations by crowdsourcing and best–worst scaling. In *Proceedings of the 2016 Conference of the North American Chapter of the Association for Computational Linguistics: Human Language Technologies*, pages 811–817. Association for Computational Linguistics.

Svetlana Kiritchenko and Saif M. Mohammad. 2016c. Sentiment composition of words with opposing polarities. In *Proceedings of the 2016 Conference of the North American Chapter of the Association for Computational Linguistics: Human Language Technologies*, pages 1102–1108. Association for Computational Linguistics.

Jordan J. Louviere, Terry N. Flynn, and A. A. J. Marley. 2015. *Best-Worst Scaling: Theory, Methods and Applications*. Cambridge University Press.

Tomas Mikolov, Ilya Sutskever, Kai Chen, Greg S Corrado, and Jeff Dean. 2013. Distributed representations of words and phrases and their compositionality. In C. J. C. Burges, L. Bottou, M. Welling, Z. Ghahramani, and K. Q. Weinberger, editors, *Advances in Neural Information Processing Systems 26*, pages 3111–3119. Curran Associates, Inc.

Saif Mohammad and Felipe Bravo-Marquez. 2017a. Wassa-2017 shared task on emotion intensity. In *Proceedings of the 8th Workshop on Computational Approaches to Subjectivity, Sentiment and Social Media Analysis*, pages 34–49. Association for Computational Linguistics.

Saif Mohammad and Felipe Bravo-Marquez. 2017b. Wassa-2017 shared task on emotion intensity. In *Proceedings of the 8th Workshop on Computational Approaches to Subjectivity, Sentiment and Social Media Analysis*, pages 34–49. Association for Computational Linguistics.

Saif Mohammad, Felipe Bravo-Marquez, Mohammad Salameh, and Svetlana Kiritchenko. 2018. Semeval-2018 task 1: Affect in tweets. In *Proceedings of The 12th International Workshop on Semantic Evaluation*, pages 1–17. Association for Computational Linguistics.

Roser Morante and Caroline Sporleder. 2012. Modality and negation: An introduction to the special issue. *Computational Linguistics*, 38(2):223–260.

Nikola Mrkšić, Diarmuid Ó Séaghdha, Blaise Thomson, Milica Gašić, Lina M. Rojas-Barahona, Pei-Hao Su, David Vandyke, Tsung-Hsien Wen, and Steve Young. 2016. Counter-fitting word vectors to linguistic constraints. In *Proceedings of the 2016 Conference of the North American Chapter of the Association for Computational Linguistics: Human Language Technologies*, pages 142–148. Association for Computational Linguistics.

Maria Napoli and Miriam Ravetto. 2017. New insights on intensification and intensifiers. *Exploring Intensification: Synchronic, diachronic and cross-linguistic perspectives*, 189:1.

Terttu Nevalainen. 2008. Social variation in intensifier use: constraint on-ly adverbialization in the past? *English Language & Linguistics*, 12(2):289–315.

Terttu Nevalainen and Matti Rissanen. 2002. Fairly pretty or pretty fair? on the development and grammaticalization of english downtoners. *Language Sciences*, 24(3-4):359–380.

Carita Paradis. 1997. *Degree modifiers of adjectives in spoken British English*, volume 92 of *Lund Studies in English*. Lund University Press.

Carita Paradis. 2000. It's well weird: Degree modifiers of adjectives revisited: The nineties. *Language and computers*, 30:147–160.

Carita Paradis. 2001. Adjectives and boundedness.

Jeffrey Pennington, Richard Socher, and Christopher Manning. 2014. Glove: Global vectors for word representation. In *Proceedings of the 2014 Conference on Empirical Methods in Natural Language Processing (EMNLP)*, pages 1532–1543. Association for Computational Linguistics.

Paloma Núñez Pertejo and Ignacio M Palacios Martínez. 2014. That's absolutely crap, totally rubbish: The use of the intensifiers absolutely and totally in the spoken language of british adults and teenagers. *Functions of Language*, 21(2):210–237.

Hans Peters. 1994. *Degree Adverbs in Early Modern English*, volume 13. De Gruyter Mouton.

Matthew E. Peters, Mark Neumann, Mohit Iyyer, Matt Gardner, Christopher Clark, Kenton Lee, and Luke Zettlemoyer. 2018. Deep contextualized word representations. In *Proc. of NAACL*.

Robert Plutchik. 1980. A general psychoevolutionary theory of emotion. *Theories of emotion*, 1(3-31):4.

Jonathan Posner, James A Russell, and Bradley S Peterson. 2005. The circumplex model of affect: An integrative approach to affective neuroscience, cognitive development, and psychopathology. *Development and psychopathology*, 17(3):715–734.

R. Quirk. 1985. *A Comprehensive grammar of the English language*. General Grammar Series. Longman.

Alec Radford, Jeff Wu, Rewon Child, David Luan, Dario Amodei, and Ilya Sutskever. 2019. Language models are unsupervised multitask learners.

Johan Reitan, Jørgen Faret, Björn Gambäck, and Lars Bungum. 2015. Negation scope detection for twitter sentiment analysis. In *Proceedings of the 6th Workshop on Computational Approaches to Subjectivity, Sentiment and Social Media Analysis*, pages 99–108. Association for Computational Linguistics.

A. Stevenson and C.A. Lindberg. 2010. *New Oxford American Dictionary, Third Edition*. OUP USA.

Florian Strohm and Roman Klinger. 2018. An empirical analysis of the role of amplifiers, downtoners, and negations in emotion classification in microblogs. In *The 5th IEEE International Conference on Data Science and Advanced Analytics, Special Track on Sentiment, Emotion, and Credibility of Information in Social Data*, DSAA, Turin, Italy. IEEE.

Sali A Tagliamonte. 2006. "So cool, right?": Canadian english entering the 21st century. *Canadian Journal of Linguistics/Revue canadienne de linguistique*, 51(2-3):309–331.

Chuhan Wu, Fangzhao Wu, Junxin Liu, Zhigang Yuan, Sixing Wu, and Yongfeng Huang. 2018. Thu_ngn at semeval-2018 task 1: Fine-grained tweet sentiment intensity analysis with attention cnn-lstm. In *Proceedings of The 12th International Workshop on Semantic Evaluation*, pages 186–192. Association for Computational Linguistics.

Jinman Zhao, Sidharth Mudgal, and Yingyu Liang. 2018. Generalizing word embeddings using bag of subwords. In *Proceedings of the 2018 Conference on Empirical Methods in Natural Language Processing*, pages 601–606. Association for Computational Linguistics.

Xiaodan Zhu, Hongyu Guo, Saif Mohammad, and Svetlana Kiritchenko. 2014. An empirical study on the effect of negation words on sentiment. In *Proceedings of the 52nd Annual Meeting of the Association for Computational Linguistics (Volume 1: Long Papers)*, pages 304–313. Association for Computational Linguistics.

Enhancing the Measurement of Social Effects by Capturing Morality

Rezvaneh Rezapour, Saumil H. Shah, and **Jana Diesner**
School of Information Sciences
University of Illinois at Urbana-Champaign
{rezapou2, saumils2, jdiesner}@illinois.edu

Abstract

We investigate the relationship between basic principles of human morality and the expression of opinions in user-generated text data. We assume that people's backgrounds, culture, and values are associated with their perceptions and expressions of everyday topics, and that people's language use reflects these perceptions. While personal values and social effects are abstract and complex concepts, they have practical implications and are relevant for a wide range of NLP applications. To extract human values (in this paper, morality) and measure social effects (morality and stance), we empirically evaluate the usage of a morality lexicon that we expanded via a quality controlled, human in the loop process. As a result, we enhanced the Moral Foundations Dictionary in size (from 324 to 4,636 syntactically disambiguated entries) and scope. We used both lexica for feature-based and deep learning classification (SVM, RF, and LSTM) to test their usefulness for measuring social effects. We find that the enhancement of the original lexicon led to measurable improvements in prediction accuracy for the selected NLP tasks.

1 Introduction

User-generated text data are used in various fields to study, analyze, and extract people's culture, behavior, opinions, and emotions. The access and popularity of social media platforms such as Twitter attract individuals to participate in online discussions or share their points of view. Different beliefs and perspectives on social, political, economic, and other potentially controversial issues can lead to debates or conflicts among groups, and can result in arguments, abusive discussions, and segregated communities (Conover et al., 2011).

Given this type of behavior on online platforms, researchers have been investigating the relationship between basic principles of human values and the expression of opinions in user-generated text data by using (lexical) resources developed for this purpose and domain. This is done as part of stance analysis (Mohammad, Kiritchenko, Sobhani, Zhu, & Cherry, 2016), analysis of controversial topics (Addawood, Rezapour, Abdar, & Diesner, 2017), sentiment analysis (Wilson, Wiebe, & Hoffmann, 2005), and other standard NLP tasks. Following this line of research, in this paper, we operationalize and extract morality as a basic principle of human decision making and interaction guideline for people, e.g., when expressing themselves related to social or political topics. Our research is based on the assumption that people's backgrounds, cultures, and values affect their perception and expression of knowledge and beliefs about everyday topics. These personal idiosyncrasies and differences manifest themselves in people's social discourse and everyday use of language (Triandis, 1989), and can be helpful in analyzing or measuring people's positions or values regarding various social issues.

Concepts such as morality are challenging to measure as they require reliable operationalization and identification of regularities, and accounting for context and meaning (Bateson, 1972). To measure such concepts, we need to make sure that our results are - as much as possible - a reflection of the behavioral effect we want to study, not of the tools we use. The same is true for a wide range of social concepts that have been measured by applying lexicons to text data, such as opinion (Wiebe, Wilson, & Cardie, 2005), emotions

Proceedings of the 10th Workshop on Computational Approaches to Subjectivity, Sentiment and Social Media Analysis, pages 35–45
Minneapolis, June 6, 2019. ©2019 Association for Computational Linguistics

(Munezero, Montero, Sutinen, & Pajunen, 2014), sentiment (Pang & Lee, 2008; Rezapour, Wang, Abdar, & Diesner, 2017), and culture (Van Holt, Johnson, Carley, Brinkley, & Diesner, 2013). Moreover, natural language text data are inherently ambiguous, and signals relevant for detecting personal characteristics and social effects are sparsely distributed across text data. Therefore, we can make the basic assumption that the reliable measurement of human behavior based on text data requires robust, reliable, and transparent tools to measure any effects in a credible fashion (Diesner, 2015). This paper contributes to this challenge by improving an off-the-shelve lexicon, known as the Morality Foundations Dictionary (MFD) (Graham et al., 2013; Graham, Haidt, & Nosek, 2009), and mitigating biases in measurement by expanding and validating the lexicon (enhanced MFD) by using multiple strategies and datasets. To achieve this goal, we performed a quality-controlled, semi-automated, and human-validated expansion of the original MFD (from 324 to 4,636 syntactically disambiguated entries) (discussed in Section 4). We then used the enhanced MFD as a feature for supervised learning to predict two social effects: (1) personal stance, and (2) individual value or morality (discussed in Section 5). To make a clear distinction between the two lexicons used in this paper, from this point, we refer to the original MFD as MFDO and to the enhanced lexicon as MFDE.

For predicting stance, we used semeval 2016 Stance detection benchmark dataset (Mohammad et al., 2016). For the second task, we leveraged the Baltimore protest benchmark dataset (Mooijman, Hoover, Lin, Ji, & Dehghani, 2017) created for predicting people's morality in tweets. The stance detection task is relevant to our assumption since individual differences in stance may relate to cultural differences. Therefore, we believe that the MFDE can be of assistance in improving the predictability of stance in user-generated texts. Regarding the second dataset, we found the Baltimore dataset relevant to our task since the dataset comes from the same domain, annotated on morality, and can show the usefulness of the MFDE lexicon.

The results of our prediction models show that using the MFDE as a feature outperformed prediction compared to MFDO. Using morality as a feature increased the performance of both classical feature-based (93%) and deep learning models (85.7%) in the majority of test cases. From that, we conclude that morality can be a useful feature for detecting social effects in text data. In addition, we observed that lexicon expansion is worthwhile as it improves prediction accuracy in the majority of experiments on both morality and stance prediction.

This study makes several contributions. First, we introduce and operationalize morality as a feature for NLP tasks, and show that incorporating this information can lead to measurable improvements in prediction accuracy of social effects such as stance. Second, we apply the morality lexicon not only for morality prediction, but also for stance prediction, and this out-of-domain test enhances the robustness of our findings. Third, we improve the accuracy and transparency of measuring morality based on text data, and provide a rigorous and reusable strategy for lexicon expansion and validation.

2 Literature Review

Moral Foundations Theory (MFT), introduced by Graham and Haidt, considers four sources of individual moral judgment: 1) innate features, 2) human learning, based on the cultural context in which people are embedded, 3) judgment based on situational intuition, and 4) pluralism of moral primitives (Graham et al., 2013; Graham et al., 2009; Haidt & Graham, 2007). Based on the MFT, the Moral Foundations Questionnaire (MFQ) was developed to facilitate measuring people's spontaneous morality (Graham et al., 2013). Such standardized questionnaires are often used by researchers to conceptualize morality and elicit information about moral reasoning from individuals in a lab or remote settings. Socio-demographic characteristics (e.g., age, gender) and personal characteristics (e.g., educational level, political orientation, religiosity) were often used to aggregate and compare the results of these questionnaires. While questionnaires and lab experiments provided valuable information, they entail some shortcomings such as high costs, limited scalability, mock-up setups, and reliability issues of self-reported data (Hofmann, Wisneski, Brandt, & Skitka, 2014).

Furthermore, alternative approaches like enhancement of a user study with neuro-physiological measures (Decety, Michalska, & Kinzler, 2012), AI-based simulations (Pereira & Saptawijaya, 2007), and extracting signals about morality from text data were used to address these shortcomings. In addition, text-mining techniques have been used to study user-generated, empirical data while eliminating issues with artificial lab settings and self-reported data.

The majority of prior studies that use NLP to study morality has focused on analyzing rhetorical aspects. Sagi and Dehghani (2014) used the MFDO to measure the moral loading of news data by analyzing articles about socio-political conflicts (World Trade Center before and after 1993 and 9/11 attacks, Ground-Zero Mosque and abortion) from the New York Times. In another study, Kaur and Sasahara (2016) leveraged a combination of the MFDO and latent semantic analysis to measure morality in tweets about different social issues, such as homosexuality and immigration. They found two dimensions, namely purity and care, to be dominant in conversations focused on immorality. Moral values have also been predicted using background knowledge and textual features. Lin and colleagues (2018) proposed a context-aware framework to aggregate external knowledge with text and improve morality prediction by 13.3% compared to the baseline. Garten and colleagues (2018) used a Distributed Dictionary Representations (DDR) approach to measure semantic similarity between dictionaries and text instead of using word counts. The DDR model was further used for predicting moral values of Twitter data related to Hurricane Sandy. Mooijman and colleagues (2017) evaluated the relation between online moral rhetoric and violent protests by applying Recurrent Neural Networks (RNN) and Long Short-Term Memory (LSTM) to a Baltimore Protests dataset. Dehghani and colleagues (2016) used the MFT to understand homophily, and found that people whose tweets are highly indicative of purity tend to be more like-minded. Finally, Fulgoni and colleagues (2016) leveraged the MFDO to analyze polarized debates in news sources. Their analysis showed different moral dimensions in liberals and conservatives conversations, where the former group favored care/harm and fairness, and the latter one focused on authority and loyalty.

Overall, a very few studies have extended the MFDO using variations of word embedding models and calculating the cosine similarities between moral foundation context vectors and word vectors (Kaur & Sasahara, 2016). Our work builds upon prior studies of MFDO expansions, but differs from them in that we evaluate the semi-automated and human-validated expansion of the original lexicon as a feature for NLP prediction problems. Our ultimate goal is not to improve morality prediction or stance detection (though we do, by a small margin), which are intensively studied problems in NLP. Instead, we aim to provide a rigorous strategy for lexicon expansion, and based on that a generally useful lexicon that can serve as a feature for a variety of information extraction and classification tasks. This can particularly be useful for people who want to use reliable resources.

3   Data

We used two public benchmark datasets that were previously annotated for morality (Baltimore) and stance. The Baltimore data[1] contains tweets related to the street violence that took place in Baltimore during the Freddie Gray protests (04/12/2015 to 05/08/2015). This dataset has been used to study if the rate of moral in tweets can assist in predicting violent protests (Mooijman et al., 2017). From 19 million tweets that were collected, the authors of the original paper removed those tweets for which the geolocation was not the same as the cities where protests related to the death of Freddie Gray took place. Next, they had human annotators code 5,000 tweets for moral content based on the MFT. The annotated tweets were then used to train a deep neural network-based model (RNN and LSTMs) to predict moral values from tweets; resulting in 89.01% accuracy. To get the dataset, we ran the tweet IDs through the Twitter API and were able to extract 3,793 of the tweets (around 75.8% of the original tweets) for which human labels were available.

The stance dataset was made available for SemEval 2016 (Mohammad et al., 2016). Using Twitter as a source, this dataset contains 4,870 tweets on six topics: abortion, atheism, climate change, feminism, Donald Trump, and Hillary Clinton. The tweets were hand-coded for stance, with the options being in favor, against, and none. The SemEval competition contained two tasks: Task A) was traditional supervised classification (on five topics mentioned above excluding Donald Trump), where 70% of the annotated data was used for training and the rest for testing. The highest

---

[1] https://psyarxiv.com/4bvyx/

accuracy (68.98%) was achieved by the baseline model, which used SVM and n-grams. Nineteen teams participated, and the best performing team achieved an overall accuracy (F-score) of 67.82% by using two RNN classifiers. Overall, about nine teams used some form of word embedding approaches, while some other teams leveraged publicly available lexicons (e.g., for sentiment, hashtags, and emotion), and Twitter specific features. For Task B, tweets on Donald Trump (a topic not used in Task A) were used. The highest F-score for Task B was 56.28% with nine teams participating. For our study, we combined the test and training sets from task A, and added the tweets on Donald Trump, resulting in a total of 4,870 tweets in our stance dataset.

4   Moral Foundations Lexicon Expansion

The Moral Foundation Theory (MFT) categorizes human behavior into five basic principles that characterize opposing values (virtues and vices) as shown in Table 1. To enable the measurement of this theory based on text data, the Moral Foundations Dictionary (MFD) was developed and published (Graham et al., 2013; Graham et al., 2009). In the original MFD, there is a sixth "miscellaneous" category, which is a collection of morally relevant words that were not yet mapped to any of the other categories. The MFDO associates 324 unique indicator terms (words) with the virtues and vices from the MFT. This lexical resource is highly valuable as it implements a theory. At the same time, it is limited in several ways: First, the number of entries is small and therefore might not capture all (variations of) terms indicative of morality in text data. This can lead to limited results, which may become part of our presumably valid knowledge about human morality. This problem can be mitigated through quality-controlled lexicon expansion as presented in this paper.

Second, we do not know based on what texts the MFDO was built, and even if we knew, these texts might be different from the ones to which researchers want to apply the MFDO. In NLP, this problem is known as domain adaptation. Several solutions to this problem have been developed (Daumé, 2007; Glorot, Bordes, & Bengio, 2011; Satpal & Sarawagi, 2007). Given that the MFT aims to measure basic principles of human behavior, one could aim to build a generally valid, i.e., robust and validated resources with broad term

Category	Virtue	Vice
Protecting versus hurting others	Care	Harm
Cooperation/ trust/ just versus cheating in interaction with objects and people	Fairness	Cheating
In-group commitment (to coalitions, teams, brands) versus leaving a group	Loyalty	Betrayal
Playing by the rules of a hierarchy versus challenging hierarchies	Authority	Subversion
Behavioral immune system versus spontaneous reaction	Purity	Degradation

Table 1: Moral foundations theory

coverage, which can then be used as is or further be adapted to domains, contexts, and culture. We chose the second strategy as it results in an improved general resource for others (and us) to use, and present our solution to this problem in this paper.

In addition, the entries in the MFDO are not syntactically disambiguated, which can also limit the results, e.g., by capturing false positives. For example, one entry in the MFDO is *"safe,"* which represents the virtue of care. In a text, *"safe"* can occur as a noun, which is probably not the intended meaning, or as an adjective, which is more likely to be the intended meaning. This problem can be solved by adding the part of speech that represents the intended sense to each dictionary entry. We solve this problem as well.

The outlined limitations of the MFDO in terms of size, scope, and syntactic ambiguity can lead to flawed analysis results. We fixed these issues as described in the remainder of this section and tested the benefit of this work as described in the next section (Method).

To expand the lexicon, we first sorted the words from the "miscellaneous" category (which we named "general") into virtues and vices. Next, we manually annotated each lexicon entry with one or more best fitting parts of speech (POS). We then manually added variations of the original words and sense, such as grammatical inflections to the lexicon. All variations were added to the same category as the original root word. This expansion resulted in 1,085 words over 12 categories.

We then added synonyms, antonyms, and (direct) hypernyms of all original entries automatically by using WordNet (Fellbaum, 1998; Walenz & Didion, 2008); a word graph of broad scope and general applicability. To evaluate and adjust the new additions, we trained two human annotators to analyze every word entry for its POS and morality category assignment. Their initial intercoder-agreement was 65% (Kappa). After that, we went through all entries again, resolved annotation disagreements, and removed the words that the annotators found not suitable for any predefined category.

In the MFDO, some words occurred in multiple categories, which can confuse classifiers and make data analysis less robust. Therefore, we made the word to category assignment exclusive by assigning each redundant entry to only the best fitting category. To justify these assignments, we asked the human annotators to study each applicable term and choose the most suitable dimension for the words by considering their common meaning. Finally, we expanded nouns with their plural or singular form, adjectives with comparatives and superlative, and lemmatized the verbs (following the MPQA subjectivity lexicon (Wiebe et al., 2005)). Overall, our enhanced lexicon (MFDE) consists of 4,636 syntactically disambiguated, exhaustively expanded, and carefully pruned entries. Is this work worth the effort? To answer this question, we designed and ran experiments as described in the next sections. Our Enhanced Morality Lexicon can be accessed and downloaded at
https://doi.org/10.13012/B2IDB-3805242_V1

5 Method

To analyze the impact of using the morality lexicons on predicting social effects, we built upon previous work in this domain. We assessed the performance of the lexicon and its expansion as features for both traditional feature-based and deep learning machine learning models. To test their impact on measuring social effects, we first created baseline models, and then added the original and enhanced MFD to the baseline to test if morality is a useful feature and if the learning with MFDE outperforms MFDO.

5.1 Data Preprocessing

Tweets are noisy in that they do not follow conventional spelling schemes, and therefore require extensive data cleaning and preprocessing. To prepare our datasets for analysis, we removed all URLs, mentions (usernames), hashtag symbols, punctuations, and numbers from the tweets. We then expanded contracted words by automatically converting them to their assumed intended form (e.g., "I've" to "I have"). Finally, we lowercased all words.

5.2 Classic Machine Learning

Figure 1 shows the overall experimental design used for this approach.

Feature Selection: We use morality words as additional attributes on top of the baseline models. We consider three types of counting to aggregate morality words per tweet: morality type count, morality dimension count, and morality polarity count.

Morality dimension count represents the number of words per tweet that match any of the five morality dimensions plus the general category, resulting in six attributes (each horizontal row in Table 1).

Morality type count represents the number of words per tweet that match words in the vice or virtue category of each morality dimension (each box in the last two columns of Table 1). Using the MFDO, this results in 11 additional attributes, and for MFDE in 12 (since we divided the general category into vice and virtue).

Morality polarity count represents the number of words per tweet that match any virtue or vice category regardless of the morality dimension (each of the last two columns in Table 1), resulting in two additional attributes.

We then test each counting approach with four feature sets: baseline (no morality feature), original morality, enhanced morality with POS, and enhanced morality without POS; all of which are explained next.

1) Baseline Model (BM): We replicated the baseline method from the SemEval competition from which we re-used the stance detection dataset. In the original SemEval competition, the best performing model was the baseline, which only used word level features, namely n-grams (Mohammad et al., 2016). To re-create that, we divided the dataset into its original sub-topics (feminism, climate change, atheism, Hillary Clinton, and abortion), and created one model for each sub-topic. We then replicated the unigram bag-of-words approach. To reduce the redundancy of the features, unlike in the original model, we removed stop words as well as words that appeared in less than 5 and more than 99% of the tweets. For the Baltimore dataset, we created a simple baseline

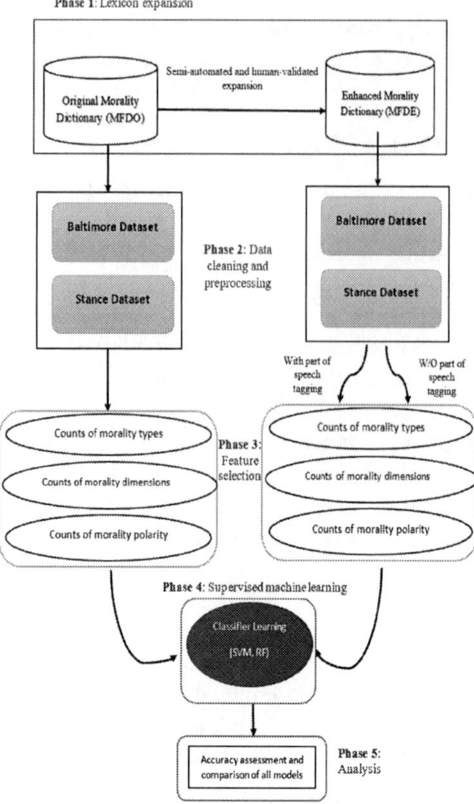

Figure 1: Experimental design and workflow of the classic machine learning approach

by extracting unigrams from the dataset and using the counts of words to create feature vectors.

We found that different numbers of tweets returned through the Twitter API as well as a lack of transparency for the original models, such as preprocessing steps and metrics, limited our ability to reproduce the original works.

2) Original Morality Model (OM): The MFDO consists of five dimensions that are further divided into virtue and vice and a sixth "miscellaneous" dimension. To aggregate the number of words per tweet, we used three types of counting as explained earlier. For the morality dimension, we added 6 attributes on top of the baseline (OM6), for the morality types, we added 11 attributes (OM11), and for morality polarity, we added two attributes to the baseline model (OM2).

3) Enhanced Morality Model with POS (EM): We used the Python NLTK library to tokenize the tweets and tag each token with a POS (Bird & Loper, 2004). We then used all matches between the texts and the MFDE if they agreed in POS as features. Finally, we aggregated the extracted words using the three counting methods explained above.

4) Enhanced Morality Model without POS (EMNP): To not only test the impact of dictionary expansion in size but also of word sense disambiguation based on syntax, we built a set of models where any word from tweets that matched the MFDE was considered regardless of its POS. This model results in a higher number of words in the BOW than the EM model since the grammatical agreement restriction was lifted from string matching. Again, we aggregated the extracted words using three count methods.

Classification: We used Support Vector Machine (SVM) and Random Forest (RF) as classification algorithms as implemented in the Python Scikitlearn package (Pedregosa et al., 2011).

For the stance dataset, we replicated the approach from the original SemEval task, i.e., we used a 70%-30% split for training and testing. For the Baltimore dataset, we conducted 5-fold cross-validation. To test the performance of our models, we (1) built the baseline model by using the full set of unigrams (BOW), (2) added attributes created from MFDO to the baseline model, and (3) added attributes created from MFDE with POS and (4) without POS to the baseline model for each of the two datasets. For each model, we tested the previously explained counting options (morality dimension, type, and polarity).

For assessing prediction accuracy, we used the standard metrics of overall accuracy, precision, recall, and F-score. Due to page limitation, we only report accuracy of the models (Table 2).

5.3 Deep Learning Models

We further investigated the usefulness of using lexicons using a recurrent neural network (RNN) with bidirectional long short-term memory (LSTM) (Hochreiter & Schmidhuber, 1997). The advantage of LSTM compared to other RNNs is its ability to consider the whole context since it is capable of bridging long time lags between inputs. To implement the models, we used Keras (Chollet, 2018). For the stance dataset, we used a 70%-30% split for training and testing, and for the morality dataset, we used 5-fold cross-validation.

Baseline LSTM: To create the embedding layer, we leveraged the 200-dimensional word embedding from GloVe Twitter trained on two billion tweets (Pennington, Socher, & Manning,

2014). The embedding layer was followed by a Bidirectional LSTM of size 100, a hidden layer with Sigmoid activation function and an output layer with Softmax activation function. We further used Adam (Kingma & Ba, 2014) to optimize the parameters, and used cross-entropy as the loss function.

Enhanced LSTM with Morality Lexicon: To create the enhanced model, we first created the embedding layers of the lexicon words for (1) the MFDO (OM), (2) the MFDE with POS (EM), and (3) the MFDE without POS (EMNP). Moreover, we first found the words that intersected between the lexicon and datasets, and then created the embedding layers using the 200-dimensional GloVe Twitter (Pennington et al., 2014) without considering the morality dimensions, type, or polarity.

After that, we concatenated the output of the baseline Bidirectional LSTM (as explained above) with the embedding of the morality words to build three types of models: (1) OM, (2) EM, and (3) EMNP. After concatenating the LSTM output and lexicon embedding, we used a hidden layer with Sigmoid activation function and an output layer with Softmax activation function. We further used Adam (Kingma & Ba, 2014) to optimize the parameters, and used cross-entropy as the loss function.

One challenge in implementing neural network models is finding the best number of layers and settings (because there is no standard way of building the models). Since we are comparing different models, we found it challenging to choose a common set of numbers as the best hyperparameters, e.g., neurons, for both baseline and enhanced models. While we found one hidden layer to work best for our models, to increase transparency, we report the performance of our models with two sets of neuron sizes: 150 and 100. Table 3 shows the output of the LSTM models.

6 Results

Table 2 and 3 shows the result of predicting stance and morality. In both tables, the highest performance for each set of experiments (OM, EM and EMNP) is marked with bold text, and gray cells indicate the highest accuracy per model (per column).

The results for the ***classic machine learning models*** are shown in Table 2. For the Baltimore dataset (originally annotated for morality, last two columns in Table 2), using a simple set of basic unigram feature and classic machine learning models resulted in a baseline accuracy of 85.20% accuracy for SVM. Adding the simplest morality model (OM11) led to a small decrease (about 0.02%) with SVM. For the RF model, adding OM11 increased the performance by about 0.21%. Adding information about morality-relevant words in more sophisticated ways, (EMs and EMNPs) increased accuracy for both RF and SVM. As shown in Table 2, the best result for RF was achieved using EM2 (85.31%), and for SVM by using EM6 (85.71%).

	Experiments	Stance Dataset												Baltimore	
		Abortion		Atheism		Climate		Clinton		Feminist		Trump			
		SVM	RF	SVM	RF	SVM	RF	SVM	RF	SVM	RF	SVM	RF	SVM	RF
Baseline	BM	66.42	62.5	69.54	64.54	61.76	**68.23**	60.81	60.13	58.94	60.7	51.17	45.07	85.20	83.91
Morality Types	OM11	66.42	62.5	**71.81**	65.0	**63.52**	**67.05**	61.14	57.77	**61.05**	**59.29**	50.7	49.29	85.18	84.12
	EM12	**67.85**	62.85	71.36	62.72	**63.52**	60.58	**64.18**	58.78	57.19	57.19	51.64	47.88	**85.60**	**84.73**
	EMNP12	66.07	**63.21**	71.36	**66.81**	62.35	62.94	62.38	**61.48**	58.94	**59.29**	**52.58**	**52.58**	85.31	84.12
Morality Dimension	OM6	**68.21**	**63.57**	70.45	**69.09**	**62.35**	64.7	59.79	58.1	59.29	60.7	51.17	46.94	85.31	**84.73**
	EM6	**68.21**	62.5	**71.36**	66.81	60.58	64.11	62.83	57.43	58.94	58.59	52.58	**53.99**	**85.71**	84.44
	EMNP6	**68.21**	62.5	70.45	60.0	60.0	**66.47**	**64.52**	**59.12**	**60.00**	**62.45**	**54.92**	50.7	85.55	84.10
Morality Polarity	OM2	67.14	63.21	69.09	**69.54**	**62.94**	65.29	62.83	57.09	58.24	56.84	52.58	**50.23**	85.31	84.99
	EM2	**67.85**	**64.28**	**72.27**	66.81	**62.94**	61.17	**63.17**	58.78	57.19	**61.05**	50.7	43.19	**85.60**	**85.31**
	EMNP2	67.14	63.92	71.81	64.54	61.17	**67.05**	**63.17**	**60.13**	**59.29**	56.49	**53.52**	49.29	85.49	84.84

Table 2: Result of predicting stance (first 12 columns) and morality (last two columns) with SVM and RF for stance and Baltimore datasets (Accuracy) (highest performance per set of experiments (OM, EM, and EMNP - each half column) in bold, highest accuracy per each model (each column) in gray)

#Neurons in Hidden Layer	Stance Dataset							Baltimore
	Experiments	Abortion	Atheism	Climate	Clinton	Feminist	Trump	
N = 150	BM	62.500	68.181	67.647	58.445	57.192	51.643	84.2391
	(1) OM	**68.214**	68.636	65.882	56.081	**57.894**	50.704	85.504
	(2) EM	67.500	72.272	**70.00**	**63.851**	**57.894**	50.234	**86.163**
	(3) EMNP	65.714	**73.181**	68.823	57.432	57.543	**54.929**	84.634
N = 100	BM	65.714	65.454	**70.588**	59.121	**58.596**	51.173	84.845
	(1) OM	64.642	66.363	69.411	**60.472**	56.842	51.643	85.900
	(2) EM	**67.142**	70.909	69.411	59.797	54.385	**53.521**	**86.612**
	(3) EMNP	64.642	**71.363**	67.647	56.756	58.245	49.765	83.580

Table 3: Result of predicting stance (first 7 columns) and morality (last column) with LSTM model for stance and Baltimore datasets (Accuracy) (highest performance per set of experiments (OM, EM, and EMNP – each half column) in bold, highest accuracy per each model (each column) in gray)

For the stance datasets, the results are shown in the first 12 columns of Table 2. Depending on the sub-topic, our baseline accuracy ranged from 45.07% (RF, Trump, stance hardest to predict) to 69.54% (SVM, atheism, stances easiest to predict). As observed for the Baltimore data, adding lexical morality features to stance increased accuracy over our baseline in all but one case (Climate, RF) cases.

The results for the *LSTM model for both datasets* are shown in Table 3. As mentioned before, we used two sets of neuron sizes for the hidden layer. For the Baltimore dataset, using the MFDE achieved better performance in both implemented models. The highest accuracy was obtained by the enhanced LSTM model using enhanced morality words (EM), 86.61% (N=100). For the stance dataset, adding morality embedding to the output of LSTM (baseline) resulted in outperforming the baseline in 83.33% of cases (10 out of 12).

Does using morality as a lexical feature improve prediction accuracy for the selected NLP tasks? Comparing the baseline to any models that include morality, we conclude that adding morality as a lexical feature increases accuracy in 13 out of 14 cases (93%) for feature-based learning (considering RF and SVM models for each topic) and in 12 out of 14 cases (85.7%) for deep learning (considering experiments with two sets of neurons for each topic). This finding suggests that using the morality as a feature is helpful for standard NLP tasks - and possibly other tasks as well, which would need to be explored in future work.

Does expanding the MFDO pay off? We find that for feature-based learning (Table 2), in 29 out of 42 cases (69.05%), the accuracy with any MFDE feature outperforms the models with MFDO features, in 21.43% of the cases, MFDO outperforms MFDE, and in 9.52% of the cases, both versions of the dictionary lead to equal results.

For the LSTM, 9 out of 14 models (64.28%) had better performance when using MFDE, while 14.28% of models (2 models) worked better with MFDO (Table 3). From that, we conclude that lexicon expansion is worthwhile as it improves prediction accuracy in the majority of our experiments, especially for feature-based learning.

Does disambiguating word sense in the MFDO via POS pay off? Based on the results in Table 2 and 3, we found that syntactic disambiguating of lexicon entries leads to only minor quantitative improvements. We believe that the usefulness of POS tags can be further tested with other types of user-generated data that follow more conventional grammatical rules. In addition, beyond what we measured in this paper, this additional layer of information might further boost the quality of the data.

Based on the results of all implemented models, highlighted in Table 2 and 3, we found that using MFDE results in higher performance compared to other models (MFDO and BM).

7   Discussion and Conclusion

In this paper, we investigated the usefulness of leveraging morality as an NLP feature for predicting two selected social effects (morality and stance). In addition, we showed how investments in the quality and general nature of lexical auxiliary tools and the rigorous evaluation of these investments improve the predictability of these social effects, thereby reducing biases in algorithmic solutions. This work matters as personal values and social effects (which are often measured as the aggregation of personal values) are abstract and complex constructs, and their measurement requires researchers to find reliable and robust ways to operationalize these concepts. The validity of such research hinges on the trustworthiness of our methods for capturing these effects in digital traces of human behavior. Hence, our work is based on the assumption that people's personal values, which might be impacted by their cultural contexts, are reflected in their language use (Bateson, 1972; Milroy & Milroy, 1985; Triandis, 1989), and that we can capture these values in user-generated text data.

Enhancing lexicons is expensive, as it requires trained human coders to assess each entry and its meta-data (in our case, category assignment and part of speech). This might help to increase the reliability of social computing research, but does this effort make a difference for improving the accuracy of NLP tasks? In order to answer this question, we evaluated the usefulness of using no lexicon, a basic lexicon, and an enhanced lexicon for capturing morality in text data to measure two different social effects (morality and stance) based on public benchmark datasets. We found that using the lexicons we tested, namely the Moral Foundations Dictionary, does increase prediction accuracy in the majority of cases, especially when used for feature-based machine learning. Moreover, we found that the semi-automated and human-validated verification and advancement of this lexical resource led to measurable improvements in capturing social effects in text data.

Our work has several limitations. For deep learning models, while using the enhanced morality lexicon yielded better overall accuracy, we still need to investigate more parameters and settings to find the most robust models. We plan to investigate these settings in the future. Moreover, the benchmark data we used were too small for this purpose. In addition, we only worked with tweets, which is just one out of many types of user-generated text data. The robustness of our evaluation might be further improved by working with texts from other genres and of higher formality, such as debates, congressional speeches, product reviews, and news articles.

Acknowledgments

This research is sponsored by the Army Research Laboratory and was accomplished under Cooperative Agreement Number W911NF-17-2-0196. The views and conclusions contained in this document are those of the authors and should not be interpreted as representing the official policies, either expressed or implied, of the Army Research Laboratory or the U.S. Government. The U.S. Government is authorized to reproduce and distribute reprints for Government purposes notwithstanding any copyright notation here on. We appreciate Jessica Schmiederer, Tiffany Lu, Craig Evans and Max McKittrick for their great help in expanding and evaluating the morality lexicon. We also thank Chieh-Li (Julian) Chin, Shubhanshu Mishra and Ly Dinh for their assistance.

References

Aseel Addawood, Rezvaneh Rezapour, Omid Abdar, and Jana Diesner. 2017. Telling apart tweets associated with controversial versus non-controversial topics. In Proceedings of the *Proceedings of the Second Workshop on NLP and Computational Social Science*, (pp. 32-41).

Gregory Bateson. 1972. *Steps to an ecology of mind: Collected essays in anthropology, psychiatry, evolution, and epistemology*: University of Chicago Press.

Steven Bird, and Edward Loper. 2004. NLTK: the natural language toolkit. In Proceedings of the *Proceedings of the ACL 2004 on Interactive poster and demonstration sessions*, (pp. 31), Association for Computational Linguistics.

François Chollet. 2018. Keras: The python deep learning library. *Astrophysics Source Code Library*.

Michael D Conover, Jacob Ratkiewicz, Matthew Francisco, Bruno Gonçalves, Filippo Menczer, and Alessandro Flammini. 2011. Political polarization on twitter. In Proceedings of the *Fifth international AAAI conference on weblogs and social media*.

Hal Daumé. 2007. Frustratingly easy domain adaptation. In Proceedings of the *45th Annual Meeting of the Association of Computational Linguistics (ACL)*, (pp. 256–263), (Vols. 45), Prague, Czech Republic.

Jean Decety, Kalina J Michalska, and Katherine D Kinzler. 2012. The contribution of emotion and cognition to moral sensitivity: a neurodevelopmental study. *Cerebral Cortex, 22*(1), 209-220.

Morteza Dehghani, Kate Johnson, Joe Hoover, Eyal Sagi, Justin Garten, Niki Jitendra Parmar, . . . Jesse Graham. 2016. Purity homophily in social networks. *Journal of Experimental Psychology: General, 145*(3), 366.

Jana Diesner. 2015. Small decisions with big impact on data analytics. *Big Data & Society, 2*(2), 2053951715617185.

Christiane Fellbaum. 1998. *WordNet: An electronic lexical database*. Cambridge, MA: MIT Press.

Dean Fulgoni, Jordan Carpenter, Lyle H Ungar, and Daniel Preotiuc-Pietro. 2016. An Empirical Exploration of Moral Foundations Theory in Partisan News Sources. In Proceedings of the *LREC*.

Justin Garten, Joe Hoover, Kate M Johnson, Reihane Boghrati, Carol Iskiwitch, and Morteza Dehghani. 2018. Dictionaries and distributions: Combining expert knowledge and large scale textual data content analysis. *Behavior research methods, 50*(1), 344-361.

Xavier Glorot, Antoine Bordes, and Yoshua Bengio. 2011. Domain Adaptation for Large-Scale Sentiment Classification: A Deep Learning Approach. *Proceedings of the 28th International Conference on Machine Learning*, 513-520.

Jesse Graham, Jonathan Haidt, Sena Koleva, Matt Motyl, Ravi Iyer, Sean P Wojcik, and Peter H Ditto. 2013. Moral foundations theory: The pragmatic validity of moral pluralism. *Advances in Experimental Social Psychology, 47*, 55-130.

Jesse Graham, Jonathan Haidt, and Brian A Nosek. 2009. Liberals and conservatives rely on different sets of moral foundations. *Journal of personality and social psychology, 96*(5), 1029-1046.

Jonathan Haidt, and Jesse Graham. 2007. When morality opposes justice: Conservatives have moral intuitions that liberals may not recognize. *Social Justice Research, 20*(1), 98-116.

Sepp Hochreiter, and Jürgen Schmidhuber. 1997. Long short-term memory. *Neural computation, 9*(8), 1735-1780.

Wilhelm Hofmann, Daniel C Wisneski, Mark J Brandt, and Linda J Skitka. 2014. Morality in everyday life. *Science, 345*(6202), 1340-1343.

Rishemjit Kaur, and Kazutoshi Sasahara. 2016. Quantifying moral foundations from various topics on Twitter conversations. In Proceedings of the *Big Data (Big Data), 2016 IEEE International Conference on*, (pp. 2505-2512), IEEE.

Diederik P Kingma, and Jimmy Ba. 2014. Adam: A method for stochastic optimization. *arXiv preprint arXiv:1412.6980*.

Ying Lin, Joe Hoover, Gwenyth Portillo-Wightman, Christina Park, Morteza Dehghani, and Heng Ji. 2018. Acquiring background knowledge to improve moral value prediction. In Proceedings of the *2018 IEEE/ACM International Conference on Advances in Social Networks Analysis and Mining (ASONAM)*, (pp. 552-559), IEEE.

James Milroy, and Lesley Milroy. 1985. Linguistic change, social network and speaker innovation. *Journal of Linguistics, 21*(2), 339-384.

Saif Mohammad, Svetlana Kiritchenko, Parinaz Sobhani, Xiaodan Zhu, and Colin Cherry. 2016. Semeval-2016 task 6: Detecting stance in tweets. In Proceedings of the *10th International Workshop on Semantic Evaluation (SemEval-2016)*, (pp. 31-41).

Marlon Mooijman, Joseph Hoover, Ying Lin, Heng Ji, and Morteza Dehghani. 2017. When protests turn violent: The roles of moralization and moral convergence.

Myriam D Munezero, Calkin Suero Montero, Erkki Sutinen, and John Pajunen. 2014. Are they different? Affect, feeling, emotion, sentiment, and opinion detection in text. *IEEE transactions on affective computing, 5*(2), 101-111.

Bo Pang, and Lillian Lee. 2008. Opinion mining and sentiment analysis. *Foundations and trends in information retrieval, 2*(1-2), 1-135.

Fabian Pedregosa, Gaël Varoquaux, Alexandre Gramfort, Vincent Michel, Bertrand Thirion, Olivier Grisel, . . . Vincent Dubourg. 2011. Scikit-learn: Machine learning in Python. *Journal of machine learning research, 12*(Oct), 2825-2830.

Jeffrey Pennington, Richard Socher, and Christopher Manning. 2014. Glove: Global vectors for word representation. In Proceedings of the *Proceedings of the 2014 conference on empirical methods in natural language processing (EMNLP)*, (pp. 1532-1543).

Luís Moniz Pereira, and Ari Saptawijaya. 2007. Modelling morality with prospective logic *Progress in Artificial Intelligence* (pp. 99-111): Springer.

Rezvaneh Rezapour, Lufan Wang, Omid Abdar, and Jana Diesner. 2017. Identifying the overlap between election result and candidates' ranking based on hashtag-enhanced, lexicon-based sentiment analysis. In Proceedings of the *2017 IEEE 11th*

International Conference on Semantic Computing (ICSC), (pp. 93-96), IEEE.

Eyal Sagi, and Morteza Dehghani. 2014. Measuring moral rhetoric in text. *Social science computer review, 32*(2), 132-144.

Sandeepkumar Satpal, and Sunita Sarawagi. 2007. Domain adaptation of conditional probability models via feature subsetting *Knowledge Discovery in Databases: PKDD 2007* (pp. 224-235). Springer-Verlag, Berlin: Springer.

Harry C Triandis. 1989. The self and social behavior in differing cultural contexts. *Psychological review, 96*, 506.

Tracy Van Holt, Jeffrey C Johnson, Kathleen M Carley, James Brinkley, and Jana Diesner. 2013. Rapid ethnographic assessment for cultural mapping. *Poetics, 41*(4), 366-383.

Brett Walenz, and John Didion. (2008). JWNL: Java WordNet library.

Janyce Wiebe, Theresa Wilson, and Claire Cardie. 2005. Annotating expressions of opinions and emotions in language. *Language resources and evaluation, 39*(2-3), 165-210.

Theresa Wilson, Janyce Wiebe, and Paul Hoffmann. 2005. Recognizing contextual polarity in phrase-level sentiment analysis. In Proceedings of the *Proceedings of Human Language Technology Conference and Conference on Empirical Methods in Natural Language Processing.*

Using Structured Representation and Data: A Hybrid Model for Negation and Sentiment in Customer Service Conversations

Amita Misra, Mansurul Bhuiyan, Jalal Mahmud, and Saurabh Tripathy
IBM-Research, Almaden
San Jose, CA, USA
`amita.misra1|mansurul.bhuiyan|jumahmud|Saurabh.Tripathy2@ibm.com`

Abstract

Twitter customer service interactions have recently emerged as an effective platform to respond and engage with customers. In this work, we explore the role of negation in customer service interactions, particularly applied to sentiment analysis. We define rules to identify true negation cues and scope more suited to conversational data than existing general review data. Using semantic knowledge and syntactic structure from constituency parse trees, we propose an algorithm for scope detection that performs comparable to state of the art BiLSTM. We further investigate the results of negation scope detection for the sentiment prediction task on customer service conversation data using both a traditional SVM and a Neural Network. We propose an antonym dictionary based method for negation applied to a CNN-LSTM combination model for sentiment analysis. Experimental results show that the antonym-based method outperforms the previous lexicon-based and neural network methods.

1 Introduction

Negation has been described as a polarity influencer (Wilson et al., 2009) and therefore it has to be taken into consideration while designing a sentiment prediction system, but how important it is in twitter customer service conversations? For example, both the customer service tweets in Table 1 have an explicit negation cue but the effect of cue words on the polarity differ. The first tweet has a negation cue [*don't*] that changes the positive polarity of the words in the scope [*think you do understand*]. Additionally, tweet 1 has a hashtag [*Misleading*] which could be a strong negative signal on its own. The second tweet has a cue word [*not*] but it does not negate the words in that sentence or change their polarity. The negation cue

[*not*] in the second tweet is not a true negation cue, and hence it has no scope.

S.No	Tweet	Sentiment
1	@Username I *don't* think you do understand. Buyers and Sellers deserve to know facts,User actively prevents accurate feedback. #Misleading.	Negative
2	@Username Sorry to hear this. Have you had a chance to call/chat us? If *not*, we can look into options:	Positive

Table 1: Customer Service Conversation.

Negation can be expressed in different ways in natural language. It may be through the use of explicit negation cues such as *no, not and never* that have a morphologic indication of a negative meaning. This also includes a group of broad or semi negatives words (e.g. barely, hardly, and seldom) that have a negative meaning but are without any morphological negative. This has been also referred to as clausal or syntactic negation (Quirk et al., 1985; Givón, 1993). These cue words are often used to negate a statement or an assertion that expresses a judgment or an opinion. However in some contexts, these cue words function as exclamations, and not as true negation cues. These false cues do not change the sentiment polarity of the following expression, and hence do not have any associated scope. We define rules to identify true negation cues and their scopes more suited to conversational data than existing general review data.

The impact of negation has been studied in domains such as biomedical, literary texts, and online reviews (Szarvas et al., 2008; Morante et al., 2008; Councill et al., 2010; Reitan et al., 2015; Konstantinova et al., 2012); however, none of the previous corpora are conversational in nature. Scope definitions may depend on the domain. Reitan et al. (2015) showed that negation scope algo-

Proceedings of the 10th Workshop on Computational Approaches to Subjectivity, Sentiment and Social Media Analysis, pages 46–56
Minneapolis, June 6, 2019. ©2019 Association for Computational Linguistics

rithm trained on a twitter domain struggled when tested on a medical domain. Majority of the previous work in scope detection has been dominated by SVMs or Neural Networks, which require expensive annotated training data. Scope annotation is costly and time-intensive as all the scope conflicts have to be resolved by mutual discussion amongst expert annotators. Our main motivation is to create a system that does not require a huge amount of training data for scope detection, but has comparable performance to machine learning models that require annotated training data. The proposed method uses constituency parse trees and semantic knowledge to predict scope. The results in Table 7 show that the method is comparable to state of the art BiLSTM model from (Fancellu et al., 2016) on gold negation cues for scope prediction. Since our method does not need expensive training data, we could also use this method to predict on other negation data sets. However, our aim here was first to test if the predicted negation scope improves sentiment in conversations.

For a real time sentiment prediction system, we need both a cue prediction system to determine the true negation cues, and scope detection. As a first step, we use a data based approach to train an SVM to predict true negation cues. It's much faster and simpler to get annotated data for cue prediction, a binary task as compared to scope detection, which is a sequence labeling task. This is followed by a second step of constituency tree-based negation scope detection for predicted cues. The last step applies negation prediction coupled with antonym dictionary to improve the sentiment performance for a combination CNN-LSTM model.

The contributions of this paper are:

- Negation scope rules more suited to conversational data.

- A constituency-tree based approach for scope detection that uses both semantic and structural information, and does not require annotated data for scope.

- An antonym based negation applied to a combination CNN-LSTM model for sentiment prediction in conversations.

We begin with a discussion of related work in Section 2, followed by negation corpus in Section 3, and negation cue and scope detection experiments in Section 4. Next, we show the effect of introducing negation detection for the sentiment task in Section 5. We then compare and contrast the twitter conversational sentiment data to previous datasets in Section 6. Finally, Section 7 presents the conclusions and future directions.

2 Related Work

Initial studies on negation scope detection were performed in Biomedical domain including medical reports, biological abstracts, and papers (Szarvas et al., 2008). Morante and Daelemans (2009) used a 2 step approach: first, a decision tree to predict negation cues, followed by a CRF meta-learner to predict negation scope. The model used a combination of k-nearest neighbors, a support vector machine, and a CRF. The research in this field was further enhanced by a shared SemEval 2012 negation and scope resolution task (Morante and Blanco, 2012). The organizers released a cue and scope annotated corpus of Conan Doyle stories.

Read et al. (2012) described both, a rule-based and a data driven approach for scope resolution. Both the methods were driven by the hypothesis that syntactic units correspond to scope annotations. The rule-based approach used heuristic rules based on POS tags and constituent category labels, while machine learning used SVM based ranking of syntactic constituents. Limited rule based system obtained similar results to the data-driven system on a held-out set. This result was particularly note-worthy since getting sufficient scope annotation training data for every new domain is quite expensive, and requires trained annotators. A comparison of these results motivated us to further develop the rule-based system for the conversational domain using both semantic information and syntactic structure. (Councill et al., 2010; Lapponi et al., 2012; Reitan et al., 2015) used CRF-based sequence labeling using features from dependency tree. Packard et al. (2014) used hand-crafted heuristics to traverse Minimal Recursion Semantics (MRS). However, if a reliable representation for a sentence could not be created, their system used a fall back mechanism based on Read et al. (2012). Fancellu et al. (2016) showed that a neural network based model using a BiLSTM outperformed the previously developed classifiers on both scope token recognition and exact scope matching for in domain testing but not on a different domain. The authors noted that when tested on a different test set from Wikipedia, White (2012)'s model built on constituency-based features performed better.

A survey on the role of negation in sentiment analysis was done by (Wiegand et al., 2010) stating that negation expressions are ambiguous i.e. in some contexts do not function as a negation and, therefore, need to be disambiguated. Rules of composition were defined by Moilanen and Pulman (2007) on the syntactic representation of a sentence to account for negation and the modeling paradigm could be applied to determine the sub-sentential polarity of the sentiment expressed. (Councill et al., 2010) showed that a CRF based negation enhanced classifier improved the F-score of positive on-line reviews by 29.5% and 11.4% for negative. Much recent progress in the field has been in connection with the "The International Workshop on Semantic Evaluation" (SemEval) (Nakov et al., 2013). Since 2013 the workshop has included shared tasks on "Sentiment Analysis in Twitter". Most of the top performing systems submitted used just a simple punctuation model that assigns a negation cue scope over all the terms to the next punctuation (Tang et al., 2014; Miura et al., 2014; Mohammad et al., 2013). (Kiritchenko et al., 2014a) reported an improvement of up to 6.5 percentage points when handling negated context on the SemEval-2013 test set. Using the simple punctuation model for scope detection, an improvement of upto 6% was reported by (Reitan et al., 2015).

With the recent advances in deep learning and use of embeddings, the CNN and LSTM based models have shown to outperform traditional SVM and lexicon based methods for sentiment in twitter and review domain. Kim (2014) applied a CNN based model to numerous document classification tasks, and improved the sentiment state of the art using a CNN architecture with one layer of convolution trained using word vectors obtained from Mikolov et al. (2013) on 100 billion words of Google News. Yin and Schütze (2015) combined different word embeddings using multichannel CNN. Wang et al. (2016) showed that a combination CNN-LSTM outperformed CNN for sentiment task. Shin et al. (2017) integrated sentiment embeddings in a CNN to build simpler high-performing models with much smaller word em-

beddings. However, none of the previous work has explored negation coupled with antonyms to get a better sentence representation for sentiment prediction.

3 Conversational Negation Corpus

hardly	lack	lacking	lacks	neither
no	nobody	none	nothing	nowhere
cant	arent	dont	doesnt	didnt
havent	isnt	mightnt	mustnt	neednt
shouldnt	wasnt	werent	wouldnt	without
seldom	scarcely	wont	never	aint
barely	nor	not	hadnt	rather
hasnt	shant			

Table 2: Negation cue lexicon.

We selected conversations from the Twitter customer service pages of different companies and downloaded 89552 customer service tweets in total[1]. A lexicon of explicit cue words that may act as indicators of negation was primarily adopted from (Councill et al., 2010; Reitan et al., 2015). It was further extended to include semi negative words. The final set of cues used is shown in Table 2. We then extracted 23243 tweets containing explicit negation cues giving a frequency of 26%. In contrast, the equivalent numbers for BioScope corpus (Szarvas et al., 2008) and for Twitter corpus (Reitan et al., 2015) are 13.8 % and 13.5% respectively. Tottie (1991) presented a comprehensive taxonomy of English negations and stated that frequency of negation is 12.8% in written English. In another statistical study on negation, (Biber, 1999) reported that negation is much more frequent in conversation as compared to written discourse. Since we had a lot more negation cue occurrences, we divided the tweets into 5 different groups based on the number of negation cues present in each tweet. A random sample was selected from each group based on the number of instances in each group giving a dataset of 2000 tweets. A separate set of 100 tweets was used as a development set to help formulate the rules and study negation patterns. Every tweet was annotated by a pair of annotators. To test the robustness of guidelines, we measured inter-annotator agreements (IAA) for each pair of raters using the token level and full scope measures as used in previous work (Reitan et al., 2015). The token level is the percentage of tokens annotators agreed upon.

---

[1] Comapny names are anonymous for annotation

Since the average number of tokens in scope is far less than the number outside the scope, this is a skewed measure. For full scope, it is the percentage of scopes that have a complete and exact match amongst annotators (PCS). After an initial annotation phase of 1000 tweets, the average token level agreement was 0.95 and full scope was 0.78. All the scope conflicts were mutually resolved after discussion. Corpus statistics are shown in Table 3. The average number of tokens per tweet is 22.3, per sentence is 13.6 and average scope length is 2.9.

Total negation cues	2921
True negation cues	2674
False negation cues	247
Average scope length	2.9
Average sentence length	13.6
Average tweet length	22.3

Table 3: Cue and token distribution in the conversational negation corpus.

3.1 Annotation Guidelines

We define rules to identify true negation cues and their scopes more suited to twitter customer service conversational data than existing general review data, which has its own characteristics such as brevity and skewed distribution towards negative polarity (Sec. 6). The guidelines described here were adapted from Councill et al. (2010) but modified for customer service conversations. Nouns and adjectives are key indicators of sentiment (Hu and Liu, 2004; Pang and Lee, 2008) and hence we had a more restricted scope for noun and adjectives as compared to verbs and adverbs. In the following examples, the cue is underlined and the scope is marked in bold.

- Annotating the negation cue.

    - False Negation: Some negation cues can be used in multiple senses and hence the mere presence of an explicit cue in a sentence does not imply that it functions as a negator, (e.g., *He could _not_ help me more*). Reitan et al. (2015) reported that in the twitter corpus the cue word _no_ often occurs as an exclamation leading to erroneous predictions. Such cues should be marked as false negations.
    - Negation cues are not part of the scope.

- Annotating the Scope

    - Annotate the minimal span for scope.
    - Scope is continuous.
    - A noun or an adjective negated in a noun phrase: If only the noun or adjective is being negated then do not annotate the entire clause. Consider each term separately, (e.g., *There are _no_ **details** on the return page*).
    - A verb or an adverb phrase: By and large, the entire phrase is annotated, (e.g., *I do _not_ **want to update it anymore** *).

We used a different scheme for annotating nouns and adverbs as compared to (Councill et al., 2010). Our nouns have a more restricted scope contrary to the previous work where typically the entire phrase is negated in a noun phrase.

4 Negation Cue and Scope Detection Experiments

We divided the dataset into train and test sets giving a training set of 2317 cues and test set of 604 cues to train both a cue detection and BiLSTM scope prediction.

4.1 Negation Cue Detection

The task of cue detection system is to determine if the potential cue word negates a concept in the sentence. It is based on the state-of-the-art cue classifier described by (Read et al., 2012; Velldal, 2011; Enger et al., 2017). A binary SVM classifier is used to disambiguate the cue for only the known cue words, considering the set of cue words as a closed class. Our baseline system uses the features and implementation as described in Enger et al. (2017). The features used are the word form, POS and lemma of the token, and lemmas for previous and next position. Adding simple features such as position of the cue word in the sentence, POS bigrams improves the F-score of false negation from a **0.61** baseline to **0.68** on a test set containing 47 false and 557 actual negation cues. See Table 4.

	F-Score		
	Baseline	**Proposed**	**Support**
False cues	0.61	0.68	47
Actual cues	0.97	0.98	557

Table 4: Cue classification on the test set.

4.2 Negation Scope Detection

Syntactic structure of the sentence has been often used to determine the scope of negation using supervised classifiers (Morante and Daelemans, 2009; Councill et al., 2010; Reitan et al., 2015; Read et al., 2012; Carrillo de Albornoz et al., 2012). Our work is inspired by the previous rule-based approach using constituency tree (Read et al., 2012; Carrillo de Albornoz et al., 2012; Velldal et al., 2012). We build on that work by adding rules based on semantic information, the position of the negation cue in the tree and the projection of its parent based on phrase structure. The syntax tree is obtained using Stanford CoreNLP (Manning et al., 2014). It is possible that the negation marker may be present in the main clause but semantically belong to the embedded clause. (Gotti et al., 2008) mention that semantic content of copula verbs is subsidiary to that of subject complement, (e.g., *A drunken worker does not become rich*, the negation marker "not" negates the subject complement "rich" rather than the copula verb "become"). Neg-raising is a linguistic phenomenon where certain predicates such as *think, believe* and *seem* occur in the main clause but may be interpreted to negate the complement clause (Fillmore, 1963; Horn, 1989). We move ahead in a linear order on either finding a copula verb or neg-raising predicates (NRPs). Table 5 contains the list of such verbs used. At this point, the algorithm branches based on POS tag of the token. We traverse the tree in an upward direction until we find a parent with the desired phrase tag as determined by the POS tag of the token. This method differs from the previous work that finds the first common ancestor enclosing the negation cue and the word immediately after it, and assumes all descendant leaf nodes to the right as its scope (Read et al., 2012). Our detailed algorithm for finding the scope is presented in Figure 1.

think	believe	seem	appear	feel
grow	look	prove	remain	smell
sound	become	might	are	am
been	has	were	was	is

Table 5: Neg-raising predicates (NRP) and copula verb.

Though we use SBAR* tags from syntax tree to determine the clause boundaries but it cannot detect all boundaries. We therefore also used explicit

1. Traverse the tokens in linear order and stop on finding any cue from the explicit cue lexicon.
2. Find the next first occurrence of noun, verb, adverb, adjective.
3. If the verb is an instance of copula verb or neg-raising, move to step2 else go to step4.
4. Branch depending upon POS tag of the token found in step2.
   (a) For nouns and adjectives:
      - Traverse the tree in upward direction level by level until you reach an ancestor with a tag of NP, VP, ADJP, SBAR* or S* for adjectives. For nouns, stop at NP, SBAR* or S*.
      - If a PP, VP, ADVP, SQ, SINV or SBAR* is a right child of the ancestor, then remove that child.
      - Get all the descendant leaves as scope.
   (b) For verbs and adverbs:
      - Traverse the tree in upward direction level by level until you reach an ancestor with a tag of VP, SBAR* or S*.
      - If there exists an SBAR*, SQ, or SINV tag as a right child of the ancestor then remove that child.
      - Get all the descendant leaves as scope.
5. Apply post-processing rules to align the scopes.

Figure 1: Negation scope detection .

discourse connectives that signal a contrast relation, or a coordination to limit the scope. These connectives act as a boundary for an idea expressed in one clause. For example, *To be honest I am not angry but upset*, the scope of <u>not</u> as per the rules given in Figure 1, would be **angry but upset**. Once we find this scope, we use the discourse connective *'but'* to delimit the scope. The list of connectives used is given in Table 6. Morante and Blanco (2012) reported that for the SemEval shared task on negation scope detection, most of the systems were post processed to improve their performance. Read et al. (2012) formulated a set of slackening heuristics by removing certain constituents at the beginning or end of a scope. This improved the alignment of scopes from an initial 52.42% to 86.13%. Following a similar approach, the post-processing rules were designed and are given in Figure 2.

because	while	until	however	what
but	though	although	nothing	nowhere
whenever	&	and	nonetheless	whereas
whose	why	where	wherever	

Table 6: Prune-connective list

- If the scope contains a connective from the prune-connective list then delimit the scope before the connective.
- If the scope contains a punctuation then delimit the scope before the punctuation marker.
- Remove the negation cue from the scope.
- Remove the scope words before the cue word, if any.
- If no scope is found after using these rules then predict a default scope as all the tokens up to the first noun, adjective or verb.
- Include the tokens after the negation cue, upto the beginning of the predicted scope.

Figure 2: Post-processing heuristic rules.

4.3 Negation Scope Detection Evaluation

The algorithm is evaluated using two different measures; *token-level* and *scope-level*. Every token can be either in-scope or out of scope. We report the F-score for both in-scope and out-of-scope tokens. Since the output is a sequence, F-score metrics may be insufficient as it just considers individual tokens. We also report percentage of correct scopes (PCS). Results are given in Table 7. The out-of-scope token has a higher F-score

	Punctuation	BiLSTM	Proposed
In-scope (F)	0.66	0.88	0.85
Out-scope (F)	0.87	0.97	0.97
PCS	0.52	0.72	0.72

Table 7: Negation classifier performance for scope detection with gold cues and scope.

as compared to in-scope. This is expected since scope tokens are restricted and less in number as compared to out-of-scope (See Table 3). The in-scope F-score is more important for the downstream task of sentiment as we apply negation on predicted in-scope tokens for sentiment. The results show that our proposed model is comparable to the BiLSTM model for sentences with gold cues that have an annotated scope, but our model does not require annotated data. For BiLSTM, we used the implementation provided by the authors [2]. We also implemented a punctuation model that marks as negated all terms from a negation cue to the next punctuation. Fancellu et al. (2017) mentioned punctuation alone as a strong predictor for negation scope detection task for a majority previous of negation corpora. Notably, it performs poorly on our data as our scope is more restricted. We next

show that having a restricted scope is beneficial to the antonym based negation sentiment prediction.

5 Sentiment with Negation Detection Pipeline

Here we show the integration of predicted negation scope in sentiment prediction pipeline. We begin with an overview of the data preprocessing, features and modeling, followed by our experimental setup and results. Finally, a comparison of the prediction performance of different systems is presented.

5.1 Experimental Method

From our tweet collection, we discarded tweets containing images and Non-English characters and anonymized all user and company handles, giving a dataset of 21746 tweets. A sentiment annotation task was run on a data annotation platform. Each tweet was initially annotated by 5 annotators using a 4 point (0 to 3) Likert scale (Likert, 1932) indicating `Not-At-All`, `Slight`, `Moderate` and `Very` about their perception on the sentiment for a given tweet. We used a set of gold standard questions to filter out the bad annotators, computed the average score for each label, and assigned the maximum score. A tweet is assigned a sentiment label if the maximum score for that label is greater than 1 else it is discarded from the study, giving a labeled dataset of 17779 tweets. To compute the inter-annotator agreement, first we measured what percentage of the annotators out of 5 contributed to the final sentiment label and then took the average over all the tweets giving a 78.8% inter-annotator agreement.

5.1.1 Data Pre-processing

A cleaning module is incorporated to reduce sparsity when generating word-based features. We replaced all links/URL by a keyword URL, removed # from the hashtags, replaced all @*mentions*, and replaced emojis and emoticons with the word explanation. An entity recognition module is run to replace the identified entity using a keyword "ENT".

5.1.2 Features

TFIDF-based unigram features.
Existence of consecutive question and exclamation marks and capitalized words.
Emotion lexicon features: A count of the number of words in each of the 8 emotion classes from

---

[2]https://github.com/ffancellu/NegNN

the NRC emotion lexicon (Mohammad and Turney, 2010)

Sentiment lexicons used:
Bing Liu's Opinion Lexicon (Ding et al., 2008); *The MPQA Subjectivity Lexicon* (Wilson et al., 2005); *Sentiment140 Lexicon* (Kiritchenko et al., 2014b); *NRC Hashtag Sentiment Lexicon* (Kiritchenko et al., 2014b);

For a given tweet, we computed minimum, maximum, average and summation of positive and negative scores of the words in the tweet that lies within a negation scope, and the average sentiment score of the last word in the tweet.

Negation handling: Append "NOT_" to each word in the scope.

5.1.3 SVM Evaluation

Libsvm (Chang and Lin, 2011) is used to implement the SVM classifier. The tweet annotated dataset was divided into a train and test set (see Table 8 for the distribution). The training set was further split into a ratio of 85:15 for the validation set. The three parameters w1, w2 and C were tuned using the validation set. The variables w1 and w2 are the penalty associated to a class and C is the regularization. Table 8 shows the evaluation metric using Precision, Recall and F measure for each class in the test set.

We do not find a major difference for SVMs(w/o negation). This is in spite of using the standard features such as prefixing the tokens in scope with a keyword *NOT_* and changing the polarity of the sentiment-bearing words using sentiment lexicons as described in previous work. A possible reason is that customer service domain is more negative as compared to general review domain See Section 6 for detailed analysis.

5.2 Neural Network Evaluation

Baseline 1: Our first baseline is a single layer CNN as used in (Kim, 2014). The model consists of a 1D convolution layer of window size 2 and 64 different filters. The convolution layer takes as input the GloVe embeddings. Max pooling layer is used to reduce the output dimensionality but keep the most salient information.

Baseline 2: (Wang et al., 2016) presented a jointed CNN and LSTM architecture. The features generated from convolution and pooling operation can be viewed as local features similar to ngrams but cannot handle long term dpendencies. LSTM can handle CNN's limitation by preserving historical information for a long period of time. Using this as a motivation, we included a convolutional layer and max pooling layer before the input is fed into an LSTM. A bidirectional LSTM layer is stacked on the convolutions layer and the tweet representation is taken to the fully connected network.

Proposed Negation + Antonym CNN-LSTM : We modified the sentence representation learned by replacing a word in the negation scope with it's antonym. Using antonyms would reduce the Out-of-Vocabulary words as compared to prefixing a word with "NOT_" for learning word representations. Replacing all the words upto punctuation with antonyms could entirely change the sentence meaning and hence this required a more restricted and accurate scope detection. We get the predicted scopes from the scope detection model described in Section 4. The antonym list is obtained from AntNET (Rajana et al., 2017)

For the NN-based approaches, 20% data is used for validation and we save the model weights only if the validation accuracy improves. The outputs of the LSTM are fed through a sigmoid layer for binary classification. Regularization is performed by using a drop-out rate of 0.2 in the drop-out layer. The model is optimized using the (Kingma and Ba, 2014) optimizer. The deep network was implemented using the Keras package (Chollet et al., 2015). Hyper-parameter optimization for the neural network is performed using Hyperas, a python package, based on hyperopt (Bergstra et al., 2015). Results in Table 8 show that the antonym based learned representations are more useful for sentiment task as compared to prefixing with NOT_. The proposed CNN-LSTM-Our-neg-Ant improves upon the simple CNN-LSTM-w/o neg. baseline with F1 scores improving from 0.72 to 0.78 for positive sentiment and from 0.83 to 0.87 for negative sentiment. Hence Negation coupled with antonyms improves the sentiment prediction for a customer service domain.

6 Discussion

In this section, we aim to show the particularities of our dataset, suggesting the reasons why negation detection did not improve the performance of the lexicon-based SVM when previous work had seen huge performance gains, and intuitions on how the antonym based method gives improvement.

- Class Distribution

Classifier	Positive Sentiment		
	Precision	Recall	Fscore
SVM-w/o neg.	0.57	0.72	0.64
SVM-Punct. neg.	0.58	0.70	0.63
SVM-our-neg.	0.58	0.73	0.65
CNN	0.63	0.83	0.72
CNN-LSTM	0.71	0.72	0.72
CNN-LSTM-Our-neg-Ant	**0.78**	**0.77**	**0.78**

Classifier	Negative Sentiment		
	Precision	Recall	Fscore
SVM-w/o neg.	0.78	0.86	0.82
SVM-Punct. neg.	0.78	0.87	0.83
SVM-Our neg.	0.80	0.87	0.83
CNN	0.88	0.72	0.79
CNN-LSTM.	0.83	0.83	0.83
CNN-LSTM-our-neg-Ant	**0.87**	**0.87**	**0.87**

	Train	Test
Positive tweets	5121	1320
Negative tweets	9094	2244

Table 8: Sentiment classification evaluation, using different classifiers on the test set.

Our customer service dataset has a much larger number of negative tweets while the benchmark sentiment dataset used in most of the previous systems has positive class as the majority class (Kiritchenko et al., 2014b; Reitan et al., 2015; Nakov et al., 2013; Mohammad et al., 2013; Tang et al., 2014). Additionally, Reitan et al. (2015) reported that the classifier struggles with negative class prediction. A F-measure of 0.533 and 0.323 is reported by Reitan et al. (2015) and Councill et al. (2010) respectively, on negative class prediction. In contrast, our baseline classifier achieves a much higher F score of 0.82 on the negative class.

- Cue Word Distribution.
The conversation negation corpus is annotated for both actual negation cues and sentiment. To see if there exists some correlation between the number of cues and sentiment, we calculated the percentage of positive and negative tweets with more than one cue. 19% of positive tweets contain more than one negation cue while for the negative class it is 48%. Though we need more evidence to support, but it is possible that the number of negation cues in these conversations is a strong indicator of negative class, hence the SVM based classifier had better

prediction on negative class detection.

- Sarcasm and Irony
Results in Table 8 show that the classifier struggles with positive class precision. A sentiment study on user-generated content by (Sarmento et al., 2009; Carvalho et al., 2009) has similar class distribution and results to ours. The sentences expressing negative opinions is almost the double of those expressing positive opinions and the precision of identifying negative opinions ($\approx 89\%$) is significantly higher than the precision of identifying positive opinions ($\approx 60\%$). They confirm the relevance of irony for sentiment analysis by an error analysis of their present classifier stating that a large proportion of misclassifications ($\approx 35\%$) derive from their system's inability to account for irony. We then performed some manual error analysis on the incorrect positive predictions for SVM and observed that some of the incorrect predictions were actually sarcastic, see Table 9. To get an insight on how our method improves these types of predictions, consider the example in Row2 in Table 9. It was predicted as positive by SVM, CNN and LSTM due to the positive word "Awesome". Our method detects negation cue word **"not"** with **"able"** in it's scope. The antonym dictionary then is used to replace **"able"** with **"incapable"**. Having a strong negative word corrects the prediction to negative. These results indicate that there is room for improvement for the positive class but negation handling may not be enough. A combination of negation and sarcasm may be a useful direction to explore in future for customer service conversations.

S.No	Tweet
1	Hi @username - Love u. I'd recommend not displaying the early bird button in the app if it's broken and not working
2	looks like I won't be able to vote because the train is running late. Awesome

Table 9: Negative sarcastic examples.

7 Conclusion and Future Work

This paper presented an approach to negation cue and scope detection in customer service interactions on Twitter and the impact of using this component for sentiment detection. We refined the annotation guidelines for scope representation, gathering a dataset of 2000 labeled tweets. Our rule based approach based on syntactic constituents does not require annotated scope data for training, but performs comparable to state of the art BiLSTM. To evaluate the effectiveness of negation modeling on sentiment detection, we performed experiments using both an SVM and CNN-LSTM Architecture. There was no significant improvement between the two lexicon based SVMs (with/without negation handling). The proposed antonym based negation for CNN-LSTM outperformed both a CNN and a combination CNN-LSTM that did not handle negation. The result and error analysis shows that customer service interactions have higher frequency of negation cues, are more skewed towards negative class, and are sometimes sarcastic. In future, we plan to study other language phenomenon such as sarcasm in combination with negation.

References

James Bergstra, Brent Komer, Chris Eliasmith, Dan Yamins, and David D Cox. 2015. Hyperopt: a python library for model selection and hyperparameter optimization. *Computational Science and Discovery*, 8(1):014008.

D. Biber. 1999. *Longman Grammar of Spoken and Written English*. Grammar Reference Series. Longman.

Jorge Carrillo de Albornoz, Laura Plaza, Alberto Díaz, and Miguel Ballesteros. 2012. UCM-I: A rule-based syntactic approach for resolving the scope of negation. In *Proceedings of the First Joint Conference on Lexical and Computational Semantics, *SEM 2012, June 7-8, 2012, Montréal, Canada.*, pages 282–287. Association for Computational Linguistics.

Paula Carvalho, Luís Sarmento, Mário J. Silva, and Eugénio de Oliveira. 2009. Clues for detecting irony in user-generated contents: Oh...!! it's "so easy" ;-). In *Proceedings of the 1st International CIKM Workshop on Topic-sentiment Analysis for Mass Opinion*, TSA '09. ACM.

Chih-Chung Chang and Chih-Jen Lin. 2011. Libsvm: A library for support vector machines. *ACM Trans. Intell. Syst. Technol.*, 2(3):27:1–27:27.

François Chollet et al. 2015. Keras. https://keras.io.

Isaac G. Councill, Ryan McDonald, and Leonid Velikovich. 2010. What's great and what's not: Learning to classify the scope of negation for improved sentiment analysis. In *Proceedings of the Workshop on Negation and Speculation in Natural Language Processing*, NeSp-NLP '10, pages 51–59, Stroudsburg, PA, USA. Association for Computational Linguistics.

Xiaowen Ding, Bing Liu, and Philip S Yu. 2008. A holistic lexicon-based approach to opinion mining. In *Proceedings of the 2008 international conference on web search and data mining*, pages 231–240. ACM.

Martine Enger, Erik Velldal, and Lilja Øvrelid. 2017. An open-source tool for negation detection: a maximum-margin approach. In *Proceedings of the EACL workshop on Computational Semantics Beyond Events and Roles (SemBEaR)*, pages 64–69, Valencia, Spain.

Federico Fancellu, Adam Lopez, Bonnie Webber, and Hangfeng He. 2017. *Detecting negation scope is easy, except when it isn't*, pages 58–63. Association for Computational Linguistics.

Federico Fancellu, Adam Lopez, and Bonnie L. Webber. 2016. Neural networks for negation scope detection. In *Proceedings of the 54th Annual Meeting of the Association for Computational Linguistics, ACL 2016, August 7-12, 2016, Berlin, Germany, Volume 1: Long Papers*. The Association for Computer Linguistics.

C.J. Fillmore. 1963. The position of embedding transformations in a grammar. *Word*, 19.

T. Givón. 1993. *English grammar: a function-based introduction*. Number v. 2 in English Grammar: A Function-based Introduction. J. Benjamins Pub. Co.

M. Gotti, M. Dossena, and R. Dury. 2008. *English Historical Linguistics 2006: Selected papers from the fourteenth International Conference on English Historical Linguistics (ICEHL 14), Bergamo, Volume 1: Syntax and Morphology*. English Historical Linguistics 2006. John Benjamins Publishing Company.

Laurence Horn. 1989. *A Natural History of Negation*. University of Chicago Press.

Minqing Hu and Bing Liu. 2004. Mining and summarizing customer reviews. In *Proceedings of the Tenth ACM SIGKDD International Conference on Knowledge Discovery and Data Mining*, KDD '04. ACM.

Yoon Kim. 2014. Convolutional neural networks for sentence classification. In *Proceedings of the 2014 Conference on Empirical Methods in Natural Language Processing, EMNLP 2014, October 25-29, 2014, Doha, Qatar, A meeting of SIGDAT, a Special Interest Group of the ACL*, pages 1746–1751.

Diederik P. Kingma and Jimmy Ba. 2014. Adam: A method for stochastic optimization. *CoRR*, abs/1412.6980.

Svetlana Kiritchenko, Xiaodan Zhu, and Saif M. Mohammad. 2014a. Sentiment analysis of short informal texts. *J. Artif. Intell. Res.*, 50:723–762.

Svetlana Kiritchenko, Xiaodan Zhu, and Saif M Mohammad. 2014b. Sentiment analysis of short informal texts. *Journal of Artificial Intelligence Research*, 50:723–762.

Natalia Konstantinova, Sheila CM De Sousa, Noa P Cruz Díaz, Manuel J Mana López, Maite Taboada, and Ruslan Mitkov. 2012. A review corpus annotated for negation, speculation and their scope. In *LREC*, pages 3190–3195.

Emanuele Lapponi, Erik Velldal, Lilja Ovrelid, and Jonathon Read. 2012. Uio2: Sequence-labeling negation using dependency features. In *Proceedings of the First Joint Conference on Lexical and Computational Semantics - Volume 1: Proceedings of the Main Conference and the Shared Task, and Volume 2: Proceedings of the Sixth International Workshop on Semantic Evaluation*, SemEval '12. Association for Computational Linguistics.

Rensis Likert. 1932. A technique for the measurement of attitudes. *Archives of psychology*.

Christopher D. Manning, Mihai Surdeanu, John Bauer, Jenny Finkel, Steven J. Bethard, and David McClosky. 2014. The Stanford CoreNLP natural language processing toolkit. In *Association for Computational Linguistics (ACL) System Demonstrations*.

Tomas Mikolov, Ilya Sutskever, Kai Chen, Gregory S. Corrado, and Jeffrey Dean. 2013. Distributed representations of words and phrases and their compositionality. In *Advances in Neural Information Processing Systems 26: 27th Annual Conference on Neural Information Processing Systems 2013. Proceedings of a meeting held December 5-8, 2013, Lake Tahoe, Nevada, United States.*, pages 3111–3119.

Yasuhide Miura, Shigeyuki Sakaki, Keigo Hattori, and Tomoko Ohkuma. 2014. Teamx: A sentiment analyzer with enhanced lexicon mapping and weighting scheme for unbalanced data. In *Proceedings of the 8th International Workshop on Semantic Evaluation (SemEval 2014)*, pages 628–632. Association for Computational Linguistics.

Saif Mohammad, Svetlana Kiritchenko, and Xiaodan Zhu. 2013. Nrc-canada: Building the state-of-the-art in sentiment analysis of tweets. In *Proceedings of the 7th International Workshop on Semantic Evaluation, SemEval@NAACL-HLT 2013, Atlanta, Georgia, USA, June 14-15, 2013*, pages 321–327. The Association for Computer Linguistics.

Saif M Mohammad and Peter D Turney. 2010. Emotions evoked by common words and phrases: Using mechanical turk to create an emotion lexicon. In *Proceedings of the NAACL HLT 2010 workshop on computational approaches to analysis and generation of emotion in text*, pages 26–34. Association for Computational Linguistics.

Karo Moilanen and Stephen Pulman. 2007. Sentiment composition. In *Proceedings of Recent Advances in Natural Language Processing (RANLP 2007)*, pages 378–382.

Roser Morante and Eduardo Blanco. 2012. *sem 2012 shared task: Resolving the scope and focus of negation. In *Proceedings of the First Joint Conference on Lexical and Computational Semantics - Volume 1: Proceedings of the Main Conference and the Shared Task, and Volume 2: Proceedings of the Sixth International Workshop on Semantic Evaluation*, SemEval '12, pages 265–274, Stroudsburg, PA, USA. Association for Computational Linguistics.

Roser Morante and Walter Daelemans. 2009. A metalearning approach to processing the scope of negation. In *Proceedings of the Thirteenth Conference on Computational Natural Language Learning*, CoNLL '09, pages 21–29, Stroudsburg, PA, USA. Association for Computational Linguistics.

Roser Morante, Anthony M. L. Liekens, and Walter Daelemans. 2008. Learning the scope of negation in biomedical texts. In *2008 Conference on Empirical Methods in Natural Language Processing, EMNLP 2008, Proceedings of the Conference, 25-27 October 2008, Honolulu, Hawaii, USA, A meeting of SIGDAT, a Special Interest Group of the ACL*, pages 715–724. ACL.

Preslav Nakov, Sara Rosenthal, Zornitsa Kozareva, Veselin Stoyanov, Alan Ritter, and Theresa Wilson. 2013. Semeval-2013 task 2: Sentiment analysis in twitter. In *Second Joint Conference on Lexical and Computational Semantics (* SEM), Volume 2: Proceedings of the Seventh International Workshop on Semantic Evaluation (SemEval 2013)*, volume 2, pages 312–320.

Woodley Packard, Emily M. Bender, Jonathon Read, Stephan Oepen, and Rebecca Dridan. 2014. Simple negation scope resolution through deep parsing: A semantic solution to a semantic problem. In *Proceedings of the 52nd Annual Meeting of the Association for Computational Linguistics*, pages 69–78, Baltimore, USA.

Bo Pang and Lillian Lee. 2008. Opinion mining and sentiment analysis. *Found. Trends Inf. Retr.*

Randolph Quirk, Sidney Greenbaum, Geoffrey Leech, and Jan Svartvik. 1985. *A Comprehensive Grammar of the English Language*. Longman, London.

Sneha Rajana, Chris Callison-Burch, Marianna Apidianaki, and Vered Shwartz. 2017. Learning antonyms with paraphrases and a morphology-aware neural network. In *Proceedings of the 6th Joint Conference on Lexical and Computational Semantics (*SEM 2017)*, pages 12–21. Association for Computational Linguistics.

Jonathon Read, Erik Velldal, Lilja Øvrelid, and Stephan Oepen. 2012. Uio1: Constituent-based discriminative ranking for negation resolution. In *Proceedings of the First Joint Conference on Lexical and Computational Semantics, *SEM 2012, June 7-8, 2012, Montréal, Canada.*, pages 310–318. Association for Computational Linguistics.

Johan Reitan, Jorgen Faret, Bjorn Gamback, and Lars Bungum. 2015. Negation scope detection for twitter sentiment analysis. In *WASSA@EMNLP*.

Luís Sarmento, Paula Carvalho, Mário J. Silva, and Eugénio de Oliveira. 2009. Automatic creation of a reference corpus for political opinion mining in user-generated content. In *Proceedings of the 1st International CIKM Workshop on Topic-sentiment Analysis for Mass Opinion*, TSA '09, pages 29–36, New York, NY, USA. ACM.

Bonggun Shin, Timothy Lee, and Jinho D. Choi. 2017. Lexicon integrated CNN models with attention for sentiment analysis. In *Proceedings of the 8th Workshop on Computational Approaches to Subjectivity, Sentiment and Social Media Analysis, WASSA@EMNLP 2017, Copenhagen, Denmark, September 8, 2017*, pages 149–158.

György Szarvas, Veronika Vincze, Richárd Farkas, and János Csirik. 2008. The bioscope corpus: Annotation for negation, uncertainty and their scope in biomedical texts. In *Proceedings of the Workshop on Current Trends in Biomedical Natural Language Processing*, BioNLP '08, pages 38–45, Stroudsburg, PA, USA. Association for Computational Linguistics.

Duyu Tang, Furu Wei, Bing Qin, Ting Liu, and Ming Zhou. 2014. Coooolll: A deep learning system for twitter sentiment classification. In *Proceedings of the 8th International Workshop on Semantic Evaluation, SemEval@COLING 2014, Dublin, Ireland, August 23-24, 2014.*, pages 208–212.

Gunnel Tottie. 1991. *Negation in English speech and writing : a study in variation.* San Diego : Academic Press. (Quantitative analyses of linguistic structure series).

Erik Velldal. 2011. Predicting speculation: A simple disambiguation approach to hedge detection in biomedical literature. *Journal of Biomedical Semantics*, 2(5). Supplement to the Fourth International Symposium on Semantic Mining in Biomedicine.

Erik Velldal, Lilja Øvrelid, Jonathon Read, and Stephan Oepen. 2012. Speculation and negation: Rules, rankers, and the role of syntax. *Computational Linguistics*, 38(2):369–410.

Xingyou Wang, Weijie Jiang, and Zhiyong Luo. 2016. Combination of convolutional and recurrent neural network for sentiment analysis of short texts. In *COLING 2016, 26th International Conference on Computational Linguistics, Proceedings of the Conference: Technical Papers, December 11-16, 2016, Osaka, Japan*, pages 2428–2437.

James Paul White. 2012. Uwashington: Negation resolution using machine learning methods. In **SEM 2012: The First Joint Conference on Lexical and Computational Semantics – Volume 1: Proceedings of the main conference and the shared task, and Volume 2: Proceedings of the Sixth International Workshop on Semantic Evaluation (SemEval 2012)*, pages 335–339. Association for Computational Linguistics.

Michael Wiegand, Alexandra Balahur, Benjamin Roth, Dietrich Klakow, and Andrés Montoyo. 2010. A survey on the role of negation in sentiment analysis. In *Proceedings of the Workshop on Negation and Speculation in Natural Language Processing*, NeSp-NLP '10, pages 60–68, Stroudsburg, PA, USA. Association for Computational Linguistics.

Theresa Wilson, Janyce Wiebe, and Paul Hoffmann. 2005. Recognizing contextual polarity in phrase-level sentiment analysis. In *Proceedings of the Conference on Human Language Technology and Empirical Methods in Natural Language Processing*, HLT '05, pages 347–354, Stroudsburg, PA, USA. Association for Computational Linguistics.

Theresa Wilson, Janyce Wiebe, and Paul Hoffmann. 2009. Recognizing contextual polarity: An exploration of features for phrase-level sentiment analysis. *Comput. Linguist.*, 35(3):399–433.

Wenpeng Yin and Hinrich Schütze. 2015. Multichannel variable-size convolution for sentence classification. In *Proceedings of the 19th Conference on Computational Natural Language Learning, CoNLL 2015, Beijing, China, July 30-31, 2015*, pages 204–214.

Deep Learning Techniques for Humor Detection in Hindi-English Code-Mixed Tweets

Sushmitha Reddy Sane*[1]   **Suraj Tripathi*[2]**   **Koushik Reddy Sane[1]**   **Radhika Mamidi[1]**

[1]International Institute of Information Technology, Hyderabad
[2]Indian Institute of Technology, Delhi

{sushmithareddy.sane, koushikreddy.sane}@research.iiit.ac.in,
surajtripathi93@gmail.com, radhika.mamidi@iiit.ac.in

Abstract

We propose bilingual word embeddings based on word2vec and fastText models (CBOW and Skip-gram) to address the problem of Humor detection in Hindi-English code-mixed tweets in combination with deep learning architectures. We focus on deep learning approaches which are not widely used on code-mixed data and analyzed their performance by experimenting with three different neural network models. We propose convolution neural network (CNN) and bidirectional long-short term memory (biLSTM) (with and without Attention) models which take the generated bilingual embeddings as input. We make use of Twitter data to create bilingual word embeddings. All our proposed architectures outperform the state-of-the-art results, and Attention-based bidirectional LSTM model achieved an accuracy of 73.6% which is an increment of more than 4% compared to the current state-of-the-art results.

1 Introduction

In the present day, we observe an exponential rise in the number of individuals using Internet Technology for different purposes like entertainment, learning and sharing their experiences. This led to a tremendous increase in content generated by users on social networking and micro-blogging sites. Websites like Facebook, Twitter, and Reddit (Danet and Herring, 2007) act as a platform for users to reach large masses in real-time and express their thoughts freely and sometimes anonymously amongst communities and virtual networks. These natural language texts depict various linguistic elements such as aggression, irony, humor, and sarcasm. In recent years, automatic detection of these elements (Davidov et al., 2010) has become a research interest for both organizations and research communities.

The advancement in computer technologies places increasing emphasis on systems and models that can effectively handle natural human language. So far, the majority of the research in natural language processing and deep learning is focused on the English language as individuals across the world use it widely. But, in multilingual geographies like India, it is a natural phenomenon for individuals to use more than one language words in speech and in social media sites like Facebook and Twitter (Cárdenas-Claros and Isharyanti, 2009; Crystal, 2002). Data shows that in India, there are about 314.9 million bilingual speakers and most of these speakers tend to mix two languages interchangeably in their communication. Researchers (Myers-Scotton, 1997) defined this linguistic behavior as Code-mixing - the embedding of linguistic units such as phrases, words, and morphemes of one language into an utterance of another language which produces utterances consisting of words taken from the lexicons of different languages.

The primary challenge with the code-mixed corpus is the lack of data in general text-corpora, (Nguyen and Doğruöz, 2013; Solorio and Liu, 2008a,b) for conducting experiments. In this paper, we take up the task of detecting one critical element of natural language (Kruger, 1996) which plays a significant part in our linguistic, cognitive, and social lives, i.e., Humor. Martin (Martin and Ford, 2018) extensively studied the psychology of humor and stated that it is ubiquitous across cultures and it is a necessary part of all verbal communication. The classification of some text as humor can be very subjective. Also, capturing Humor in higher order structures (de Oliveira et al., 2017) through text processing is considered as a challenging natural language problem. Pun detection in one-liners (Kao et al., 2016) and detection of humor in Yelp reviews (de Oliveira et al., 2017)

---

https://en.wikipedia.org/wiki/Multilingualism_in_India

Proceedings of the 10th Workshop on Computational Approaches to Subjectivity, Sentiment and Social Media Analysis, pages 57–61
Minneapolis, June 6, 2019. ©2019 Association for Computational Linguistics

have also been studied in recent years.

Deep learning techniques (LeCun et al., 2015) have contributed to significant progress in various areas of research, including natural language understanding. Convolutional neural network based networks have been used for sentence classification (Kim, 2014), bidirectional LSTM networks (biLSTM) were used for sequence tagging (Huang et al., 2015), and attention based bidirectional LSTM networks were used for relational classification (Zhou et al., 2016) and topic-based sentiment analysis (Baziotis et al., 2017). In this work, we propose three deep learning networks using bilingual word embeddings as input and compare it against the classification models presented in (Khandelwal et al., 2018) using their annotated corpus to detect one of the playful domains of language: Humor. An example from the corpus:

"Subha ka bhula agar sham ko wapas ghar aa jaye then we must thank GPS technology.."
"(If someone is lost in the morning and returns home in the evening then we must thank GPS technology.)

This tweet is annotated as humorous. In particular, we are focused on code-mixed data as it lacks the presence of bilingual word embeddings, commonly used, to train any deep learning model which is essential for understanding human behavior, events, reviews, studying trends as well as linguistic analysis (Vyas et al., 2014).

1.1 Corpus creation for Bilingual Word Embeddings

The corpus used for training the bilingual word embeddings is created using Twitter's API. Around 200k tweets are extracted using 1000 most common words from the training corpus after removing stop words. Preprocessing is done on the sentences, and Twitter handles starting with "@" or words that have any special symbol are removed. URLs are replaced with the word "URL".

1.2 Word2Vec

Code-mixed (Hindi-English) data need vector representations of its words to train a deep learning based model. However, our corpus being bilingual in nature prohibits the use of any pre-trained word2vec (Mikolov et al., 2013) representations. As mentioned earlier, we used the collected Twitter data to train the bilingual word embedding model. We experimented with various hyperparameters like embedding size, window length, and

negative sampling. Based on the results, we finalized the following set of values for our main task - humor detection.

- Embedding size: 300, Window length: 10, Negative sampling

1.3 FastText

One of the limitations of word2vec model is the inability to handle words with very low frequency in the training corpus and out-of-vocabulary words which might be present in the unseen text instances. Example: people on social media write words like "happppyyyyy", "lolll", etc. These kinds of new words can't have pre-trained word embeddings. To address this problem in the bilingual scenario, we analyzed the performance of fastText (Bojanowski et al., 2017) word embedding model, which considers subword information, for generating word embeddings. FastText learns character n-gram (Joulin et al., 2016) representations and represents words as the sum of the n-gram vectors, where n is a hyperparameter. We kept hyperparameters like embedding size, window length, etc., same as in word2vec model to compare their results.

1.4 Model Architecture

We propose three different deep learning architectures for the task of humor detection based on CNN and biLSTM networks which take bilingual word embeddings as input. We used cross-entropy loss function and Adam optimizer for training all our proposed architectures.

1.4.1 Model 1 - Convolutional Neural Network (CNN)

We propose a CNN-based model, refer to Figure 1, which takes bilingual word embeddings as input. CNN based model makes use of a set of 4 parallel 1D convolution layers to extract features from the input embeddings. Features derived from the convolution layer are then fed into the global max-pool layer, which extracts one feature per filter. The extracted features from max-pool layer are then flattened and passed to multiple fully connected (FC) layers. Finally, classification is performed using a softmax layer. We have used various training techniques such as dropout (.25 to .75) (Srivastava et al., 2014) and batch-normalization (Ioffe and Szegedy, 2015) that helps in reducing overfitting and sensitivity towards initial weights respectively. With the use of batch-normalization, we also observed improvement in the convergence rate.

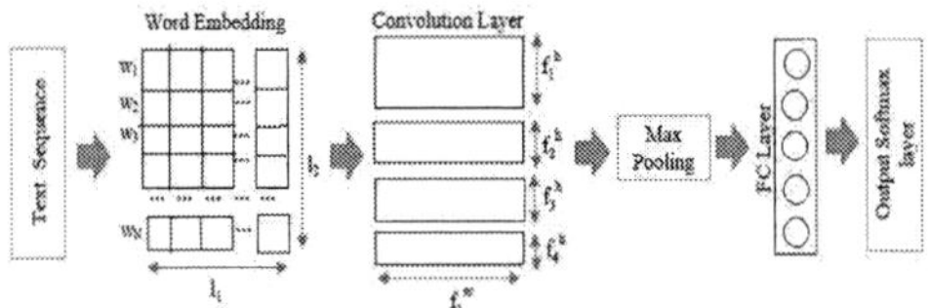

Figure 1: Proposed CNN architecture

The model uses four parallel instances of convolution layer with varying kernel sizes. We experimented with various values for hyperparameters such as the number of kernels, kernel sizes and finalized following values based on the performance on the validation set:

- Kernel size:

$$f_1^h = 3, f_2^h = 6, f_3^h = 9, f_4^h = 12$$

- Number of kernels = 200, Stride = 1.

We analyzed the performance of the proposed CNN based network with both word2vec and fast-Text generated bilingual word embeddings and presented their results in Table 2. Here, Model 1(a) refers to CNN with word2vec and Model 1(b) refers to CNN with fastText based word representations respectively.

1.4.2 Model 2 - Bidirectional LSTM Network

Bidirectional LSTM architectures have been proved to be very useful to model word sequences and are robust to learn on data with long-range temporal dependencies. We use the bidirectional LSTM network on the input bilingual word embeddings to capture the compositional semantics for the bilingual texts in our experiments.

The sentiment of each word in the sentence depends on the context in which the word is used, where context includes content in front of the word as well as behind the word. To model these scenarios, we make use of bidirectional LSTM network which has been successfully applied in generating context-dependent hidden representations as well as capturing long-term dependencies in text classification tasks (Wang et al., 2016). We experimented with a different number of hidden layers and number of hidden units in each hidden layer

and finalized the value of 1 and 200 respectively based on the results on the validation set. We used similar architecture as showed in Figure 2 with no attention mechanism and used concatenated $\overrightarrow{h_t}$ and $\overleftarrow{h_1}$ as input to the dense layer (#hidden units = 200) which is followed by the final softmax layer. To analyze the effect of different bilingual word embeddings, we make use of both word2vec, and fastText generated embeddings. In Table 2, Model 2(a) refers to the use of word2vec with Model 2 and Model 2(b) refers to the use of fastText with Model 2.

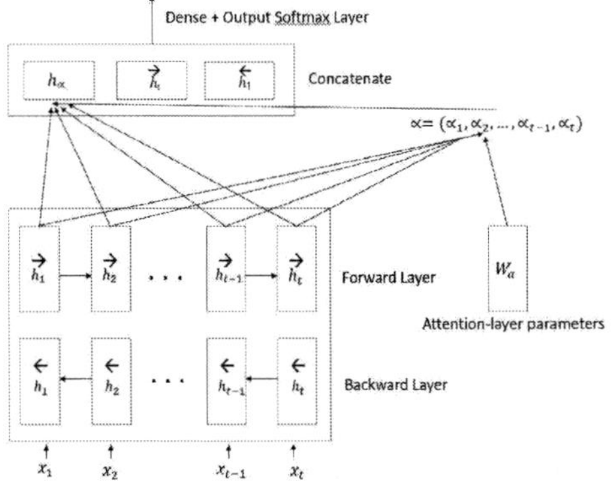

Figure 2: Proposed Attention based BiLSTM Model

1.4.3 Model 3 - Attention-based Bidirectional LSTM Network

We further propose an attention-based mechanism for the bidirectional LSTM network. The word-level attention model learns which words in a given sentence are more critical for determining the overall emotion (humorous / non-humorous) of the sentence. These words act as decisive points. Some parts in sentences create noise, and this mechanism helps to filter out those noises.

Input sentence $x_1, x_2, ..., x_{t-1}, x_t$ represents bilingual word embedding of the input text utterance, which is fed into the hidden layer of the proposed bidirectional LSTM network as input. As presented in Figure 2, bidirectional LSTM architecture makes use of both forward and backward hidden states at each time step. We used well-known standard LSTM units for our architecture and thus omitted the equations related to the cell units. At each time step i, $h_i = [\overrightarrow{h_i}; \overleftarrow{h_i}]$ represents complete hidden state representation. We make use of the hidden state of each step to calculate the weights for each word and weighted summation of all time steps. h_α is used as an input to the classifier in combination with $\overrightarrow{h_t}$ and $\overleftarrow{h_1}$. Concatenated hidden states are passed on to a single dense layer, followed by output softmax layer. We used the same hyperparameter settings for hidden representation and dense layer size as mentioned in Model 2 to analyze the effect of adding attention to the proposed model. We experimented with both word2vec and fastText generated bilingual word embeddings, and results are presented in Table 2. Here, Model 3(a) refers to the use of word2vec and Model 3(b) refers to the use of fastText with Model 3 respectively.

Word-Hi	Word-En	Word2Vec	FastText
pyaar	love	0.64	0.78
nafrat	hate	0.71	0.73
ldai	fight	0.74	0.85
majak	funny	0.62	0.71
gussa	angry	0.78	0.76

Table 1: Similar meaning Hindi and English words similarity scores with word2vec and fastText models

2 Results

The benchmark dataset that is published online by (Khandelwal et al., 2018) is used for evaluating the effectiveness of bilingual word embeddings and proposed deep learning models. It contains 3543 annotated tweets where 1755 are labeled humorous and 1698 as non-humorous. We make use of 5-fold cross-validation for generating our experimental results. Using all the features (Khandelwal et al., 2018), the baseline systems: kernel SVM, random forest, extra tree, and naive Bayes presented the best accuracy of 69.3%. Going forward, to the best of our knowledge, we are the first to experiment with deep learning architectures using bilingual word embedding for detecting humor in code-mixed data. All of our models showed better accuracies than current state-of-art-results, and our proposed Attention-based bidirectional LSTM achieved the best accuracy of 73.6%.

The challenges in this task are the linguistic complexity of code-mixed data and lack of clean data. To address phrasal repetitions, short and simple constructions, non-grammatical words and spelling errors in the data, larger corpora need to be built and annotated in the geographies and communities where multilingualism is observed.

In Table 1, we analyzed the generated bilingual word embeddings by comparing the similar-

Model	Accuracy
Random Forest*	65.2
Naive Bayes*	67.2
Extra tree*	67.8
Kernel SVM*	69.3
Model 1(a)	70.8
Model 1(b)	71.3
Model 2(a)	71.5
Model 2(b)	72.2
Model 3(a)	**72.8**
Model 3(b)	**73.6**

Table 2: Detailed accuracies achieved on the benchmark dataset by different models. *Random Forest, Naive Bayes, Extra tree, and kernel SVM accuracies are from (Khandelwal et al., 2018)

ity scores of Hindi and English words with similar meaning. We observed that fastText model showed better similarity scores than word2vec model which indicates that bilingual word embeddings do get better with subword information which is used in learning fastText word representations. In Table 2, we presented the results of our proposed deep learning based architectures which takes bilingual words embeddings generated from word2vec and fastText skip-gram model. We also experimented with CBOW versions of both learning strategies and achieved similar results.

3 Conclusion

In this paper, we address the problem of humor detection in code-mixed Hindi-English data generated by bilingual users. We propose three different deep learning based models which take bilingual word embeddings as input. Both word2vec and fastText based models are used for learning bilingual word representations and also to demonstrate the effectiveness of these techniques by presenting similarity scores of words with similar meaning in Hindi and English languages. The proposed attention-based biLSTM model worked best with an accuracy of 73.6%. Compared to the state-of-the-art models all our proposed deep learning models performed better at detecting humor in code-mixed data. For future work, we will generate aligned multilingual word embeddings and compare them with vectors aligned with MUSE, and pre-aligned fastText embeddings.

---

https://github.com/facebookresearch/MUSE

References

Christos Baziotis, Nikos Pelekis, and Christos Doulk-eridis. 2017. Datastories at semeval-2017 task 4: Deep lstm with attention for message-level and topic-based sentiment analysis. In *Proceedings of the 11th International Workshop on Semantic Evaluation (SemEval-2017)*, pages 747–754.

Piotr Bojanowski, Edouard Grave, Armand Joulin, and Tomas Mikolov. 2017. Enriching word vectors with subword information. *Transactions of the Association for Computational Linguistics*, 5:135–146.

Mónica Stella Cárdenas-Claros and Neny Isharyanti. 2009. Code-switching and code-mixing in internet chatting: Betweenyes, ya,andsi-a case study. *The Jalt Call Journal*, 5(3):67–78.

David Crystal. 2002. Language and the internet. *IEEE Transactions on Professional Communication*, 45(2):142–144.

Brenda Danet and Susan C Herring. 2007. *The multilingual Internet: Language, culture, and communication online*. Oxford University Press on Demand.

Dmitry Davidov, Oren Tsur, and Ari Rappoport. 2010. Semi-supervised recognition of sarcastic sentences in twitter and amazon. In *Proceedings of the fourteenth conference on computational natural language learning*, pages 107–116. Association for Computational Linguistics.

Zhiheng Huang, Wei Xu, and Kai Yu. 2015. Bidirectional lstm-crf models for sequence tagging. *arXiv preprint arXiv:1508.01991*.

Sergey Ioffe and Christian Szegedy. 2015. Batch normalization: Accelerating deep network training by reducing internal covariate shift. *arXiv preprint arXiv:1502.03167*.

Armand Joulin, Edouard Grave, Piotr Bojanowski, and Tomas Mikolov. 2016. Bag of tricks for efficient text classification. *arXiv preprint arXiv:1607.01759*.

Justine T Kao, Roger Levy, and Noah D Goodman. 2016. A computational model of linguistic humor in puns. *Cognitive science*, 40(5):1270–1285.

Ankush Khandelwal, Sahil Swami, Syed S Akhtar, and Manish Shrivastava. 2018. Humor detection in english-hindi code-mixed social media content: Corpus and baseline system. *arXiv preprint arXiv:1806.05513*.

Yoon Kim. 2014. Convolutional neural networks for sentence classification. *arXiv preprint arXiv:1408.5882*.

Arnold Kruger. 1996. The nature of humor in human nature: Cross-cultural commonalities. *Counselling Psychology Quarterly*, 9(3):235–241.

Yann LeCun, Yoshua Bengio, and Geoffrey Hinton. 2015. Deep learning. *nature*, 521(7553):436.

Rod A Martin and Thomas Ford. 2018. *The psychology of humor: An integrative approach*. Academic press.

Tomas Mikolov, Ilya Sutskever, Kai Chen, Greg S Corrado, and Jeff Dean. 2013. Distributed representations of words and phrases and their compositionality. In *Advances in neural information processing systems*, pages 3111–3119.

Carol Myers-Scotton. 1997. *Duelling languages: Grammatical structure in codeswitching*. Oxford University Press.

Dong Nguyen and A Seza Doğruöz. 2013. Word level language identification in online multilingual communication. In *Proceedings of the 2013 Conference on Empirical Methods in Natural Language Processing*, pages 857–862.

Luke de Oliveira, ICME Stanford, and Alfredo Láinez Rodrigo. 2017. Humor detection in yelp reviews.

Thamar Solorio and Yang Liu. 2008a. Learning to predict code-switching points. In *Proceedings of the Conference on Empirical Methods in Natural Language Processing*, pages 973–981. Association for Computational Linguistics.

Thamar Solorio and Yang Liu. 2008b. Part-of-speech tagging for english-spanish code-switched text. In *Proceedings of the Conference on Empirical Methods in Natural Language Processing*, pages 1051–1060. Association for Computational Linguistics.

Nitish Srivastava, Geoffrey Hinton, Alex Krizhevsky, Ilya Sutskever, and Ruslan Salakhutdinov. 2014. Dropout: a simple way to prevent neural networks from overfitting. *The Journal of Machine Learning Research*, 15(1):1929–1958.

Yogarshi Vyas, Spandana Gella, Jatin Sharma, Kalika Bali, and Monojit Choudhury. 2014. Pos tagging of english-hindi code-mixed social media content. In *Proceedings of the 2014 Conference on Empirical Methods in Natural Language Processing (EMNLP)*, pages 974–979.

Yequan Wang, Minlie Huang, Li Zhao, et al. 2016. Attention-based lstm for aspect-level sentiment classification. In *Proceedings of the 2016 conference on empirical methods in natural language processing*, pages 606–615.

Peng Zhou, Wei Shi, Jun Tian, Zhenyu Qi, Bingchen Li, Hongwei Hao, and Bo Xu. 2016. Attention-based bidirectional long short-term memory networks for relation classification. In *Proceedings of the 54th Annual Meeting of the Association for Computational Linguistics (Volume 2: Short Papers)*, volume 2, pages 207–212.

How do we feel when a robot dies? Emotions expressed on Twitter before and after hitchBOT's destruction

Kathleen C. Fraser
National Research Council Canada
Ottawa, Canada
kathleen.fraser@nrc-cnrc.gc.ca

Frauke Zeller
Ryerson University
Toronto, Canada
fzeller@ryerson.ca

David Harris Smith
McMaster University
Hamilton, Canada
dhsmith@mcmaster.ca

Saif M. Mohammad
National Research Council Canada
Ottawa, Canada
saif.mohammad@nrc-cnrc.gc.ca

Frank Rudzicz
University of Toronto and Vector Institute
Toronto, Canada
frank@spoclab.com

Abstract

In 2014, a chatty but immobile robot called hitchBOT set out to hitchhike across Canada. It similarly made its way across Germany and the Netherlands, and had begun a trip across the USA when it was destroyed by vandals. In this work, we analyze the emotions and sentiments associated with words in tweets posted before and after hitchBOT's destruction to answer two questions: Were there any differences in the emotions expressed across the different countries visited by hitchBOT? And how did the public react to the demise of hitchBOT? Our analyses indicate that while there were few cross-cultural differences in sentiment towards hitchBOT, there was a significant negative emotional reaction to its destruction, suggesting that people had formed an emotional connection with hitchBOT and perceived its destruction as morally wrong. We discuss potential implications of anthropomorphism and emotional attachment to robots from the perspective of robot ethics.

1 Introduction

A small group of Canadian researchers created the hitchBOT project in 2014, intersecting art, social robotics, and social science (Zeller and Smith, 2014; Smith and Zeller, 2017b). Its purpose was to kindle the public's engagement in arts and science, as well as spark discussions about our societies' attitudes towards robotics and technology. To this end, hitchBOT, shown in Figure 1, was designed to hitchhike alone across Canada (from Halifax to Victoria), relying on the kindness of strangers since it could not move on its own.

Figure 1: The hitchBOT robot.

The physical form of hitchBOT consisted of 'pool noodle' flotation devices for arms and legs, rubber boots, a plastic bin wrapped in solar panels for a body, and LED screens with facial animation on its head. GPS and 3G wireless allowed hitchBOT to communicate location and other diagnostics to the home server, and enabled speech recognition and automated dialogue via Cleverscript servers (Existor, 2016). Roughly the size of a five-year-old child, hitchBOT was designed to appear playful and non-threatening (Smith and Zeller, 2017a).

To a large extent, hitchBOT was successful. It traversed Canada, over 10,000 kilometres in 26 days, with no damage or adverse events, and gained broad international interest. With more than 35,000 followers on Twitter, 48,000 Likes on Facebook, and 12,000 followers on Instagram, hitchBOT incited a substantial level of engagement on social media. Moreover, hitchBOT at-

Proceedings of the 10th Workshop on Computational Approaches to Subjectivity, Sentiment and Social Media Analysis, pages 62–71
Minneapolis, June 6, 2019. ©2019 Association for Computational Linguistics

tracted significant international media interest, encompassing all traditional media forms (TV, radio, print media).

In 2015, a twin hitchBOT traveled Germany, the Netherlands, and the USA. The latter journey began on 17 July in Marblehead, MA, but abruptly ended in wilful destruction on 1 August, in Philadelphia, PA, only 500 km away.

In this paper, we examine the emotional connotations of the words used in the Twitter discourse around hitchBOT, using existing crowd-sourced lexicons for emotion and sentiment. Others have started to investigate the emotional connections people build through personal interactions with robots (Young et al., 2009; Hirth et al., 2011; Hwang et al., 2013; Damiano et al., 2015). However, hitchBOT was exceptional in that the vast majority of its many Twitter followers would never meet it. In this sense, hitchBOT was similar to a public figure, or celebrity, and its destruction was a news-worthy event. As such, this represents a unique opportunity to measure widespread public opinion about robots and their treatment at the hands of humans, without the complicating factor of personal ownership. Darling (2016) argues that the degree of emotional connection we feel towards non-human entities, and specifically the emotional distress we feel when they are abused, is a major factor in whether we agree as a society to grant those entities legal protections beyond the simple property rights of the owner. Therefore it stands to reason that a better understanding of public sentiment could help to inform the debate over potential policies and regulations relating to robots and their use (e.g., Lin et al. (2011)).

We specifically explore two questions here:

(1) Were there differences in the type or scale of emotions expressed in each of the host countries? We compare the percentages of words associated with different emotions from the tweets produced during each trip, to examine any cultural factors in the public reaction to hitchBOT.

(2) What emotions were triggered when hitchBOT was destroyed? We compare the percentages of different emotion words and the distribution of positive and negative words produced before and after hitchBOT's destruction, to determine the dominant emotional responses to the event.

We begin with an overview of the related work studying human emotions towards robots, and then describe the corpus of tweets and the word–emotion association lexicons used in this work. We then present our findings, and conclude by discussing some examples from the data in relation to issues of anthropomorphism, emotion, and the question of how the ethical codes that govern our behaviour toward humans and animals may (or may not) apply to robots.

2 Background and related work

As robots become more common in our everyday lives, there is a growing need to understand the factors influencing interactions between humans and robots, including the emotional component. One active area of research focuses on developing robots that can express emotion (Kühnlenz et al., 2013); here, in contrast, we consider the emotions expressed by humans towards robots. How do robots make us feel? Many robots are designed to promote anthropomorphism and zoomorphism (the attribution of human or animal characteristics to a non-human/animal entity), and it has been shown that the degree to which we anthropomorphize a robot affects our emotional connection with it (Riek et al., 2009). However, even robots with little physical resemblance to a human or animal can induce emotional attachments (Sung et al., 2007).

Our sentiments towards robots may depend partly on cultural differences. Bartneck et al. (2007a) administered a questionnaire on negative attitudes towards robots to 467 participants from seven different countries, including Germany, the Netherlands, and the USA. The questionnaire was divided into three subscales focusing on interaction, social influence, and emotion. In general, participants from the USA showed the most positive attitudes towards robots, particularly in their openness to interacting with robots, although they were more negative than the German or Dutch on the topic of robot emotion.

Social media has proven to be a rich source of data for sentiment and emotion analysis on a variety of topics, using lexicon-based and machine learning methods (e.g. Rosenthal et al. (2015); Giachanou and Crestani (2016); Mohammad et al. (2018)). However, very little work has focused on the emotions expressed towards robots. Friedman et al. (2003) analyzed 3,119 forum posts relating to the AIBO robot dog. They developed a coding scheme to categorize posts as affirming or negating the following characteristics in AIBO robots: life-like essences, technological essences, mental states, social rapport, and moral standing. Interestingly, while most users affirmed aspects of life-like essences, mental states, and social rapport, only 12% expressed that the AIBO dogs have moral standing (e.g. a right not to be mistreated). Mubin et al. (2016) annotated 235 Twitter posts relating to the Nao robot, using a similar coding scheme, finding that over half the tweets expressed life-like essences and/or social rapport. Fink et al. (2012) compared forum posts about AIBO dogs, Roomba robot vacuum cleaners, and iPad tablets for topic and degree of anthropomorphism. They characterized anthropomorphic language as an attribution to the device of: life-likeness, emotional states or feelings, gender, personality, intention, names, or status as a family member. They found a generally higher frequency of anthropomorphic language in posts which also expressed a feeling or attitude towards the device, again supporting a link between anthropomorphism and emotion.

Other work on social media has focused specifically on users' interactions with chatbots, such as the infamous Tay chatbot. Tay was launched by Microsoft in 2016 and promptly shut down a day later, after her interactions with Twitter users resulted in her learning to generate toxic and offensive content. Neff and Nagy (2016) analyzed user responses to the incident and found that most reactions fell into two categories: those who saw Tay as a helpless victim of human behaviour, and those who viewed her as a threat or an example of technology spinning out of control. More generally, we expect that there will be individual differences in the degree to which artificial intelligence technologies are seen as useful and progressive versus threatening and dangerous, and this may be reflected in the emotional responses observed.

The questions of how we feel when a robot is harmed are open for debate. Friedman et al. (2003) describe the outrage and disgust expressed by some online forum users when an AIBO robot dog was thrown into the garbage on live TV; some Twitter users also expressed discomfort or sadness in response to a video of a Boston Dynamics employee kicking a robot dog (Parke, 2015).

The 'death' of a robot can be even more emotional. In Japan, when robot dogs break down permanently, they are sometimes honoured with Bud-dhist funerals (Burch, 2018). Other work has explored the attachments that soldiers develop with military robots, and the sense of loss that can follow their destruction in battle (Carpenter, 2016). Even the break-down of a Roomba can elicit "surprising" levels of emotional distress (Sung et al., 2007).

The prospect of 'killing' a robot can also be disturbing to many people. Bartneck et al. (2007b) report a study in which participants first interacted with a robot, and were then asked to destroy it with a hammer. Participants described feelings of guilt and uneasiness (although, notably, it appears that they all complied). Darling et al. (2015) reported that, when faced with a similar task, participants hesitated longer when the robot had been given a name and personified back-story.

To summarize the related work as it applies to our questions: we expect to see evidence for different attitudes towards hitchBOT across countries, with the USA expressing more positive sentiment and openness towards the robot (Bartneck et al., 2007a). After hitchBOT's destruction, we expect to see an increase in negative emotion, including sadness at the loss of hitchBOT and anger and disgust towards the perpetrator(s). However, people who feel distrustful of technology or artificial intelligence may express opinions supporting hitchBOT's destruction.

3   Methodology

In this section we first present the Twitter data collected for the analysis, then discuss our methodology for emotion analysis through the use of two large, publicly-available lexicons for sentiment and emotion.

3.1   Twitter data

The raw dataset comprises 188,082 tweets containing the token *@hitchBOT*, with the first tweet posted on 29 May, 2014, two months before hitch-BOT's first trip, and the last tweet posted on 16 November, 2015, 3.5 months after its destruction.

We first remove all retweets with no additional content (73,050 tweets), and all exact duplicates (30,334 tweets). We also remove all tweets from hitchBOT's own Twitter account[1] (494 tweets). We determine the language of a tweet using the Python `langdetect` library.[2] The vast majority

---

[1] Tweets from this account were written by a human.
[2] `https://pypi.org/project/langdetect/`

of tweets are written in English; to better capture the emotions in the countries through which hitchBOT travelled, we also include all tweets written in French (one of Canada's official languages), German, and Dutch. We exclude those written in any other languages (20,132 tweets). We then pre-process the tweets by replacing links, usernames, and RT tokens with $\langle URL \rangle$, $\langle @USERNAME \rangle$, and $\langle RT \rangle$, respectively. After this step, any tweets containing only links, usernames, and retweet tokens are also removed (435 tweets). As a result, we include 63,632 tweets in the final dataset.

3.2 Emotion analysis

There are different theories regarding the categorization and definition of emotions. In one view, there is a finite set of universal emotions. In pioneering work, Ekman et al. (1969) proposed a set of six culturally-universal emotions (joy, sadness, disgust, fear, anger, and surprise); Plutchik (1984) later developed a set of eight basic emotions (adding trust and anticipation).

An alternative theory seeks to describe emotions in terms of their underlying factors, or dimensions. Russell (2003) argues in favour of three largely independent dimensions, namely: valence (positive versus negative), arousal (active versus passive), and dominance (powerful versus weak).

In this work, we conduct our analysis from both the categorical and dimensional perspectives by using two lexicons: the NRC Emotion Lexicon (Mohammad and Turney, 2013), and the NRC Valence-Arousal-Dominance (VAD) Lexicon (Mohammad, 2018). Both lexicons were collected by crowd-sourcing annotations of emotional associations with words, and are publicly available.[3] The NRC lexicons offer wider coverage than most existing lexicons, and the use of best-worst scaling in the VAD Lexicon has been shown to lead to more reliable annotations than those obtained using rating scales (Mohammad, 2018). The NRC lexicons have been extensively validated for Twitter emotion and sentiment analysis (Tang et al., 2014; Yu and Wang, 2015; Chikersal et al., 2015).

Briefly, the Emotion Lexicon contains emotion labels for 14,182 unigrams. The labels are binary, indicating whether a word is associated with (a) any of Plutchik's eight basic emotions, and (b) positive or negative sentiment. The VAD Lexicon contains scores for 20,007 words along the dimensions of valence, arousal, and dominance. The scores are real-valued and range from 0 to 1 along each of the VAD dimensions. Note that the scores do not have intrinsic meaning; rather, they represent the relative rankings of words along each axis.

In both cases, the lexicons were originally created for English words; multi-lingual versions of the lexicons are also available, but were obtained by simply translating the English words to other languages. This can lead to some ambiguity, as one word may have multiple possible translations, and words may have different emotional connotations in different languages and cultures. However, Mohammad et al. (2016) showed that when words were automatically translated from English to Arabic, 90% of the Arabic words had the same sentiment associations as the original English word, and Afli et al. (2017) reported similar results for Irish.

In our analysis, the tweets are first tokenized using the NLTK tweet tokenizer. We ignore all words from the Cornell stoplist,[4] as well as the word token *robot*, which occurs in 30% of all tweets. From the remaining word tokens, we include only the subset of words which are listed in both the Emotion and VAD lexicons. For the basic emotions, we measure the percentage of words associated with that emotion (i.e. out of every 100 words, how many are associated with sadness, joy, etc.). For the VAD analysis, we focus primarily on valence, and report the average valence of all words (which are present in the lexicons), as well as the distributions of valence values.

The number of tweets and word tokens for each phase, as well as the number of word tokens which are represented in the lexicons, are given in Table 1. The 'Other' row includes tweets written before hitchBOT's destruction, but while it was not actively travelling (e.g. between trips). The 'Post-USA' row includes tweets posted after hitchBOT's destruction which ended the USA trip.

4 Analyses

4.1 A contrast of nations

In the first analysis, we aimed to compare the emotion words produced during each of the four trips (i.e., the first four rows in Table 1). However,

---

[3] http://saifmohammad.com/WebPages/lexicons.html

[4] http://www.lextek.com/manuals/onix/stopwords2.html

Phase	Tweets	Tokens	Lex.
1 Canada	8,490	131,846	21,843
2 Germany	1,625	23,171	3,457
3 Netherlands	211	2,970	478
4 USA	2,703	44,565	7,415
5 Other	5,316	82,090	13,430
6 Post-USA	45,287	714,441	116,752
Total	*63,632*	*999,083*	*163,375*

Table 1: Number of tweets and word tokens in the various phases of hitchBOT's existence, after pre-processing. The 'Lex.' column indicates the number of tokens appearing in both lexicons.

due to the relatively small number of tweets available for the Netherlands trip, we exclude these data and compare only Canada, Germany, and the USA (note that the USA data includes only those tweets produced *before* hitchBOT's destruction). This corresponds to lines 1, 2, and 4 in Table 1.

Only a small fraction of tweets are labelled with location information, and so for each country we include all tweets posted within the duration of hitchBOT's visit to that country, with the assumption that much of the Twitter content will be generated from inside the country of interest. There is some evidence to support this: during the Germany trip, 75% of tweets were written in German (compared to 7% during the Canada trip 1% during the USA trip).

Figure 2 shows the percentage of words associated with each emotion during each phase. Qualitatively, the distributions are similar across the trips, with Twitter users in all countries producing more positive than negative emotion words, and more words associated with anticipation and joy than anger, disgust, fear, and sadness. However, there are some differences as well. To determine whether the differences between countries are significant, we first perform a χ^2 test for each emotion, comparing the observed word counts for each emotion for each of the three countries to the expected counts under the null hypothesis of no difference between the countries. The χ^2 test is appropriate in the case of unequal sample sizes, as we have here. Since we repeat this test 10 times, we use a Bonferroni-adjusted α of 0.005 as the significance threshold. In cases where a significant difference is observed, we conduct a post-hoc pairwise proportion test to determine between which countries the relevant differences occur. Since the pairwise procedure involves three comparisons, we use $\alpha = 0.016$ as the threshold for significance.

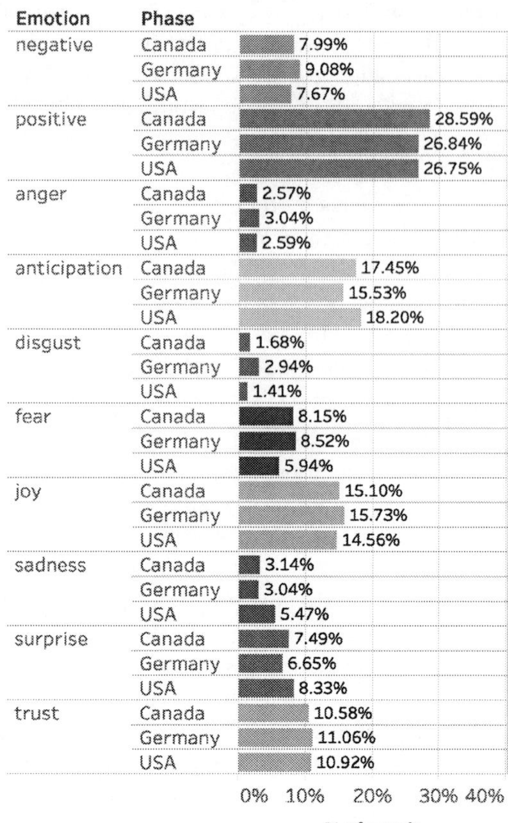

Figure 2: A comparison of the emotions expressed in tweets while hitchBOT travelled through different countries. For all words in the tweets which are contained in the emotion lexicon, we show the percentage of those words that are associated with the various emotions, by country.

Considering first the overall sentiment, there is no significant different in the percentage of negative words produced in the three countries. Canada produces the highest percentage of positive words, although the difference is only significant compared to the USA ($p = 9.8 \times 10^{-5}$).

For the basic emotions, there are no significant differences between the countries on anger, anticipation, joy, surprise, or trust. For disgust, Germany has a significantly higher percentage than both Canada ($p = 6.6 \times 10^{-5}$) and the USA ($p = 7.0 \times 10^{-6}$). The USA has the lowest percentage of fear words, significantly lower than both Canada ($p = 2.2 \times 10^{-8}$) and Germany ($p = 6.1 \times 10^{-5}$). Finally, the USA has the highest percentage of words associated with sadness compared to both Canada ($p = 4.2 \times 10^{-18}$) and Germany

$(p = 6.8 \times 10^{-6})$.

While it is not possible here to analyze each of these trends in detail, we do consider two illustrative examples of what kinds of words are driving these differences:

Why were people sadder during the USA trip, even before hitchBOT's death? This pattern turns out to be driven by multiple discouraged tweets around the start of hitchBOT's American journey, when the robot did not manage to leave its starting point for a week, e.g. *hitchhiking robot's cross-country trek off to a **sluggish** start* and *a cross-country hitchhike is **tough** if no one will help you **leave** massachusetts*. Since hitchBOT's destruction cut the trip short after only two weeks, these early tweets have a larger impact than if the trip had been completed as expected.

Why were people more disgusted during the Germany trip? The most frequent word associated with disgust during the Germany trip is the German *schade*, which in the NRC lexicons is translated as the English *bummer*, which is associated with disgust. However, *schade* could also be translated as *shame* or *pity*; in the Emotion Lexicon, *shame* is also associated with disgust, but *pity* is not. This illustrates how different translations of the same word may have slightly different emotional connotations. (A manual review of the German tweets reveals that most occurrences of this word correspond to the sense of "what a pity," rather than explicit disgust towards hitchBOT.)

While these differences certainly merit further investigation, the overall impression is of remarkably similar emotional profiles in each of the three countries visited.

4.2   The death of hitchBOT

In the second analysis, we partition the dataset into those tweets written before and after hitchBOT's destruction (lines 1–5 versus line 6 from Table 1). For convenience, we refer to these time periods as *Life* and *Death*, respectively. Note that these tweets could have been posted from anywhere in the world, as long as they were written in English, French, German, or Dutch. Figure 3 shows the percentages of words associated with the eight basic emotions as well as positive and negative sentiment. The difference in emotion word percentages between life and death is significant for every emotion and sentiment (according to a χ^2 test and

corrected for multiple comparisons).

Most trends are as expected, with increases in anger, disgust, fear, sadness, surprise, and negative sentiment after hitchBOT's death. Similarly, we observe a decrease in anticipation, joy, and positive sentiment. Counter-intuitively, the percentage of trust words shows a small but significant increase after death. An examination of the data suggests multiple reasons for this, including: the negation of trust words (e.g. *hitchhiking not **safe** for robots either in us*), irony (e.g. *welcome to the city of **brotherly** love*), and word-sense ambiguity (e.g. *adorable hitchhiking hitchbot **found** mutilated*).

In terms of the magnitude of the changes, the greatest relative difference is seen in the emotions of anger (4.7 times greater after death) and disgust (3.8 times greater), followed by sadness (3.6 times greater). This pattern seems reasonable, given the deliberate nature of the destruction.

Emotion	Phase	% of words
negative	Life	8.02%
	Death	24.88%
positive	Life	27.84%
	Death	21.22%
anger	Life	2.78%
	Death	13.06%
anticipation	Life	17.05%
	Death	13.32%
disgust	Life	1.96%
	Death	7.40%
fear	Life	7.15%
	Death	16.87%
joy	Life	14.47%
	Death	11.35%
sadness	Life	4.08%
	Death	14.60%
surprise	Life	7.59%
	Death	10.29%
trust	Life	10.62%
	Death	12.05%

Figure 3: A comparison of the emotions expressed in tweets before and after hitchBOT's destruction. For all words in the tweets which are contained in the Emotion Lexicon, we show the percentage of those words that are associated with the various emotions.

We then consider the valence distribution of the words produced before and after hitchBOT's destruction. Valence is similar in some ways to the positive-negative sentiments discussed above, but contains much richer information about the inten-

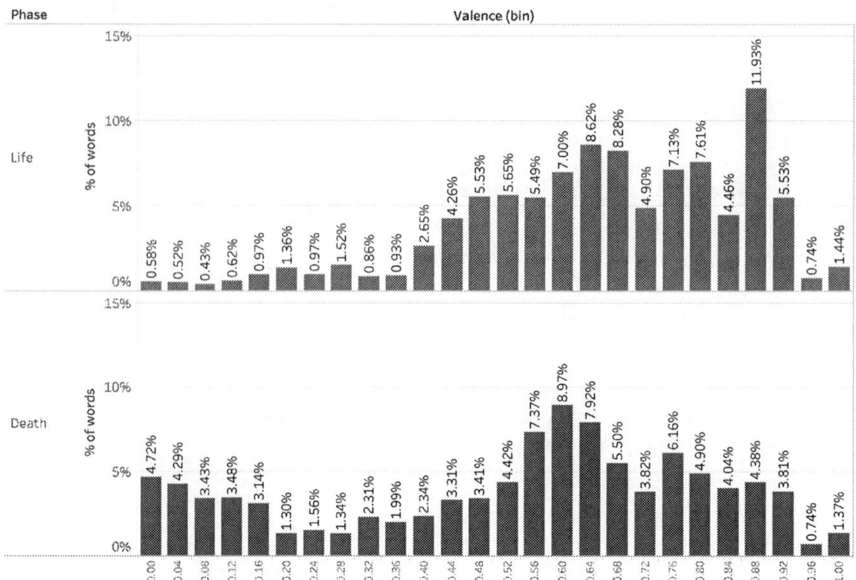

Figure 4: The valence distribution before/after hitchBOT's destruction, for words contained in the VAD lexicon.

sity of the emotion. If we consider only the mean valence, we do see a reduction from 0.67 in life, to 0.55 in death. However, Figure 4 offers a more detailed picture of how the valence distribution changes. A Kolmogorov–Smirnov test indicates that the two distributions are significantly different ($p < 0.001$). Specifically, we observe a substantial increase in the lowest-valence words (i.e. those expressing strong negative emotion) after death.[5]

To qualitatively examine the words which are found in these lowest-valence bins, the most highly-frequent words in the three lowest bins are given in Table 2. An interesting feature of these words is how many of them reflect some level of anthropomorphism and/or moral judgment. For example, words like *die*, *death*, *demise*, *killing*, and *kill*, imply the end of a life, at least metaphorically. The word *murder* is even stronger, since it denotes specifically the unlawful ending of a *human* life. In terms of moral judgments, the high frequency of words such as *blame*, *shame*, *terrible*, and *wrong* suggest the belief that there was something ethically wrong with destroying the robot. The word *crime* is also significant in this context, implying that this action was not just ethically but also legally unacceptable.

However, these views are far from universal. We also observe many words which are not usually associated with actions against animate beings, such as *destroyed* and *destruction*, as well as *broken* and *wrecked* (not visible in Table 2, with frequencies of 55 and 53, respectively). Furthermore, we note an apparent dissociation between the degree of anthropomorphism expressed in the tweet, and the polarity of the sentiment regarding hitchBOT's destruction. For example, among tweets expressing dismay at the incident, some mourn the loss of hitchBOT merely as a piece of technical equipment in a science experiment:

> *so a canadian robotics students' long, successful experiment in trust ended a few weeks after entering the states :(*

while others attribute personality and mental state to hitchBOT, and even refer to it with a nickname:

> *oh 'merica, what did you do to our sweet, sweet @hitchbot poor little hitchy.*

Tweets which celebrate hitchBOT's destruction are in a minority, but there are several, and they similarly range from describing hitchBOT simply as an object (albeit, an object that could be 'killed'):

---

[5] The distributions for arousal and dominance, as well as interactive visualizations for all the figures in this paper, can be accessed at `http://saifmohammad.com/WebPages/hitchbot.html`

to attributing gender and personality:

Attributing human-like characteristics to a robot, but then not ascribing it moral standing (e.g. the right not to be harmed), has interesting parallels to the findings of Friedman et al. (2003) with respect to AIBO dogs, and may also relate to the observations of Neff and Nagy (2016) that Tay the chatbot was sometimes viewed as a threat to, rather than a victim of, humanity. However, the examples here are merely anecdotal and additional work will be required to annotate the data for these various attitudes before we can draw further conclusions.

5   Discussion

There is a potential gap between what people write on Twitter and how they truly feel about robots and their destruction. On such a platform, there may be a tendency to use emotionally provocative language to attract attention and retweets. Even ignoring this effect, clearly we can say, for example, that a battery is 'dead' without thinking that it was ever really alive. Friedman et al. (2003) also discuss this disconnect between language and belief, observing that in many cases, anthropomorphic language is used playfully and as an informal shorthand (even in this paper, we find it simpler to refer to hitchBOT's *life* rather than *the period of time prior to hitchBOT's destruction*). In their work, Friedman et al. (2003) conclude that, "we are not saying AIBO owners believe literally that AIBO is alive, but rather that AIBO evokes feelings *as if* AIBO were alive." Similarly, we certainly do not propose that the use of anthropomorphic language indicates that Twitter users actually believed hitchBOT was a living thing, but rather that their lexical choices reflect an emotional connection with the robot, and subsequent empathetic reaction to its destruction, akin in some ways to that which might be evoked by a living being.

The human tendency towards anthropomorphism can have far-reaching consequences in terms of what we view as ethical behaviour. In

Freq.	Token	Freq.	Token	Freq.	Token
3061	destroyed	214	shame	127	blame
1477	demise	205	shit	124	terrible
739	death	185	hate	119	hell
417	destruction	178	wrong	105	die
413	murder	175	tragic	104	dangerous
360	kill	156	destroying	101	crime
277	mutilated	155	upset	93	violence
234	doomed	147	damn	91	war
228	killing	143	violent	87	sadly
216	fake	132	hurt	85	incident

Table 2: The highest frequency words in the lowest valence bins after hitchBOT's destruction.

a thought-provoking discussion of whether social robots should be extended any type of legal protection, Darling (2016) argues that many of our existing laws protecting animals from abuse are based on our anthropomorphism and emotional connection with animals, rather than, e.g., biological factors (the fact that it is legal to slaughter a cow for food but not a horse seems based primarily in our cultural emotional connection to horses). Darling (2016) also writes that one interpretation of the purpose of law is to codify a social contract: "We construct behavioural rules that most of us agree on, and we hold everyone to the agreement." From that perspective, it is important to start gathering data on the nature and extent of society's emotional attachments to robots of various kinds.

The current analysis is limited in a number of ways. Emotion is analyzed on the word level, rather than the sentence level, and as such we do not take into account negations or any other context, nor do we attempt to detect sarcasm. In particular, we cannot ensure that hitchBOT is the actual entity to which the emotion is attached (e.g., *when he comes to this **great** nation's **beautiful** capital, i want to be able to drive him through it.*). Furthermore, the amount of data in each phase is not balanced, with the majority of tweets occurring after hitchBOT's destruction, and the particularly small number during the trip to the Netherlands limited our cross-cultural analysis.

Nonetheless, while somewhat exploratory in nature, these preliminary analyses suggest several avenues for future research. By analyzing tweets on the sentence-level and conducting a topic analysis, we can get a better sense of what attitudes and beliefs are underlying people's emotional word choices. Additionally, by manually annotating tweets for attributions to hitchBOT of life-likeness, emotional states, intention, and so on (following the work of Fink et al. (2012)), we can start to draw a clearer link between anthropomorphic language and emotional attachment. In future work we also plan to look more specifically into different cultures and their perceptions, using various lexicons. We can also consider machine learning approaches to emotion analysis, as well as recent advances in lexicon-based approaches (Buechel and Hahn, 2016). Finally, although the corpus is not currently publicly available, we do plan to release the data to other researchers in the future.

6 Conclusion

We have presented an analysis of the emotion words produced by Twitter users about hitchBOT. When comparing tweets written during each of hitchBOT's trips across Canada, Germany, and the United States, the emotion word percentages were generally similar, although some significant differences were observed, with Canadians expressing the most positive sentiment, and Americans expressing the least fear and the most sadness. While Germans expressed significantly more disgust than the others, this effect may be due to a near-synonym translation with a different emotional connotation than the original German word.

When examining the tweets written before and after hitchBOT's 'death', significant differences were observed in all of the basic emotions, with marked increases in the percentage of words associated with anger, disgust, and sadness. The proportion of words with very low valence scores (i.e. those expressing negative sentiment) also increased dramatically. A qualitative analysis of these low-valence words suggests that Twitter users perceived the actions of the vandals as morally corrupt, with an intensity of emotion that seems incommensurate with an interpretation of the event as simple property damage. These findings will hopefully provoke future questions probing how humans should behave towards robots and towards discussions around robot ethics.

References

Haithem Afli, Sorcha McGuire, and Andy Way. 2017. Sentiment translation for low resourced languages: Experiments on Irish general election tweets. In *18th International Conference on Computational Linguistics and Intelligent Text Processing*.

Christoph Bartneck, Tomohiro Suzuki, Takayuki Kanda, and Tatsuya Nomura. 2007a. The influence of people's culture and prior experiences with Aibo on their attitude towards robots. *AI & Society*, 21(1-2):217–230.

Christoph Bartneck, Marcel Verbunt, Omar Mubin, and Abdullah Al Mahmud. 2007b. To kill a mockingbird robot. In *Proceedings of the ACM/IEEE International Conference on Human-Robot Interaction*, pages 81–87. ACM.

Sven Buechel and Udo Hahn. 2016. Emotion analysis as a regression problemdimensional models and their implications on emotion representation and metrical evaluation. In *Proceedings of the Twenty-second European Conference on Artificial Intelligence*, pages 1114–1122. IOS Press.

James Burch. 2018. In Japan, a Buddhist funeral service for robot dogs. *National Geographic*. [Online; accessed 20-November-2018].

Julie Carpenter. 2016. *Culture and human-robot interaction in militarized spaces: A war story*. Routledge.

Prerna Chikersal, Soujanya Poria, and Erik Cambria. 2015. SeNTU: Sentiment analysis of tweets by combining a rule-based classifier with supervised learning. In *Proceedings of the 9th International Workshop on Semantic Evaluation (SemEval 2015)*, pages 647–651.

Luisa Damiano, Paul Dumouchel, and Hagen Lehmann. 2015. Towards human–robot affective co-evolution overcoming oppositions in constructing emotions and empathy. *International Journal of Social Robotics*, 7(1):7–18.

Kate Darling. 2016. Extending legal protection to social robots: The effects of anthropomorphism, empathy, and violent behavior towards robotic objects. In Ryan Calo, Michael Froomkin, and Ian Kerr, editors, *Robot Law*. Edward Elgar Publishing.

Kate Darling, Palash Nandy, and Cynthia Breazeal. 2015. Empathic concern and the effect of stories in human-robot interaction. In *Robot and Human Interactive Communication (RO-MAN), 2015 24th IEEE International Symposium on*, pages 770–775. IEEE.

Paul Ekman, E Richard Sorenson, and Wallace V Friesen. 1969. Pan-cultural elements in facial displays of emotion. *Science*, 164(3875):86–88.

Existor. 2016. Cleverscript - turn scripts into bots. `http://www.cleverscript.com`. [Online; accessed 7-February-2016].

Julia Fink, Omar Mubin, Frédéric Kaplan, and Pierre Dillenbourg. 2012. Anthropomorphic language in online forums about Roomba, AIBO and the iPad. In *Proceedings of the IEEE International Workshop on Advanced Robotics and its Social Impacts (ARSO 2012)*, pages 54–59.

Batya Friedman, Peter H Kahn Jr, and Jennifer Hagman. 2003. Hardware companions?: What online AIBO discussion forums reveal about the human-robotic relationship. In *Proceedings of the SIGCHI Conference on Human Factors in Computing Systems*, pages 273–280. ACM.

Anastasia Giachanou and Fabio Crestani. 2016. Like it or not: A survey of Twitter sentiment analysis methods. *ACM Computing Surveys (CSUR)*, 49(2):1–41.

Jochen Hirth, Norbert Schmitz, and Karsten Berns. 2011. Towards social robots: Designing an emotion-based architecture. *International Journal of Social Robotics*, 3(3):273–290.

Jihong Hwang, Taezoon Park, and Wonil Hwang. 2013. The effects of overall robot shape on the emotions invoked in users and the perceived personalities of robot. *Applied Ergonomics*, 44(3):459–471.

Barbara Kühnlenz, Stefan Sosnowski, Malte Buß, Dirk Wollherr, Kolja Kühnlenz, and Martin Buss. 2013. Increasing helpfulness towards a robot by emotional adaption to the user. *International Journal of Social Robotics*, 5(4):457–476.

Patrick Lin, Keith Abney, and George Bekey. 2011. Robot ethics: Mapping the issues for a mechanized world. *Artificial Intelligence*, 175(5-6):942–949.

Saif M. Mohammad. 2018. Obtaining reliable human ratings of valence, arousal, and dominance for 20,000 English words. In *Proceedings of The Annual Conference of the Association for Computational Linguistics (ACL)*, pages 174–184, Melbourne, Australia.

Saif M. Mohammad, Felipe Bravo-Marquez, Mohammad Salameh, and Svetlana Kiritchenko. 2018. Semeval-2018 Task 1: Affect in tweets. In *Proceedings of International Workshop on Semantic Evaluation (SemEval-2018)*, New Orleans, LA, USA.

Saif M Mohammad, Mohammad Salameh, and Svetlana Kiritchenko. 2016. How translation alters sentiment. *Journal of Artificial Intelligence Research*, 55:95–130.

Saif M. Mohammad and Peter D. Turney. 2013. Crowdsourcing a word-emotion association lexicon. *Computational Intelligence*, 29(3):436–465.

Omar Mubin, Aila Khan, and Mohammad Obaid. 2016. #naorobot: Exploring Nao discourse on Twitter. In *Proceedings of the 28th Australian Conference on Computer-Human Interaction*, pages 155–159. ACM.

Gina Neff and Peter Nagy. 2016. Talking to bots: Symbiotic agency and the case of Tay. *International Journal of Communication*, 10:4915–4931.

Phoebe Parke. 2015. Is it cruel to kick a robot dog? *CNN*. [Online; accessed 20-November-2018].

Robert Plutchik. 1984. Emotions: A general psycho-evolutionary theory. *Approaches to emotion*, pages 197–219.

Laurel D Riek, Tal-Chen Rabinowitch, Bhismadev Chakrabarti, and Peter Robinson. 2009. How anthropomorphism affects empathy toward robots. In *Proceedings of the 4th ACM/IEEE international Conference on Human Robot Interaction*, pages 245–246. ACM.

Sara Rosenthal, Preslav Nakov, Svetlana Kiritchenko, Saif Mohammad, Alan Ritter, and Veselin Stoyanov. 2015. Semeval-2015 task 10: Sentiment Analysis in Twitter. In *Proceedings of the 9th International Workshop on Semantic Evaluation (SemEval 2015)*, pages 451–463.

James A Russell. 2003. Core affect and the psychological construction of emotion. *Psychological Review*, 110(1):145–172.

David Harris Smith and Frauke Zeller. 2017a. The death and lives of hitchBOT: The design and implementation of a hitchhiking robot. *Leonardo*, 50(1):77–78.

David Harris Smith and Frauke Zeller. 2017b. hitchBOT: The risks and rewards of a hitchhiking robot. *Suomen Antropologi: Journal of the Finnish Anthropological Society*, 42(3):63–65.

Ja-Young Sung, Lan Guo, Rebecca E Grinter, and Henrik I Christensen. 2007. "My Roomba is Rambo": Intimate home appliances. In *International Conference on Ubiquitous Computing*, pages 145–162. Springer.

Duyu Tang, Furu Wei, Bing Qin, Ting Liu, and Ming Zhou. 2014. Coooolll: A deep learning system for twitter sentiment classification. In *Proceedings of the 8th International Workshop on Semantic Evaluation (SemEval 2014)*, pages 208–212.

James E Young, Richard Hawkins, Ehud Sharlin, and Takeo Igarashi. 2009. Toward acceptable domestic robots: Applying insights from social psychology. *International Journal of Social Robotics*, 1(1):95.

Yang Yu and Xiao Wang. 2015. World Cup 2014 in the Twitter world: A big data analysis of sentiments in US sports fans tweets. *Computers in Human Behavior*, 48:392–400.

Frauke Zeller and David H. Smith. 2014. The Hitchbot's guide to travelling across a continent. http://theconversation.com/ the-hitchbots-guide-to-travelling -across-a-continent-31920. [Online; accessed 27-February-2016].

"When Numbers Matter!": Detecting Sarcasm in Numerical Portions of Text

Abhijeet Dubey[*]
IIT Bombay

Lakshya Kumar[*†]
AI Research Einstein
Salesforce

Arpan Somani[*†]
Big Data Labs
American Express

Aditya Joshi
CSIRO

Pushpak Bhattacharyya
IIT Bombay

Abstract

Research in sarcasm detection spans almost a decade. However a particular form of sarcasm remains unexplored: sarcasm expressed through numbers, which we estimate, forms about **11%** of the sarcastic tweets in our dataset. The sentence *'Love waking up at 3 am'* is sarcastic because of the number. In this paper, we focus on detecting sarcasm in tweets arising out of numbers. Initially, to get an insight into the problem, we implement a rule-based and a statistical machine learning-based (ML) classifier. The rule-based classifier conveys the crux of the numerical sarcasm problem, namely, incongruity arising out of numbers. The statistical ML classifier uncovers the indicators i.e., features of such sarcasm. The actual system in place, however, are two deep learning (DL) models, CNN and attention network that obtains an F-score of **0.93** and **0.91** on our dataset of tweets containing numbers. To the best of our knowledge, this is the first line of research investigating the phenomenon of sarcasm arising out of numbers, culminating in a detector thereof.

1 Introduction

Sarcasm is a challenge to sentiment analysis because it uses verbal irony to express contempt or ridicule, thereby, potentially confusing typical sentiment classifiers. Several approaches for sarcasm detection have been reported in the recent past (Hazarika et al., 2018; Joshi et al., 2017; Ghosh and Veale, 2017; Buschmeier et al., 2014; Riloff et al., 2013). In this paper, we focus on a peculiar form of sarcasm: sarcasm expressed through numbers. In other words, the goal of this paper is the classification task where a tweet containing one or more numbers is classified as sar-

castic due to numbers or non-sarcastic. For example, the sentence *'Having 2 hours to write a paper is fun'* is sarcastic. The numeral 2 plays a key role in conveying sarcasm. Therefore, in this paper, we focus on different approaches for the detection of sarcasm due to numbers. Towards this, we first introduce the task, identify its challenges, introduce a labeled dataset and devise three approaches for the task. Our approaches are based on three prevalent paradigms of NLP: rule-based, statistical machine learning-based[1] and deep learning-based.

The contribution of the paper is as follows:

1. The paper details the purpose and challenges of the problem.

2. We introduce a labeled[2] dataset of 60949 tweets containing numbers.

3. Finally, we present approaches which will serve as strong baselines for future work in detecting sarcasm arising due to numbers.

The rest of the paper is organized as follows. In Section 2, we present our motivation. In Section 3, we discuss the related work in detail. Then, we present insights into the problem using rule-based and statistical machine learning-based approaches in Section 4. Then, in Section 5, we present two deep learning-based approaches. In Section 6, we outline the experimental setup and present the results of our experiments in Section 7. We present both qualitative as well as quantitative error analysis in Section 8. Finally, we conclude the paper and discuss future work in Section 9.

2 Motivation

The challenge that sarcastic text poses to sentiment analysis has led to research interest in com-

---

[*]Equal Contribution.
[†]The work was done when authors were doing their Masters at IIT-Bombay.

[1]This refers to statistical approaches that do not rely on deep learning.
[2]labels: sarcastic due to number, non-sarcastic.

Proceedings of the 10th Workshop on Computational Approaches to Subjectivity, Sentiment and Social Media Analysis, pages 72–80
Minneapolis, June 6, 2019. ©2019 Association for Computational Linguistics

putational sarcasm. While several approaches to detect sarcasm have been reported (González-Ibáñez et al., 2011; Joshi et al., 2015), they may fall short in case of sarcasm expressed via numbers. Consider the following three sentences:

1. *This phone has an awesome battery backup of 38 hours*

2. *This phone has a terrible battery backup of 2 hours*

3. *This phone has an awesome battery backup of 2 hours*

At the time of writing this paper, a battery backup of 38 hours is good for phones while a battery backup of 2 hours is bad. Therefore, sentences 1 and 2 are non-sarcastic because the sentiment of the adjectives ('*awesome*' and '*terrible*') conforms with the sentiment associated with the corresponding numerical values. On the contrary, the sarcasm in sentence 3 above occurs because of incompatibility/incongruity[3] between the word '*awesome*' (positive word) and '*2 hours*' (numerical value). The above examples illustrate that the sarcasm can arise due to numbers which can mislead a normal sarcasm detection system. Therefore, in this paper, we aim to solve the problem of detecting sarcasm arising due to numbers. The utility of our work lies in the fact that our system is a crucial link in a pipeline for sarcasm detection where the input tweets first pass through a general sarcasm detector, out of which the tweets labeled as non-sarcastic are then subjected to further scrutiny of the numerical sarcasm detector. Figure 1 shows the interfacing of our module with the overall sarcasm detection system.

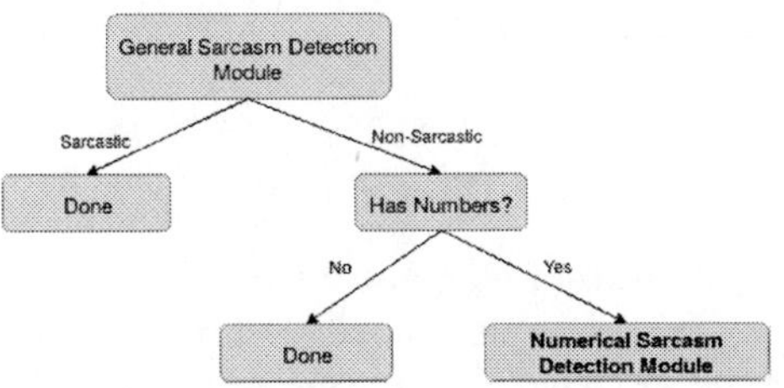

Figure 1: Interfacing of our module with the overall sarcasm detection system

---

[3]Ivanko and Pexman (2003) describe the relationship between incongruity and sarcasm.

3   Related Work

Sarcasm and irony detection has been extensively studied in linguistics, psychology, and cognitive science (Gibbs, 1986; Utsumi, 2000). Computational detection of sarcasm has become a popular area of natural language processing research in recent years (Joshi et al., 2017). Tepperman et al. (2006) present sarcasm recognition in speech using spectral (average pitch, pitch slope, etc.), prosodic and contextual cues. Carvalho et al. (2009) use simple linguistic features like an interjection, changed names, etc. for irony detection. Davidov et al. (2010) train a sarcasm classifier with syntactic and pattern-based features. González-Ibáñez et al. (2011) state that sarcasm transforms the polarity of an apparently positive or negative utterance into its opposite. Liebrecht et al. (2013) show that sarcasm is often signaled by hyperbole, using intensifiers and exclamations; in contrast, non-hyperbolic sarcastic messages often receive an explicit marker. Riloff et al. (2013) capture sarcasm as a contrast between a positive sentiment word and a negative situation. Joshi et al. (2015) show how sarcasm arises because of implicit or explicit incongruity in the sentence. Buschmeier et al. (2014) analyze the impact of different features for sarcasm/irony classification. Bouazizi and Ohtsuki (2016) propose a pattern-based approach to detect sarcasm on Twitter. As deep learning techniques gain popularity, Ghosh and Veale (2016) propose a neural network semantic model for sarcasm detection. They use Convolutional Neural Network (CNN) followed by a Long Short Term Memory (LSTM) network and finally a fully connected layer. Poria et al. (2016) propose a novel method to detect sarcasm using CNN. They use a pre-trained CNN for extracting sentiment, emotion and personality features for sarcasm detection. Amir et al. (2016) propose a deep-learning-based architecture to incorporate additional context for sarcasm detection. They propose an approach to learn user embeddings to provide contextual features, going beyond the lexical and syntactic cues. Finally, they use these user embeddings for sarcasm detection. Zhang et al. (2016) use a bi-directional Gated Recurrent Unit (GRU) followed by a pooling neural network to detect sarcasm. Ghosh and Veale (2017) propose a neural architecture that considers the speaker's mood on the basis of most recent prior tweets for sarcasm detection. Farías et al. (2016) propose a novel model using affective features based on a wide range of lexical resources available for English for detecting irony in tweets. Sulis et al. (2016) study the difference between sarcasm and irony in tweets. They propose a novel set of sentiment, structural and psycholinguistic features for distinguishing between irony and sarcasm. Peled and Reichart (2017) and Dubey et al. (2019) model sarcasm interpretation as a monolingual machine translation task. They use Moses[4], attention networks, and pointer generator networks for the task of sarcasm interpretation. Van Hee et al. (2018) present the first shared task in irony detection in tweets. Recently, Hazarika et al. (2018) propose a hybrid approach for sarcasm detection in online social media discussions. They extract contextual information from the discourse of a discussion thread. They also use user embeddings that encode stylometric and personality features of users and content-based feature extractors such as CNN and show a significant improvement in classification performance on a large Reddit corpus.

4 Getting Insight into the Problem

End-to-end deep learning (DL) architectures are very popular for solving NLP problems these days. However, DL approaches do not give insight into the problem. To better understand the "numerical sarcasm problem" (detecting sarcasm arising due to numbers in tweets), we first implement a rule-based and statistical machine learning-based approach before embarking on the deep learning-based approach. In this section, we introduce a rule-based approach that conveys the crux of the numerical sarcasm problem, namely, incongruity arising out of numbers. We also present a statistical machine learning-based approach that conveys the importance of handcrafted features for decision making.

4.1 Rule-based Approach

Figure 2 shows our rule-based system. This approach considers noun phrases in the tweet as candidate contexts and determines the optimal threshold of a numerical measure for each context.

We divide tweets into two sets, namely sarcastic and non-sarcastic repository. We represent each tweet in the form of a tuple containing tweet index number, noun phrase vector, numerical value, and unit of measurement. For example, assume

<hr>

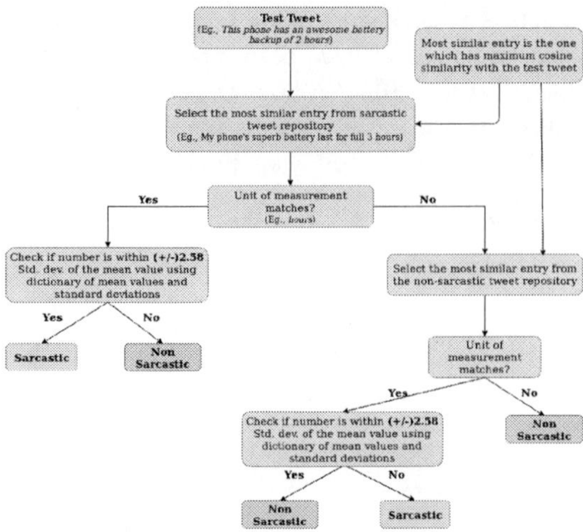

Figure 2: Rule-Based Approach

that the 14th instance in the dataset is the sarcastic tweet *'This phone has an awesome battery backup of 2 hours'*. This tweet contains two noun phrases: *'phone'* and *'awesome battery backup'*. The words in these two noun phrases are *'phone'*, *'awesome'*, *'battery'*, *'backup'*. We first convert these words into 200-D word vectors (initialized using GloVe (Pennington et al., 2014) and fine-tuned on our dataset). Then we sum up word vectors of words in the noun phrase list and normalize them by the length of the noun phrase list. We call this the noun phrase vector. Given these entities, the tweet representation is: *(14, Noun Phrase Vector, 2, 'hours')*. Since the tweet is sarcastic, it is stored in the sarcastic repository. In addition to tweet entries, both sarcastic and non-sarcastic repositories also maintain two dictionaries: (a) Dictionary of mean values where each entry is a key-value pair where key is the unit of measurement and value is the average of all the numbers corresponding to that number unit and (b) Dictionary of standard deviation is created in a similar manner.

A test tweet is classified as sarcastic or non-sarcastic according to the following steps:

1. **Computation of noun phrase vector:** We create a noun phrase vector from the words in the noun phrase list of the test tweet as described above.

2. **Sarcastic repository consultation:** We compute the cosine similarity of noun phrase vectors of test tweet and tweets in sarcastic repository respectively. Then, we select

the tweet from the sarcastic repository whose noun phrase vector has the maximum cosine similarity with the noun phrase vector of the test tweet. We call this the *'most similar entry'*. If the unit of measurement in the most similar entry is same as that in the test tweet, we use the dictionary of mean values and dictionary of standard deviations to check whether the number present in the test tweet is within ± 2.58 standard deviation of the mean value for that unit of measurement. If it is, the tweet is predicted as sarcastic, otherwise, non-sarcastic.

3. **Non-Sarcastic repository consultation:** If the unit of measurement in the most similar entry from the sarcastic repository is not the same as that in the test tweet, we select the most similar entry to the test tweet from the non-sarcastic repository and proceed in a similar manner.

4. **Fall-back label assignment:** If no match is found, the test tweet is predicted as non-sarcastic.

4.2 Statistical Machine Learning-based Approach

We use two statistical machine learning-based classifiers: **SVM** and **Random-forest**. We use the following features in our statistical machine learning-based approach.

- **Sentiment-based features (S)**: Number of positive words, number of negative words[5], number of highly emotional positive words, number of highly emotional negative words (Positive/Negative word is said to be highly emotional if it is an adjective, adverb or verb).

- **Emoticon-based features (E)**: Number of positive emoticons, number of negative emoticons, contrast between word and emoticon which is a boolean feature that takes the value as 1 when either positive word and negative emoticon is present or negative word and positive emoticon is present in the tweet.

- **Punctuation-based features (P)**: Number of exclamation marks, number of dots, number of question mark, number of capital letter words and number of single quotations.

- **Numerical value (NV)**: The actual number in the tweet.

- **Numerical unit (NU)**: One-hot representation of the unit of measurement.

5 Deep Learning-based Approach

In this section, we describe two deep learning-based models.

5.1 CNN-FF Model

Figure 3 shows the architecture of CNN-FF model. We use embedding matrix $E \in \mathbb{R}^{|V| \times d}$ with $|V|$ as the vocabulary size and d as the word vector dimension. For the input tweet, we obtain an input matrix $I \in \mathbb{R}^{|S| \times d}$ where $|S|$ is the length of the tweet. I_i is the d-dimensional vector for i-th word in the tweet in the input matrix. Let k be the length of the filter, and the vector $f \in \mathbb{R}^{|k| \times d}$ is a filter for the convolution operation. For each position p in the input matrix I, there is a window w_p of k consecutive words, denoted as:

$$w_p = [I_p, I_{p+1}, ..., I_{p+k-1}] \qquad (1)$$

A filter f convolves with the window vectors (k-grams) at each position to generate a feature map $c \in \mathbb{R}^{|S|-k+1}$, each element c_p of the feature map for window vector w_p is produced as follows:

$$c_p = func(w_p \circ f + b) \qquad (2)$$

where $\circ$ is the element-wise multiplication, $b \in \mathbb{R}$ is a bias term and $func$ is a nonlinear transformation function. We use multiple convolution filters of different sizes to obtain a feature map of the given tweet. We further apply max-over-time pooling over the obtained feature map. The output from each filter is concatenated to get the final feature vector. This feature vector acts as input to the fully-connected layer. We train the entire model by minimizing the binary cross-entropy loss.

$$E(y, \widehat{y}) = \sum_{i=1}^{e} y_i \log(\widehat{y}_i) \qquad (3)$$

---

[5]Positive and negative words are selected using Senti-WordNet (Baccianella et al., 2010).

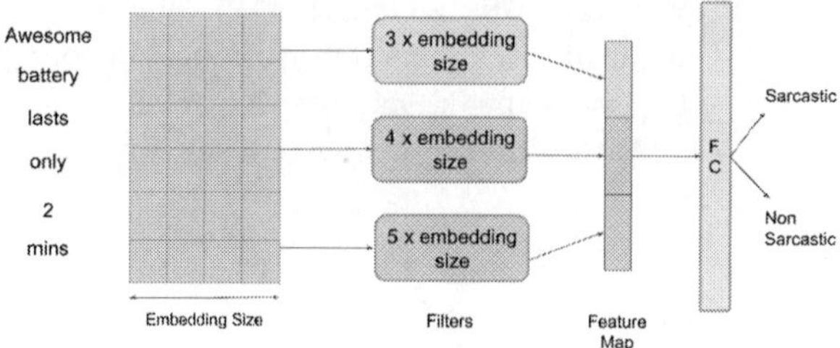

Figure 3: CNN followed by Fully Connected Layer for Numerical Sarcasm Detection

5.2 Attention Network

Figure 4 shows the architecture of our attention network. It consists of two main parts: a word encoder and a word level attention layer. We describe these two components as follows,

1. **Word Encoder:** Given an input tweet of length T with words w_t, where $t \in [1, T]$. We convert each word w_t to its vector representation x_t using the embedding matrix E. Then, we use a bidirectional LSTM to get annotations of words by summarizing information from both directions. The bidirectional LSTM contains the forward LSTM $\overrightarrow{f}$, which reads the tweet from w_1 to w_T and a backward LSTM $\overleftarrow{f}$, which reads the tweet from w_T to w_1:

$$x_t = E^T w_t, t \in [1, T] \quad (4)$$
$$\overrightarrow{h_t} = \overrightarrow{LSTM}(x_t), t \in [1, T] \quad (5)$$
$$\overleftarrow{h_t} = \overleftarrow{LSTM}(x_t), t \in [T, 1] \quad (6)$$

We finally obtain the annotation for a given word w_t by concatenating the forward hidden state $\overrightarrow{h_t}$ and backward hidden state $\overleftarrow{h_t}$, i.e., $h_t = [\overrightarrow{h_t}, \overleftarrow{h_t}]$, which summarizes the information of the whole tweet centered around w_t.

2. **Word Level Attention:** We claim that numbers play a crucial role while predicting sarcasm in tweets containing numbers. Hence, we introduce the attention network to extract information which is important to the overall meaning of the tweet. Our attention architecture is similar to the attention model introduced in Yang et al. (2016), except that we do not use hierarchical attention since tweets are short sentences and do not have a hierarchical structure.

$$u_t = tanh(W_w^T h_t + b_w) \quad (7)$$
$$\alpha_t = \frac{exp(u_t^T u_w)}{\sum_t exp(u_t^T u_w)} \quad (8)$$
$$s_i = \sum_t \alpha_t h_t \quad (9)$$
$$p = softmax(W_c^T s_i + b_c) \quad (10)$$

First, we multiply the word annotation h_t with $W_w \in \mathbb{R}^{2d \times T}$ and add to $b_w \in \mathbb{R}^{T \times 1}$, which is fed into *tanh* layer to get u_t as its hidden representation. Then, we calculate the similarity of u_t with a word level context vector u_w to measure the importance of the words. Then, we calculate normalized importance weight α_t using softmax function. The word level context vector u_w is randomly initialized and jointly learned during the training process. Finally, we aggregate this representation to form a tweet vector s_i, and multiply it with $W_c \in \mathbb{R}^{2d \times 2}$ and add to $b_c \in \mathbb{R}^{2 \times 1}$ to generate p, which is used for classification. We train this model by minimizing the binary cross-entropy loss.

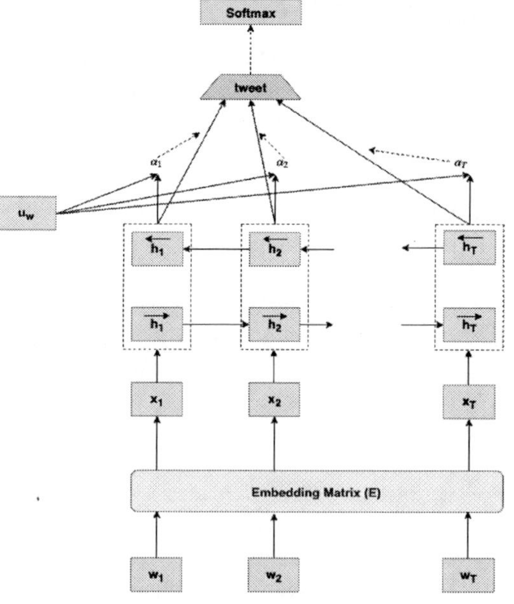

Figure 4: Attention Network for Numerical Sarcasm Detection

6 Experimental Setup

We create two datasets containing tweets as follows. We download tweets containing hashtags

Dataset	Sarcastic	Non Sarcastic
Dataset 1	100000 (28.57%)	250000 (71.43%)
Dataset 2	11024 (18.1%)	49925 (81.9%)

Table 1: Statistics of Datasets. From Dataset 1, we extract sarcastic and non-sarcastic tweets containing numbers and then manually annotate them to obtain a high quality labeled dataset of tweets containing numbers.

#sarcasm, #sarcastic, #BeingSarcastic as sarcastic, and those with #nonsarcasm, #notsarcastic as the non-sarcastic, using the Twitter-API. We eliminate duplicate tweets, retweets, remove URLs, usernames, hashtags and other Non-ASCII characters from the tweets. We call this Dataset 1 which contains a total of 350000 tweets. From Dataset 1, we select a subset of tweets which contain numerical values. Then, we remove irrelevant tweets from this subset, like the ones which contain alphabet or special character adjacent to a number like *Model34d, 4s,* < 3 (heart smiley), etc. As a final step, to improve the quality of our dataset, we give the following instructions to two annotators who independently annotate tweets to evaluate if the tweets containing numbers are really sarcastic due to the number or not. We call this Dataset 2 (Dataset of tweets containing numbers) which is a subset of Dataset 1 and contains a total of 60949 tweets.

1. Mark the tweet with *label = 1*, if it is sarcastic and the sarcasm is arising due to numbers.

2. Mark the tweet with *label = 0*, otherwise.

The value of Cohen's Kappa which measures inter-annotator agreement is **0.81**. Table 1 shows the percentage of sarcastic and non-sarcastic tweets in Dataset 1 and Dataset 2 respectively.

As baselines, we re-implement the work (by adapting features wherever necessary) reported by González-Ibáñez et al. (2011), Liebrecht et al. (2013) and Joshi et al. (2015). The choice of our baselines is based on approaches that use only the text to be classified. For statistical machine learning-based approaches, we use **SVM** with RBF kernel and $c = 1.0$ using grid-search and **Random-forest** with *number of estimators* = 10. For deep learning-based approaches, we use $200D$ tweet word embeddings, initialized using GloVe and fine tuned on our data. For CNN-FF Model, we use 128 filters each of size 3, 4 and 5,

i.e., a total 128×3 filters. We use a dropout of 0.5. We train the network using mini-batch gradient descent. Finally, we report the average 5-fold cross-validation values in Table 4.

7 Results

Table 3 shows the evidence of degradation in the performance of three previous approaches on Dataset 2 (dataset of tweets containing numbers). We observe that among the three previous approaches, features from Joshi et al. (2015) perform the best and obtain an F-score of **0.72** and **0.27** on Dataset 1 and Dataset 2 respectively. There is a **degradation of 45% points** in F-score from Dataset 1 to Dataset 2 which clearly shows that the past approaches are not able to capture the sarcasm arising due to numbers because their features are not designed to capture the incongruity arising due to numbers. This strengthens our claim. To further strengthen the importance of our approaches, we evaluate them on Dataset 1 and Dataset 2 respectively using the strategy illustrated in Figure 1. On Dataset 1, we apply our approaches on tweets that are misclassified by the best performing past approach of Joshi et al. (2015). We also evaluate our approaches on Dataset 2 and show the evidence of overall improvement in F-score in Table 4. Our CNN-FF model obtains the best F-score of **0.88** and **0.93** which is a **significant improvement of 16%** and **66%** points in F-score over the best performing past approach of Joshi et al. (2015) on Dataset 1 and Dataset 2 respectively.

To check if our results are statistically significant, we perform **Kolmogorov-Smirnov test** (Karson, 1968) and find that our results are statistically significant.

8 Error Analysis & Visualization

Table 2 shows the distribution of attention weights over input tweets and illustrates the importance of numbers while making the sarcastic/non-sarcastic decision. We also perform a qualitative analysis of errors which results in six categories:

1. **Sarcasm not due to numbers**: Sarcastic sentences which contain a number but the sarcasm is not due to the number. For example, *'phelps will be the mvp for 2014 lmao phelpshaterhere'*

Sarcastic due to numbers	Non-Sarcastic
i 'm so excited to work 14 hours during a blizzard tomorrow & get to drive home in the worst	just got done with a nice 25 min run clear air feels good
i love being wide awake at 345 in the morning	it 's 12.00 pm and im still in my pj 's god i love lazy non working days
5 hours left and am down to 50 % battery battery yea like that 's going to last x	2 finals today wish me luck : x i still have a lot to study after my first final

Table 2: Distribution of attention weights over some input tweets while making the numerical sarcastic/non-sarcastic decision. The darker the color and larger the font, the higher is the weight

Approach	Dataset 1	Dataset 2
González-Ibáñez et al. (2011)	0.68	0.17
Liebrecht et al. (2013)	0.67	0.21
Joshi et al. (2015)	**0.72**	**0.27**

Table 3: Evidence of F-score degradation of previous approaches on Dataset 2 (numerical sarcasm dataset)

Approaches	Dataset 1	Dataset 2
Rule-Based Approach	0.83	0.78
SVM	0.86	0.82
Random Forest	0.86	0.84
CNN-FF	**0.88**	**0.93**
Attention Network	0.87	0.91

Table 4: Evidence of overall improvement in F-score using our approaches

2. **Numbers enhancing sarcasm**: An interesting type of error is related to the previous. Although the sarcasm is not due to the numerical value, the number highlights the sarcastic property of the sentence, as in *'day 2 of having an adorable puppy n he already chewed up my macbook charger'*. The fact that the incident happened on the 2nd day strengthens the sarcastic expression in the sentence.

3. **Comparison of numbers**: Multiple numerical entities may result in sarcasm as in the case of *'wow..from 30$ to 25$... significant discount!'*. Our approaches are not designed to take this into account.

4. **Unseen situations**: Since numeric sarcasm is associated with situations present in the tweet, situations unseen in the training set result in errors in sarcasm detection. An example of such a tweet is *'yay it's 3 am & i'm bored with no one to talk to'*.

5. **'Special' numbers**: These include numeric tokens that should not have been considered as tokens at all. This includes the use of '2' and '4' in place of 'to' and 'for' in noisy text such as tweets.

6. **Additional context required**: These are examples where the sarcasm is understood if additional context is available. For example, *'i get to work with the worlds mos (sic) exciting person at 9 to make my day better'*.

To clearly understand the proportion of errors made by each of our approaches, we also perform quantitative analysis of errors which results in three categories: (A) Examples where the rule-based approach fails to detect sarcasm but machine learning-based approach detects it, (B) Examples where the machine learning-based approach fails to detect sarcasm but deep learning-based approach detects it, and (C) Examples where none of the approaches detect the sarcasm.

Error Category	(A)	(B)	(C)
Sarcasm not due to numbers	34	32	10
Numbers enhancing sarcasm	12	22	20
Comparison of numbers	4	12	12
Unseen situations	32	14	18
'Special' numbers	12	12	30
Additional Context Required	6	8	10

Table 5: Percentage of errors for the three configurations; (A): Rule-based approach goes wrong but statistical machine learning-based approach is correct, (B): Statistical machine learning-based approach goes wrong but the deep learning-based approach is correct, (C): All three approaches go wrong

Table 5 shows the proportion of errors in the three configurations. The ad-hoc nature of the rule-based approach reflects in percentage values. Similarly, analyzing tweets in which sarcasm is enhanced due to numbers and sarcasm arising due to a comparison between numbers appear as useful pointers for future work.

9   Conclusions & Future Work

In this paper, we present approaches to handle a special case of sarcasm: sarcasm expressed through numbers. We show that past works in sarcasm detection do not perform well for text containing numbers. We then compare our approaches with three previous works and show the significant improvements in F-score when our approaches are used on top of other approaches. To the best of our knowledge, this is the first line of research investigating the phenomenon of sarcasm arising out of numbers, culminating in a detector thereof. Our error analysis points out to specific numerical sarcasm challenges, thus creating immediate future tasks. The utility of our work lies in the fact that our system is a crucial link in a pipeline for sarcasm detection, where a tweet labeled as non-sarcastic and containing a number gets a final check of being sarcastic. Future work consists of incorporating a language model for numbers to handle unseen situations. Long term future work consists in tackling irony in general, humor and humble bragging (*'Oh my life is miserable: I have to sign 500 autographs a day'*) all of which have their genesis in incongruity.

Acknowledgement

The authors would like to thank Diptesh Kanojia, Urmi Saha, Kevin Patel, Rudra Murthy, Sandeep Mathias, Jaya Saraswati and members of the Center For Indian Language Technology, IIT Bombay. The authors would also like to thank Minali Upreti for helping with the diagrams and the anonymous reviewers for their valuable comments and feedback.

References

Silvio Amir, Byron C. Wallace, Hao Lyu, Paula Carvalho, and Mario J. Silva. 2016. Modelling context with user embeddings for sarcasm detection in social media. In *Proceedings of The 20th SIGNLL Conference on Computational Natural Language Learning*, pages 167–177. Association for Computational Linguistics.

Stefano Baccianella, Andrea Esuli, and Fabrizio Sebastiani. 2010. Sentiwordnet 3.0: An enhanced lexical resource for sentiment analysis and opinion mining. In *Proceedings of the Seventh conference on International Language Resources and Evaluation (LREC'10)*, Valletta, Malta. European Languages Resources Association (ELRA).

Mondher Bouazizi and Tomoaki Otsuki Ohtsuki. 2016. A pattern-based approach for sarcasm detection on twitter. *IEEE Access*, 4:5477–5488.

Konstantin Buschmeier, Philipp Cimiano, and Roman Klinger. 2014. An impact analysis of features in a classification approach to irony detection in product reviews. In *Proceedings of the 5th Workshop on Computational Approaches to Subjectivity, Sentiment and Social Media Analysis*, pages 42–49, Baltimore, Maryland. Association for Computational Linguistics.

Paula Carvalho, Luís Sarmento, Mário J. Silva, and Eugénio de Oliveira. 2009. Clues for detecting irony in user-generated contents: Oh...!! it's "so easy" ;-). In *Proceedings of the 1st International CIKM Workshop on Topic-sentiment Analysis for Mass Opinion*, TSA '09, pages 53–56, New York, NY, USA. ACM.

Dmitry Davidov, Oren Tsur, and Ari Rappoport. 2010. Semi-supervised recognition of sarcastic sentences in twitter and amazon. In *Proceedings of the fourteenth conference on computational natural language learning*, pages 107–116. Association for Computational Linguistics.

Abhijeet Dubey, Aditya Joshi, and Pushpak Bhattacharyya. 2019. Deep models for converting sarcastic utterances into their non sarcastic interpretation. In *Proceedings of the ACM India Joint International Conference on Data Science and Management of Data*, CoDS-COMAD '19, pages 289–292, New York, NY, USA. ACM.

Delia Irazú Hernández Farías, Viviana Patti, and Paolo Rosso. 2016. Irony detection in twitter: The role of affective content. *ACM Trans. Internet Technol.*, 16(3):19:1–19:24.

Aniruddha Ghosh and Dr. Tony Veale. 2016. Fracking sarcasm using neural network. In *Proceedings of the 7th Workshop on Computational Approaches to Subjectivity, Sentiment and Social Media Analysis*, pages 161–169. Association for Computational Linguistics.

Aniruddha Ghosh and Tony Veale. 2017. Magnets for sarcasm: Making sarcasm detection timely, contextual and very personal. In *Proceedings of the 2017 Conference on Empirical Methods in Natural Language Processing*, pages 482–491. Association for Computational Linguistics.

Raymond W Gibbs. 1986. On the psycholinguistics of sarcasm. *Journal of Experimental Psychology: General*, 115(1):3–15.

Roberto González-Ibáñez, Smaranda Muresan, and Nina Wacholder. 2011. Identifying sarcasm in twitter: A closer look. In *Proceedings of the 49th Annual Meeting of the Association for Computational Linguistics: Human Language Technologies: Short Papers - Volume 2*, HLT '11, pages 581–586, Stroudsburg, PA, USA. Association for Computational Linguistics.

Devamanyu Hazarika, Soujanya Poria, Sruthi Gorantla, Erik Cambria, Roger Zimmermann, and Rada Mihalcea. 2018. Cascade: Contextual sarcasm detection in online discussion forums. In *Proceedings of the 27th International Conference on Computational Linguistics*, pages 1837–1848. Association for Computational Linguistics.

Stacey L. Ivanko and Penny M. Pexman. 2003. Context incongruity and irony processing. *Discourse Processes*, 35(3):241–279.

Aditya Joshi, Pushpak Bhattacharyya, and Mark James Carman. 2017. Automatic sarcasm detection: A survey. *ACM Comput. Surv.*, 50:73:1–73:22.

Aditya Joshi, Vinita Sharma, and Pushpak Bhattacharyya. 2015. Harnessing context incongruity for sarcasm detection. In *Proceedings of the 53rd Annual Meeting of the Association for Computational Linguistics and the 7th International Joint Conference on Natural Language Processing (Volume 2: Short Papers)*, pages 757–762, Beijing, China. Association for Computational Linguistics.

Marvin Karson. 1968. Handbook of methods of applied statistics. volume i: Techniques of computation descriptive methods, and statistical inference. volume ii: Planning of surveys and experiments. i. m. chakravarti, r. g. laha, and j. roy, new york, john wiley; 1967, $9.00. *Journal of the American Statistical Association*, 63(323):1047–1049.

Christine Liebrecht, Florian Kunneman, and Antal Van den Bosch. 2013. The perfect solution for detecting sarcasm in tweets #not. In *Proceedings of the 4th Workshop on Computational Approaches to Subjectivity, Sentiment and Social Media Analysis*, pages 29–37. Association for Computational Linguistics.

Lotem Peled and Roi Reichart. 2017. Sarcasm sign: Interpreting sarcasm with sentiment based monolingual machine translation. In *Proceedings of the 55th Annual Meeting of the Association for Computational Linguistics (Volume 1: Long Papers)*, pages 1690–1700. Association for Computational Linguistics.

Jeffrey Pennington, Richard Socher, and Christopher Manning. 2014. Glove: Global vectors for word representation. In *Proceedings of the 2014 Conference on Empirical Methods in Natural Language Processing (EMNLP)*, pages 1532–1543, Doha, Qatar. Association for Computational Linguistics.

Soujanya Poria, Erik Cambria, Devamanyu Hazarika, and Prateek Vij. 2016. A deeper look into sarcastic tweets using deep convolutional neural networks. In *Proceedings of COLING 2016, the 26th International Conference on Computational Linguistics: Technical Papers*, pages 1601–1612. The COLING 2016 Organizing Committee.

Ellen Riloff, Ashequl Qadir, Prafulla Surve, Lalindra De Silva, Nathan Gilbert, and Ruihong Huang. 2013. Sarcasm as contrast between a positive sentiment and negative situation. In *Proceedings of the 2013 Conference on Empirical Methods in Natural Language Processing*, pages 704–714. Association for Computational Linguistics.

Emilio Sulis, Delia Iraz Hernndez Faras, Paolo Rosso, Viviana Patti, and Giancarlo Ruffo. 2016. Figurative messages and affect in twitter: Differences between irony, sarcasm and not. *Knowledge-Based Systems*, 108:132 – 143. New Avenues in Knowledge Bases for Natural Language Processing.

Joseph Tepperman, David R. Traum, and Shrikanth Narayanan. 2006. ”yeah right”: sarcasm recognition for spoken dialogue systems. In *INTERSPEECH 2006 - ICSLP, Ninth International Conference on Spoken Language Processing, Pittsburgh, PA, USA, September 17-21, 2006*.

Akira Utsumi. 2000. Verbal irony as implicit display of ironic environment: Distinguishing ironic utterances from nonirony. *Journal of Pragmatics*, 32(12):1777 – 1806.

Cynthia Van Hee, Els Lefever, and Veronique Hoste. 2018. Semeval-2018 task 3: Irony detection in english tweets. In *Proceedings of The 12th International Workshop on Semantic Evaluation*, pages 39–50, New Orleans, Louisiana. Association for Computational Linguistics.

Zichao Yang, Diyi Yang, Chris Dyer, Xiaodong He, Alex Smola, and Eduard Hovy. 2016. Hierarchical attention networks for document classification. In *Proceedings of the 2016 Conference of the North American Chapter of the Association for Computational Linguistics: Human Language Technologies*, pages 1480–1489, San Diego, California. Association for Computational Linguistics.

Meishan Zhang, Yue Zhang, and Guohong Fu. 2016. Tweet sarcasm detection using deep neural network. In *Proceedings of COLING 2016, the 26th International Conference on Computational Linguistics: Technical Papers*, pages 2449–2460. The COLING 2016 Organizing Committee.

Cross-lingual Subjectivity Detection for Resource Lean Languages

Aida Amini[1], Samane Karimi[2, 3], and Azadeh Shakery[2, 4]

[1]School of Computer Science and Engineering, University of Washington
[2]School of Electrical and Computer Engineering, College of Engineering, University of Tehran
[3]Computer Science Department, University of Houston
[4]School of Computer Science, Institute for Research in Fundamental Sciences (IPM)University of Tehran
amini91@cs.washington.edu
{samanekarimi, shakery}@ut.ac.ir

Abstract

Wide and universal changes in the web content due to the growth of web 2 applications increase the importance of user-generated content on the web. Therefore, the related research areas such as sentiment analysis, opinion mining and subjectivity detection receives much attention from the research community. Due to the diverse languages that web-users use to express their opinions and sentiments, research areas like subjectivity detection should present methods which are practicable on all languages. An important prerequisite to effectively achieve this aim is considering the limitations in resource-lean languages. In this paper, cross-lingual subjectivity detection on resource lean languages is investigated using two different approaches: a language-model based and a learning-to-rank approach. Experimental results show the impact of different factors on the performance of subjectivity detection methods using English resources to detect the subjectivity score of Persian documents. The experiments demonstrate that the proposed learning-to-rank method outperforms the baseline method in ranking documents based on their subjectivity degree.

1 Introduction

Rapid growth of web 2 applications lead to an increase in textual content generated by users such as comments, reviews and any kind of textual data reflecting peoples opinions. In text mining literature, this kind of data is known as subjective data. Consequently, many automatic methods for detecting this kind of data from objective ones and in the next step, for detecting the polarity of subjective data have been proposed. These methods form one of the main research areas in text mining called subjectivity and sentiment analysis. Most papers in this area propose methods for sentiment analysis on English whereas users of web 2 ap-

plications are from a wide range of languages so there is a serious need for making sentiment analysis possible on other languages. This goal is achieved by different approaches proposed in this research area. Some papers present methods for sentiment analysis on non-English languages such that English resources are translated to the target language using dictionaries, machine translation or other tools, then a sentiment analysis method is proposed for the non-English language using the translated resources.

Some other papers propose a cross-lingual framework for sentiment analysis. In this approach, passing the language boundaries is an internal step which is situated within the whole procedure. Some other papers address sentiment analysis on multi-lingual environments. The main goal in these papers is to employ all useful information from different languages to facilitate subjectivity detection and sentiment analysis on multi-lingual documents.

In this paper, the problem of subjectivity detection in cross-lingual case is studied to see how the sentiment resources in resource-rich languages like English can be used to achieve high performance in subjectivity detection systems of resource-lean languages like Persian. The methods employed as subjectivity detection methods in this paper are a language-model-based method and a method based on learning-to-rank techniques that are implemented in cross-lingual case.

Our experiments show that some factors including translation direction and translation unit have an impact on the performance of cross-lingual subjectivity detection methods. Furthermore, experimental results show that learning to rank approach leads to high performance in subjectivity detection task.

The rest of this paper is organized as follows. In section 2, some of the most relevant studies in

Proceedings of the 10th Workshop on Computational Approaches to Subjectivity, Sentiment and Social Media Analysis, pages 81–90
Minneapolis, June 6, 2019. ©2019 Association for Computational Linguistics

subjectivity detection and sentiment analysis area are reviewed. Section 3 describes two subjectivity detection methods implemented in this paper. Experimental results are explained in section 4. The paper is concluded by future work and conclusion section.

2 Related Work

Most of previous studies in sentiment analysis area has been applied to English data. Sentiment analysis on other languages and on multi-lingual environments and in cross-lingual settings which is using resources of one language like English to do sentiment analysis on another language, has attracted a great deal of attention in recent years so a large number of papers focus on these areas. Previous studies related to these areas are explained in the rest of this section.

2.1 Cross-lingual Sentiment analysis

Ku et al. (Ku et al., 2006) propose algorithms for opinion extraction and summarization for Chinese. To this aim, they provide the necessary Chinese sentiment lexicon by translating the available English one, namely General Inquirer. In an Italian one, Esuli and Sebastiani (Esuli and Sebastiani, 2009) propose an opinion extraction system using lexical resources to improve the performance of the proposed opinion extraction system.

Banea et al. (Banea et al., 2008) have studied the performance of automatic translation in a sentiment analysis system where training sources are in a resource-rich language and test sources are in another language. Authors have done comparative evaluations on Romanian and Spanish through three different experiments. In all three experiments, English is used as a source language which both a manually annotated corpus (MPQA) and a subjectivity analysis tool (OpinionFinder) is available.

Another paper on Spanish sentiment analysis is proposed by Brooke (Brooke et al., 2009). In this paper, a lexicon-based sentiment analysis system is adapted to Spanish such that semantic orientation of each word in Spanish is computed using the translated lexicon.

Steinberger et al. (Steinberger et al., 2011a) propose a method that starts by construction of a sentiment dictionary in two languages (English and Spanish). In the next step, parallel data from English and Spanish are translated to the third lan-

guage (Arabic, Czech, French, German, Italian and Russian) and the new sentiment dictionary is obtained from the intersection of the translations.

In another paper of Steinberger et al. (Steinberger et al., 2011b), the construction and employment of a parallel corpus with sentiment labels is studied. This paper proposes to detect the polarity of opinions that are about entities like persons, organizations and concepts across different languages. A simple method is selected for polarity detection in this paper, which adds up positive and negative scores in six-word windows around the entities. The sentiment scores of the words are computed using the sentiment dictionaries created by triangulation method (Steinberger et al., 2011a).

Bautin et al. (Bautin et al., 2008) propose a method to detect the sentiment label of news articles gathered from online newspapers in nine languages including Arabic, Chinese, English, French, German, Italian, Japanese, Korean, and Spanish. In this paper, machine translation is used to transfer textual documents into English. Then, a sentiment analysis system entitled Lydia is employed to detect the translated documents labels.

Wei and Pal (Wei and Pal, 2010) propose a cross-lingual sentiment analysis system that uses SCL(Structural Correspondence Learning) technique to find an efficient representation for documents which is shared in both languages.

One of the latest papers in this area address the aspect-based sentiment analysis in cross-lingual setting (Lambert, 2015). In this paper, Lambert propose a method which translates opinionated segments of the source language under some constraints such that their translation in target language would not be reordered.

2.2 Multi-lingual sentiment analysis

Banea et al. (Banea et al., 2014) uses classification methods for subjectivity detection in a multi-lingual environment using the alignments between word senses in different languages from wordNet, namely English and Romanian.

Balahur and Turchi (Balahur and Turchi, 2014) propose to investigate sentiment detection and classification on different languages other than English. Three languages including German, Spanish and French are selected for this aim. In this article, three machine translation systems such as Google, Bing and Moses is investigated and its results show that the machine translation method can lead to high performance in sentiment detection and classification similar to the performance in the original language (English).

In Banea et al. (Banea et al., 2010) a labeled English dataset is translated to five other languages including Romanian, Spanish, French, German and Arabic. Then some multilingual versions of the English datasets based on all possible combinations of these six languages are generated and used to train Nave Bayes classifiers with unigram features.

Wan (Wan, 2009) propose a sentiment analysis system whose idea is similar to (Banea et al., 2010). Authors in (Wan, 2009) use the multilingual views to the dataset by automatic translation of reviews. The English reviews are translated to Chinese and the paper illustrates that the proposed cross-lingual sentiment analysis system outperforms the mono-lingual one.

To evaluate the multi-lingual comparability of multi-lingual subjectivity analysis systems, Kim et al. (Kim et al., 2010) have presented an evaluation method. In this method, performance of different subjectivity analysis systems including a corpus-based method, a lexicon-based method and OpinionFinder (a well-known tool for subjectivity analysis) is measured on multi-lingual data on English, Korean, Japanese and Chinese.

3 Methodology

The main aim of this paper is to distinguish subjective text from objective ones. The task of identifying documents containing subjective text is appealing due to the fact that subjectivity detection is a preliminary step before other sentiment analysis tasks such as polarity detection. In many subjectivity detection methods there is a need for a collection of documents with two labels: subjective and objective. The main aim of this paper is to explore and investigate different methods for making the full use of labeled datasets from resource rich languages like English (as train data) to improve quality of subjectivity detection in resource lean languages like Persian (as test data).

Having both test and train datasets in the same language, would cause less ambiguities in subjectivity detection results in comparison with having them in different languages. Consequently, better subjectivity detection performance is expected when both train and test datasets are in the same language.

In cross-lingual domains, the similarity between the source and target language and the quality of translation tool are critical in the performance. Each language has its own ambiguities. For example, both words "milk" and "lion" translate to the same word in Persian or the word "pretty" has two meanings in English. Each of these ambiguities affect both monolingual and cross-lingual results. However, these effects may be more catastrophic in cross-lingual cases since we are dealing with ambiguities in both languages and the errors caused by incorrect translations. In this paper, two different approaches for crossing the language borders are investigated:

In the first approach, resources of the source language are translated to the target language, then a model is built using the translated data and finally the model is applied on the test data (source translation).

The second approach uses an inverse translation direction. In this approach, first, a model is built using the data in the source language. Simultaneously, the data in the target language is translated to the source language. Finally, the model is applied on the translated test data (target translation).

These two approaches are studied by means of two different subjectivity detection methods including a language-model based method and a learning-to-rank method. In the following sections, the details related to each of the mentioned methods are further discussed.

3.1 Cross lingual Subjectivity Detection

In cross lingual subjectivity detection, the test data is form the resource lean language(Persian) and the train data is from the resource rich languages(English). Due to the different languages of the train and test data, there is a need to cross the language borders in one of the steps of cross lingual subjectivity detection process. Translation phase adds some more challenges to the problem in terms of translation direction and unit.

Translation direction is one of the factors that affects the translation quality due to the different ambiguities in each language.

Translation unit Translation can be done in word or sentence level that leads to different results. For example, the context available in sentence level translation can help the translator solve the the ambiguity of words' different meanings. Therefore, the translation unit can be another factor to be considered. These two factors are considered in each of the proposed methods, i.e. the language-model based method and the learning-to-rank method.

3.1.1 Language-Model based method

Language modeling is an approach which has been widely used in Information retrieval recently. In this paper, we employed the language-model based subjectivity detection method proposed in (Karimi and Shakery, 2017). In (Karimi and Shakery, 2017), each test document is assigned a subjectivity score based on its similarity to the language models of subjective and objective train datasets. This score is computed from the difference of the similarity between the test document language model and the language model of subjective train dataset (subjective model), $sim_{subj}(d)$, and the similarity between the test document language model and the language model of objective train dataset (objective model), $sim_{obj}(d)$.

$$score(d) = sim_{subj}(d) - sim_{obj}(d) \quad (1)$$

The subjective and objective models are built over the unigrams of subjective and objective documents in the train dataset. Each unigram in each model is assigned a value representing the its occurrence probability in the subjective or objective documents. In this approach, the effect of each word on the subjectiveness and objectiveness of the document is measured. For example the word "opinion" would appear more frequently in subjective documents. In addition to that, the effect of neutral words(propositions or modal verbs) can be ignored with the usage of an appropriate scoring formula since these words are present almost equally in both categories. In our method, we utilize this approach to compute the subjectivity score of a document in a cross-lingual setting. The details of how the similarity values (i.e. $sim_{subj}(d)$ and $sim_{obj}(d)$) are computed in our method are explained in the rest of this section.

As mentioned before, the translation unit and translation direction are two important factors affecting cross-lingual subjectivity detection performance. The proposed language-model based method is explained considering these two factors. Words and documents are two translation units considered in this paper:

- Word level translation: In this case, the translation phase follows the training phase. The translation can be done in two directions.

From English to Persian (source translation): In this case, the translation should be applied to the reference language models, namely subjective and objective models. These models consist of unigrams and their occurrence probability, so the translation can be easily applied to the models. The translated reference language models are computed as follows.

$$p(f|\theta_{subj}) = \sum_{w} p(f|w, \theta_{subj})p(w|\theta_{subj})$$
$$\approx \sum_{w} p(f|w)p(w|\theta_{subj}) \quad (2)$$

$$p(f|\theta_{obj}) = \sum_{w} p(f|w, \theta_{obj})p(w|\theta_{obj})$$
$$\approx \sum_{w} p(f|w)p(w|\theta_{obj}) \quad (3)$$

$$p(w|\theta_{subj}) = \frac{\sum_{d \in D_{subj}} c(w, d)}{\sum_{d \in D_{subj}} |d|} \quad (4)$$

$$p(w|\theta_{obj}) = \frac{\sum_{d \in D_{obj}} c(w, d)}{\sum_{d \in D_{obj}} |d|} \quad (5)$$

where $c(w, d)$ represents the frequency of word w in document d and $|d|$ is the length of document d. D_{Subj} and D_{obj} represent the set of subjective and objective documents in the train dataset respectively. f, w and $p(f|w)$ represent a Persian word, an English word and the probability that f translates to w using the employed translation tool (i.e. translation probability) respectively. $p(w|\theta_{subj})$ and $p(w|\theta_{obj})$ stands for the occurrence probability of word w in the primal (before translation) subjective and objective language models that are calculated using the Eq. (4) and the Eq. (5). Accordingly, $p(f|\theta_{subj})$ and $p(f|\theta_{obj})$ represent the word probabilities in the translated subjective and objective language models respectively.

The outputs of the translation phase are the reference language models in the target language,

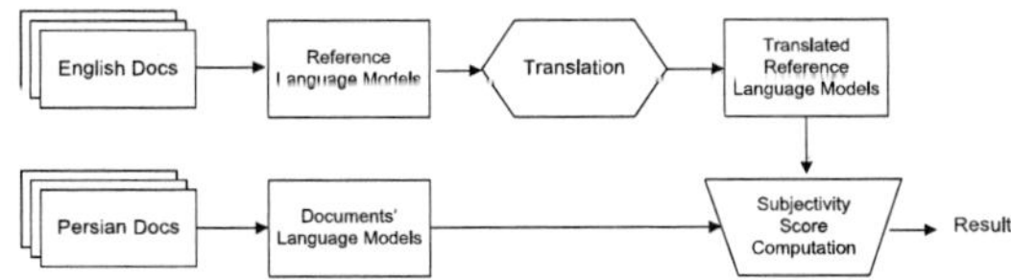

Figure 1: Language model-based subjectivity detection from English to Persian

namely, the translated subjective and objective models which can be used for computing the subjectivity score of a test document d. To this aim, first, we need to calculate the similarity between the language model of d and the subjective model, i.e. $sim_{subj}(d)$, and also the similarity between the document's language model and the objective model, i.e. $sim_{obj}(d)$. The similarity between the language models are measured using kl-divergence formula according to the Eq. (6) and the Eq. (7):

$$sim_{subj}(d) = \sum_{f \in d} -p(f|\theta_d) . \log \frac{p(f|\theta_d)}{p(f|\theta_{subj})} \quad (6)$$

$$sim_{obj}(d) = \sum_{f \in d} -p(f|\theta_d) . \log \frac{p(f|\theta_d)}{p(f|\theta_{obj})} \quad (7)$$

Figure 1 illustrates this procedure in more details.

Persian to English (target translation): In this case, the Persian unigrams are mapped to the model. For each of the Persian documents, the unigrams are derived and translated to English. Therefore, the model in the source language can be used over the translated unigram language model of the test document. In this case, the reference language models are computed the same as mono-lingual case using the Eq. (4) and the Eq. (5) and the documents language model is translated according to the Eq. (8).

$$p(w|\theta_d) = \sum_{f} p(w|f, \theta_d) p(f|\theta d))$$
$$\approx \sum_{f} p(w|f) p(f|\theta d) \quad (8)$$

where $p(w|\theta_d)$ represents the word probabilities in the translated document language model and $p(f|\theta_d)$ represents the word probabilities in the primal (before translation) document language model. Final subjectivity score is computed according to the Eq. (1).

- Document level translation: This level of translation is independent of the direction of the translation. So, the translation is applied as a preprocessing step. Then, the training and testing steps would be similar to monolingual situation.

3.1.2 Learning to rank

Learning to rank approach in information retrieval refers to a method using machine learning techniques to rank documents based on their relevance to a query. Therefore, to use this approach in subjectivity detection task a query list is needed. In this paper, for each language a list of subjective terms is specified as the query list. These lists are the subjective portion of a sentiment lexicon in each language which is specified by selecting terms with higher subjectivity weights. Then, the relevance of documents to the queries in the list is used as a measure of their subjectivity level. In other words, the learning to rank method computes the relevance degree of each test document to the query and the final result is a ranked list of documents for each query. The query set used in this paper is a sentiment lexicon constructed in (Dehdarbehbahani et al., 2014) which is employed in two manners:

- List query level: In this manner, all of the words in the sentiment lexicon are assumed to be one enormous query.

- Term query level: The assumption of having a query with the length of more than 1000 words can be inane. Therefore, in this section, each term of the lexicon is used as a separate query so the number of feature vectors would be the multiplication of the number of queries and documents. The final output should be the scores assigned to the test documents. As mentioned above, there would be q*d feature vectors, hence, q*d individual scores. To compute a single score for each test document, as the desired output of the subjectivity detection method, a weighted average over scores obtained from each query term q_i of the query q can be computed in this manner as below:

$$score(d, q) = \sum_{q_i \in q} \frac{w(q_i) . score(d, q_i)}{|q|} \quad (9)$$

where $w(q_i)$ is the weight of each query term q_i in the sentiment lexicon. $score(d, q_i)$ is the score of each test document d with query term , q_i obtained from the learning to rank method.

In this approach, the translation can be done via two procedures. These procedures are figured based on the feature set used in the learning to rank method as explained below:

- Translated Unigrams: In the first procedure which unigrams are used as query independent features, the translation phase is performed simply on the unigrams of the train dataset.

- Query dependent features: These features are computed using the probabilistic translations for query terms as described below:

  a) Term Frequency: This feature is calculated according to the following relations in cross lingual situation:

  $$TF(f_i, d_f) = c(f_i, d_f) \quad (10)$$

  $$CLTF(e_j, d_f) = \sum_{f_i} p(f_i|e_j).TF(f_i, d_f) \quad (11)$$

  $$CL\_Feat1(d, e) = \sum_{e_j \in e} \log(CLTF(e_j, d)) \quad (12)$$

  where d_f represents the document in Persian, e_j represents the query term in English and e represents the whole query, f_i represents the ith translation of e_j, $p(f_i|e_j)$ shows the translation probability of e_j to f_i and $c(f_i, d_f)$ represents the frequency of the query word f_i in document d_f.

  b) Inverse Document Frequency: This feature is calculated as below:

  $$IDF(e_j) = \frac{N}{|d \in D|e_j \in D|} \quad (13)$$

  $$CLIDF(e_j) = \sum_{f_i} p(f_i|e_j).IDF(f_i) \quad (14)$$

  $$CL\_Feat2(e) = \sum_{e_j \in e} \log(CLIDF(e_j)) \quad (15)$$

  where N represents the number of documents in the collection, d represents the test document, D represents the collection of documents, e_j represents the query term and e represents the whole query.

c) BM25: This feature provides a measurement of the relevance degree of the document to the query. This feature is calculated as below:

$$CL\_Feat3(d, q) =$$
$$\sum_{q_i \in q} CLIDF(q_i) \times \quad (16)$$
$$\frac{c(q_i, d).(k_1 + 1)}{c(q_i, d) + k_1.(1 + b - b.\frac{|d|}{avg(dl)})}$$

Where $|d|$ represents the document length and $avg(dl)$ is the average length of the documents in the collection and $c(q_i, d)$ is the frequency of query term q_i in document and d. k_1 and b are constant parameters used for determining the effect of query term frequency and normalizing the document length respectively.

d) KL-Divergence: This feature that shows the relevance degree of the document to the query is computed according to the Eq. (8) where the document language model is computed based on the probabilistic translation (Azarbonyad et al., 2012).

e) Document length: this feature shows the length of the document.

4 Experimental Results and Discussion

4.1 Datasets

The datasets used in this paper consist of documents about movies. Movie is a difficult domain to analyze since it contains a great variety of words based on the movie story while comments regarding other products can mostly be narrowed to a set of technical words that are used in the products domain. The datasets used in this paper are in two languages:

English Dataset : This dataset (Ku et al., 2006) contains 5000 movie reviews from Rotten Tomatoes that form subjective documents and 5000 movie summaries from the Internet Movie Database that form objective documents of the dataset. The average document length in this dataset is 11 words.

Persian Dataset : As there was no Persian dataset in movie domain with subjective and objective labels, it is constructed to be employed in this paper. Subjective documents are gathered from the websites containing movie critics such as: www.naghdefarsi.com, myturn.blogsky.com, yasserbayani.persianblog.ir. To ensure that all documents gathered from these websites are opinionated, only some specific URL patterns are followed. More than 7500 subjective documents are accumulated using these URLs. For the objective part of this dataset, Wikipedia is used as the main information resource. This website poses information regarding the movies that are produced over the past century so it contains objective data about movies. To ensure that none of documents contains any opinions, only the textual content under specific titles are collected. These titles are Actors/Actresses, Awards and Movie Story. All these data, if existed, are considered as one document. In addition to Wikipedia content, the paragraphs that start with movie story title from naghdefarsi website are also added to the objective dataset. In total, 3500 objective documents are gathered. The average document length in this dataset is 83.

Language Differences There are major distinctions between Persian and English languages including the difference in the sentence structure, negative and modal verb formations, and the use of adjectives. In contrast to English language, the verb in Persian appears at the end of the sentence. Negative verbs are constructed by adding *ne* to the beginning of the verb in contrast of having separate *not*. The usage of adjectives, which are also critical in subjectivity detection, are different in a way that they usually appear after the word they are describing.

4.2 Translators

Translators accuracy has a great impact on the final results. The more accurate the translator, the closer to mono lingual results would be. In addition, based on the methodology employed, different kinds of information regarding the translation are needed. For the language-model based method, Google translate is used as the translation tool. The source text is sent to this tool in packages via 100 separate threads. In word level translation, the unigrams of the dataset are submitted as input and the outcome is the list of possible translations. In this case, the first translation is considered to be the most probable translation. In the document level translation, the whole documents are extracted and sent for translation. The result would be the whole document in the target language that does not include different possible translations so the returned document is

Runs	MAP
LM-EToP-W	0.693
LM-PToE-W	0.849

Table 1: The comparison of LM-EToP-W and LM-PToE-W in terms of MAP.

used as the translated document. In the learning-to-rank method, the probabilistic translations are needed. The Moses translator is used for this purpose (Koehn et al., 2007). This translator is built over the Wikipedia corpus in Intelligent Information Systems Lab in University of Tehran. All possible translations with their probabilities are considered in our learning to rank method.

4.3 Experimental results

In this section, two different methods for cross-lingual subjectivity detection are evaluated through different experiments investigating their different characteristics. These methods are language-model based method and learning-to-rank method which are explained in section 3. In the rest of this section, experiments related to each of the methods are presented.

4.3.1 Language-model based method

In this section, experimental results of the language-model based method are represented. In this experiment, the English dataset is used to build the reference language models and the Persian dataset is used as the test data. Translation is applied on both directions, in other words on both English and Persian datasets and top translation is chosen for each word. Furthermore, translation is done on both document level and word level. In word level, based on the direction of translation, unigrams of the language models in the source language are translated to the target language and used to be compared with the other language models according to the methods formulas explained in section 3.1.1. Table 1 shows the results of this experiment which contains MAP values of the cross-lingual word level runs namely LM-EToP-W and LM-PToE-W which only differ in the direction of translation.

As shown in table 1, the Language-model based method using the word level translation performs better when the translation is from Persian to English. One of the reasons for this result is that in LM-EToP-W the unigrams in the reference language models (English dataset) are translated and

Runs	MAP
LM-EToP-D	0.800
LM-PToE-D	0.483

Table 2: The comparison of LM-EToP-D and LM-PToE-D in terms of MAP.

Runs	MAP
AD-EToP-LQ	0.675
AD-PToE-LQ	0.708
AD-EToP-TQ	0.929
AD-PToE-TQ	0.764

Table 3: The comparison of AD-EToP-LQ, AD-PToE-LQ, AD-EToP-TQ and AD-PToE-TQ in terms of MAP.

subsequently are subject to translation errors. As the methods performance basically depends on the quality of subjective and objective reference language models, the results would be reasonable.

In the next experiment, translation is applied in document level. The documents are translated to the target language in a preprocessing step and the rest of the experiment is similar to a monolingual problem. LM-EToP-D and LM-PToE-D are two runs executed in this section with document level translation from English to Persian and Persian to English respectively.

The results in Table 2 show that in document level translation, translation from English to Persian is more accurate than from Persian to English, contrary to word level translation. The reason is that the translation tool failed in translating most of the Persian documents, while in translating from English to Persian more documents are translated correctly by the machine translation tool so the MAP value of LM-EToP-D is higher than LM-PToE-D

4.3.2 Learning-to-Rank method

To obtain the results of our learning-to-rank method, a query list is needed. In this paper, the Persian query list is selected from the lexicon constructed in (Dehdarbehbahani et al., 2014). The lexicon contains 7491 terms and one tenth of it which has higher weights are selected as the Persian query list. The English query list which is selected from the Sentiwordnet (Baccianella et al., 2010) contains 156581 terms.

As explained in section 3.1.2, the queries are used via two approaches. In the first approach, the whole list is considered as one big query. In the second approach, each term in the query list is considered as an individual query and final subjectivity detection result is obtained by aggregating the results of each query weighted by the querys subjectivity weight. We employed SVM-rank (Joachims, 2006) and RankLib (Dang) to implement our learning-to-rank based method. In computations of the second feature set, BM25 feature has two parameters, including k and b, which

are set to 1.5 and 0.8 respectively.

In the following experiments, the English dataset is used as the train set and the Persian dataset as the test set, MAP value is reported and the translation is applied in word level.

In the next experiment, ADARank algorithm is executed using the RankLib tool by four runs: 1) Using the whole query list of subjective words as one query while the translation direction is from English to Persian (AD-EToP-LQ). 2) Using the whole query list as one query while the translation direction is from Persian to English (AD-PToE-LQ). 3) Using each word of the query list as an individual query while the translation direction is from English to Persian (AD-EToP-TQ) 4) Using each word of the query list as an individual query while the translation direction is from Persian to English (AD-PToE-TQ). The results of this experiment are shown in table 3.

According to Table 3, using each word of the list as a separate query leads to better results than using one big query containing all subjective words as AD-EToP-TQ and AD-PToE-TQ outperform AD-EToP-LQ and AD-PToE-LQ respectively. Since words may have different translations and the selected translation may be incorrect, in AD-PToE-TQ and AD-EToP-TQ runs, the translation error only affects the single search corresponding to that query term but in AD-PToE-LQ and AD-EToP-LQ runs, the translation error of query terms would affect the whole query and it leads to lower results in the search corresponding to the list of query terms.

In the next experiment, we compare the results of the learning-to-rank based method with a baseline method. As a baseline method for ranking documents according to their subjectivity score, the language-model based method explained in section 3.1.1 can be a good choice since:

- It provides quantitative values as subjectivity scores of documents which facilitates ranking them similar to the output of the learning to rank approach.

Runs	MAP
LM-PToE-W	0.849
AD-EToP-TQ	0.929

Table 4: The comparison of AD-EToP-TQ and LM-PToE-W in terms of MAP.

Runs	MAP
RF-EToP-TQ-rev	0.811
AD-EToP-TQ-rev	0.809
CA-EToP-TQ-rev	0.860

Table 5: The comparison of RF-EToP-TQ-rev, AD-EToP-TQ-rev and CA-EToP-TQ-rev in terms of MAP.

- In previous papers, this method has been used for detecting positive documents from negative ones (Hu et al., 2007) and also for detecting subjective documents from objective ones (Karimi and Shakery, 2017).

To do the comparison, the best results of each method obtained in the experiments is selected. According to the results reported in previous tables, the best result of the language-model based method is achieved when translation is from Persian to English and translation units are words (namely LM-PToE-W). The best result of the learning-to-rank based method is obtained when each word of the list is used as an individual query while the translation direction is from English to Persian and the ADARank algorithm is employed (namely AD-EToP-TQ). These results are shown in table 4.

According to the results in table 4, in case translation tools are available, subjectivity detection using the learning-to-rank based method outperforms the language-model based method. The next experiment is designed to check if the results are biased to the dataset. Therefore, the Persian and English datasets are used interchangeably. In other words, in this experiment, the Persian dataset is used as the train set and the English dataset is used as the test set. Hence, the direction of translation is from Persian to English and term query level is used in this experiment. In this experiment, three learning to rank algorithms using Ranklib tool including Random Forests (RF-EToP-TQ-rev), ADARank (AD-EToP-TQ-rev) and Coordinate Ascent(CA-EToP-TQ-rev) are used and the MAP values are measured. Table 5 shows the results of these three runs.

As table 5 shows, Coordinate Ascent outperforms both other algorithms while Random Forests and ADARank performs similarly.

5 Conclusion

In this paper, we propose an extensive investigation on the cross-lingual subjectivity detection problem. Our main focus is to employ of English resources to rank Persian documents based on their subjectivity degree. In this study, two methods are employed as subjectivity detection systems. The first method is a language-model based method which computes the subjectivity score of each test document based on the similarity between the statistical language model of the test document and a reference subjective model and a reference objective model. The reference subjective and objective models are built using the labeled English data. Moreover, a cross-lingual subjectivity detection method is proposed which employs learning-to-rank techniques to rank documents according to their subjectivity score. In this method, the terms of a sentiment lexicon are used as query terms and the documents of the train data with subjective labels are considered as relevant documents to the query terms. Based on these definitions, the learning-to-rank framework is employed to rank test documents in resource-lean languages benefiting from resources including sentiment lexicon or labeled data in resource-rich languages. These two methods are evaluated using various translation directions and different translation units. Experimental results show how different parameters impact on the methods performance. Experiments also demonstrate that the proposed learning-to-rank based method outperforms the language-model based approach as a baseline method of ranking document according to their subjectivity degree. One of the future works for this research is studying the impact of translation on the performance of subjectivity detection in other resource lean languages.

References

Hosein Azarbonyad, Azadeh Shakery, and Heshaam Faili. 2012. Using learning to rank approach for parallel corpora based cross language information retrieval. In *proceedings of 20th European Conference on Artificial Intelligence (ECAI)*, pages 79–84.

Stefano Baccianella, Andrea Esuli, and Fabrizio Sebastiani. 2010. Sentiwordnet 3.0: An enhanced lexical resource for sentiment analysis and opinion mining. volume 10.

Alexandra Balahur and Marco Turchi. 2014. Comparative experiments using supervised learning and machine translation for multilingual sentiment analysis. *Computer Speech & Language*, 28(1):56–75.

Carmen Banea, Rada Mihalcea, and Janyce Wiebe. 2010. Multilingual subjectivity: Are more languages better? In *Proceedings of the 23rd international conference on computational linguistics*, pages 28–36. Association for Computational Linguistics.

Carmen Banea, Rada Mihalcea, and Janyce Wiebe. 2014. Sense-level subjectivity in a multilingual setting. *Computer Speech & Language*, 28(1):7–19.

Carmen Banea, Rada Mihalcea, Janyce Wiebe, and Samer Hassan. 2008. Multilingual subjectivity analysis using machine translation. In *Proceedings of the Conference on Empirical Methods in Natural Language Processing*, pages 127–135. Association for Computational Linguistics.

Mikhail Bautin, Lohit Vijayarenu, and Steven Skiena. 2008. International sentiment analysis for news and blogs. In *ICWSM*.

Julian Brooke, Milan Tofiloski, and Maite Taboada. 2009. Cross-linguistic sentiment analysis: From english to spanish. In *RANLP*.

Van Dang. The lemur project-wiki-ranklib.

Iman Dehdarbehbahani, Azadeh Shakery, and Heshaam Faili. 2014. Semi-supervised word polarity identification in resource-lean languages. *Neural networks : the official journal of the International Neural Network Society*, 58:50–59.

Andrea Esuli and Fabrizio Sebastiani. 2009. Enhancing opinion extraction by automatically annotated lexical resources. In *Language and Technology Conference*, pages 500–511. Springer.

Yi Hu, Ruzhan Lu, Xuening Li, Yuquan Chen, and Jianyong Duan. 2007. A language modeling approach to sentiment analysis. In *Computational Science – ICCS 2007*, pages 1186–1193, Berlin, Heidelberg. Springer Berlin Heidelberg.

Thorsten Joachims. 2006. Training linear svms in linear time. volume 2006, pages 217–226.

Samaneh Karimi and Azadeh Shakery. 2017. A language-model-based approach for subjectivity detection. *Journal of Information Science*, 43(3):356–377.

Jungi Kim, Jinji Li, and Jong-Hyeok Lee. 2010. Evaluating multilanguage-comparability of subjectivity analysis systems. In *ACL*, page 595.

Philipp Koehn, Hieu Hoang, Alexandra Birch, Chris Callison-Burch, Marcello Federico, Nicola Bertoldi, Brooke Cowan, Wade Shen, Christine Moran, Richard Zens, Chris Dyer, Ondej Bojar, Alex Constantin, and Evan Herbst. 2007. Moses: Open source toolkit for statistical machine translation.

Lun-Wei Ku, Yu-Ting Liang, and Hsin-Hsi Chen. 2006. Opinion extraction, summarization and tracking in news and blog corpora. In *Proceedings of AAAI*, pages 100–107.

Patrik Lambert. 2015. Aspect-level cross-lingual sentiment classification with constrained smt. In *Proceedings of the 53rd Annual Meeting of the Association for Computational Linguistics and the 7th International Joint Conference on Natural Language Processing*, pages 781–787.

Josef Steinberger, Polina Lenkova, Mohamed Ebrahim, Maud Ehrmann, Ali Hurriyetoglu, Mijail Kabadjov, Ralf Steinberger, Hristo Tanev, Vanni Zavarella, and Silvia Vázquez. 2011a. Creating sentiment dictionaries via triangulation. In *Proceedings of the 2nd workshop on computational approaches to subjectivity and sentiment analysis*, pages 28–36. Association for Computational Linguistics.

Josef Steinberger, Polina Lenkova, Mijail A. Kabadjov, Ralf Steinberger, and Erik Van der Goot. 2011b. Multilingual entity-centered sentiment analysis evaluated by parallel corpora. In *RANLP*.

Xiaojun Wan. 2009. Co-training for cross-lingual sentiment classification. In *Proceedings of the Joint Conference of the 47th Annual Meeting of the ACL and the 4th International Joint Conference on Natural Language Processing of the AFNLP: Volume 1-volume 1*, pages 235–243. Association for Computational Linguistics.

Bin Wei and Christopher Joseph Pal. 2010. Cross lingual adaptation: An experiment on sentiment classifications. In *ACL*, pages 258–262.

Analyzing Incorporation of Emotion in Emoji Prediction

Shirley Anugrah Hayati[*] and **Aldrian Obaja Muis**[*]
Language Technologies Institute
Carnegie Mellon University
{shayati, amuis}@cs.cmu.edu

Abstract

In this work, we investigate the impact of incorporating emotion classes on the task of predicting emojis from Twitter texts. More specifically, we first show that there is a correlation between the emotion expressed in the text and the emoji choice of Twitter users. Based on this insight we propose a few simple methods to incorporate emotion information in traditional classifiers. Through automatic metrics, human evaluation, and error analysis, we show that the improvement obtained by incorporating emotion is significant and correlate better with human preferences compared to the baseline models. Through the human ratings that we obtained, we also argue for preference metric to better evaluate the usefulness of an emoji prediction system.

1 Introduction

Emoji is a set of pictograms that symbolize a lot of things from facial expressions to flags. Recently, research in emoji started to gain attention from Natural Language Processing (NLP) researchers due to its rising popularity in social media for users to express ideas, concepts, or emotion (Novak et al., 2015).

There has been some interest in tackling the task of emoji prediction (Barbieri et al., 2017, 2018a). Because of the rich expressiveness of emoji, understanding emojis will help other kinds of natural language understanding tasks such as sentiment analysis (Felbo et al., 2017) or generating or suggesting emoji for social media content (Novak et al., 2015).

Now, as noted by Wolny (2016), people use emojis to express diverse emotions. And intuitively we can see why certain emojis are used to convey certain emotions. For example, the 😭, which depicts "loudly crying face", seems highly

---

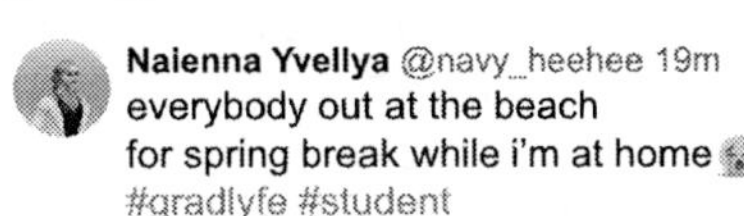

Figure 1: An example of a tweet with high emotional content (sadness) overall, while individual words do not really reflect any particular emotions.

correlated with the emotion of sadness. Figure 1 shows a tweet for which the user expresses their sadness about the event through the use of the emoji 😭. The individual words alone do not explicitly convey any sadness, but the readers will be able to get a sense of sadness from the tweet. In this case, a system that is able to recognize the emotion content of a tweet will be more likely to recommend emojis related to such emotion, hence providing better user experience.

Based on this intuition, in this work we aim to explore the incorporation of emotion content of a tweet to improve emoji prediction. Thus, the question that we would like to answer through this work is: "How can we make use of emotion content to guide emoji prediction models?"

Our contributions are as follows:

- We show more explicitly the link between certain emojis and certain emotions.
- We evaluate two simple methods to incorporate emotion information into an SVM model.
- We show, both through automatic and manual metrics, significant improvement of top emojis predicted by our emotion-aware models over the baseline models.
- We do an in-depth analysis of the dataset, the task, and give some recommendation for future directions.

Proceedings of the 10th Workshop on Computational Approaches to Subjectivity, Sentiment and Social Media Analysis, pages 91–99
Minneapolis, June 6, 2019. ©2019 Association for Computational Linguistics

- We release our crawled tweets the corpus containing human-rated tweet-emoji pairs for further analysis.[1]

2 Related Work

Barbieri et al. (2017) pioneered the task of emoji prediction by creating a dataset of 589,000 tweets containing a single mention of an emoji from the top-20 most frequent emojis. They also performed human evaluation by asking crowdworkers to give the emoji that best matches the tweet in a 5-emoji setting, and found that their systems are comparable to human performance in predicting emojis.

Cappallo et al. (2018) highlights the importance of having a balanced test set, in order to better evaluate the models' performance on rarer emojis. Bušić et al. (2018) also notice the imbalanced test set of the original dataset in Barbieri et al. (2017), and propose a more balanced dataset that is based on the top-5 and top-10 emojis in that dataset.

Çöltekin and Rama (2018) shows that SVM is better in emoji prediction than using bi-directional RNN. Wu et al. (2018) incorporated sentiment information in their neural models, and obtained small improvements in terms of overall F_1-score over the baseline models that do not use sentiment information.

Barbieri et al. (2018b) explores another metric, called *coverage error*, to account for the fact that some emojis are quite synonymous to each other (e.g., 🖤 and 💕).

3 Task Description and Data

In this paper, we begin by following Barbieri et al. (2017) on the definition of the task: given a tweet which initially contains a single emoji, predict the original emoji using just the text of the tweet. In our case, we would also like to offer a reinterpretation of the task as the task to suggest an appropriate emoji for a given tweet. This reinterpretation has a few benefits. First, it acknowledges that there is no a single correct emoji that can fit in a tweet. There could be (and there are, as we will see) multiple emojis that fit the tweet, depending on the context. Second, it makes it natural to use human ratings as evaluation metrics, instead of F_1-score, since now the systems are evaluated in how good their recommendations are.

---

[1]https://github.com/sweetpeach/semoji
As per Twitter policy, we release only the Tweet IDs, from which the actual texts can be queried using Twitter API.

Dataset	Train	Dev	Test
Barbieri	580,271	4,359	4,370
Union	597,995	74,747	75,000

Table 1: Training, development, and test set size for the two datasets in this paper.

3.1 Dataset

We use dataset from Barbieri et al. (2017), which consists of tweets retrieved between October 2015 and May 2016 containing exactly one emoji from the 20 most frequent emojis. We call this dataset Barbieri.

As also observed by Cappallo et al. (2018) and Bušić et al. (2018), there are some limitations to this dataset, namely:

- The set of 20 emojis in the dataset are not all independent; some emojis have overlapping semantics or are ambiguous. For instance, 🖤 and 💕 arguably have similar semantics and we see people using them in similar context.
- The emoji distribution is imbalanced, as also mentioned by Bušić et al. (2018) and Cappallo et al. (2018). From Table 2, we can see that the tweets labeled with 😂, 🖤, and 😜 greatly outnumber the rest.
- It contains duplicate tweets that appear both in training and test data, diluting the model analysis. Moreover, the dataset is divided into train set, development set, and test set based on the timestamp of the tweets, resulting in more disparity in the dataset. For example, in the test set, it has 757 tweets labeled with 😂 but only 3 with 🌲.

To address the first issue, we collapsed some emojis and removed some others, and we combine the dataset from Barbieri with the dataset from SemEval (Barbieri et al., 2018a) to increase the diversity of the emojis. From Barbieri, we removed 🖤 and 📷 after analyzing the tweets with those labels because the context in which they appear tends to be too broad, and the emoji 🖤 covers similar semantics.

SemEval has eight emojis which are not included in Barbieri. We select ☀️, 😊, 📷, 📸, 😎, and 😁 to be included in our data. Then, we merge {🖤, 😜, 💕} as 🖤, {📷, 📸} as 📷, and {😊, 😁} as 😊. At the end, we have 20 emojis for our new dataset.

To address the label imbalance, we improve the number of tweets with low frequency emojis like

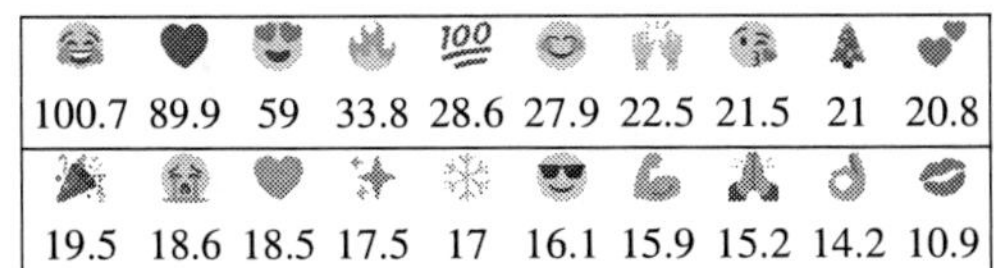

😁	❤️	😍	🙌	💯	😊	👯	📸	🌲	💕
100.7	89.9	59	33.8	28.6	27.9	22.5	21.5	21	20.8
📣	🙈	💜	✨	❄️	😎	💪	🙏	🔥	💿
19.5	18.6	18.5	17.5	17	16.1	15.9	15.2	14.2	10.9

Table 2: The 20 emojis in Barbieri et al.'s (2017) dataset with their frequencies (in thousands).

	😁	😍	🙈	❤️	💯	🙌	😎	✨	🌲	😊
All	75.0	75.0	75.0	75.0	60.4	59.5	51.9	41.0	27.8	27.6
Train	60.0	60.0	60.0	60.0	48.2	47.5	41.4	32.7	22.2	22.0
Dev	7.5	7.5	7.5	7.5	6.0	5.9	5.2	4.1	2.8	2.8
Test	7.5	7.5	7.5	7.5	6.0	5.9	5.2	4.1	2.8	2.8
	📷	👯	😭	🙏	🔥	❄️	☀️	💪	💿	📣
All	25.9	22.4	19.4	19.2	17.9	16.9	14.8	14.7	14.1	13.0
Train	20.7	17.9	15.5	15.3	14.3	13.5	11.8	11.8	11.2	10.4
Dev	2.6	2.2	1.9	1.9	1.8	1.7	1.5	1.5	1.4	1.3
Test	2.6	2.2	1.9	1.9	1.8	1.7	1.5	1.5	1.4	1.3

Table 3: The 20 emojis in UNION dataset with their frequencies (in thousands).

❄️ by including additional tweets that are crawled from February to April 2018. We follow Barbieri et al. (2017) in that we pick tweets that are geo-localized in the United States, and we pick only tweets that contain a single emoji that is in our set of 20 emojis. We also subsample the most frequent emojis so that they do not appear more than 75,000 times in this dataset.

Finally, the issue of duplicate tweets are handled in our preprocessing step, which will be described in more details in the next section.

We call our new dataset UNION. The way we construct UNION results in a much bigger validation and test data, as summarized in Table 1. The statistics for both datasets is also shown in Table 2 and Table 3.

3.2 Preprocessing

For BARBIERI dataset, we use their original dataset as is without any further modification. For UNION dataset, we preprocessed the tweets using NLTK Tweet tokenizer[2], normalizing user handles and URLs to special tokens. The tweets were tokenized and lowercased. Certain repeated punctuations are split, such as multiple exclamation marks, while others are kept, like ellipsis. Words with more than two same repeated characters are truncated into only 2 repeated characters, such as

"cooool" becoming "cool". We also removed duplicate tweets and tweets with less than three tokens after tokenization. Unlike BARBIERI which was split based on timestamps, we randomly split the UNION dataset into training, validation, and test set with 80%, 10%, 10% ratios.

4 Emotion as Features

The objective of this work is to see how emotions can be incorporated into the models for predicting emoji, and whether they can be used to improve the models' performance.

For this study, we choose the more popular Ekman et al. (1969)'s six basic emotions: anger, disgust, fear, joy, sadness, and surprise. To label our tweets with emotion categories,[3] we used Twitter Emotion Recognition (Colnerič and Demsar, 2018), which is a character-based Recurrent Neural Network (RNN) model for predicting emotion categories from English tweets, to assign emotion scores to the Twitter texts. The model was trained on tweets distantly supervised by hashtags, and is reported to achieve 71.8% micro F_1-score for classifying Ekman's six emotions under multi-class setting. Distant supervision of emotion categories using hastags in tweets has been shown to correlate well with human judgments (Mohammad, 2012).

We suppose that some emojis such as 🙈 and 😊 would have strong association with certain emotions. To validate this intuition, we extract from the emotion classifier the probabilities for each of the Ekman's six emotions for each tweet. We then aggregate these probability distributions based on the emoji labels, and measure the deviation of the probabilities from the average distribution over all tweets, representing the baseline probabilities for each emotion.[4]

More formally, let $X = \{x_1, \ldots, x_N\}$ be the collection of tweets with $Y = \{y_1, \ldots, y_N\}$ the corresponding emojis, where N is the number of tweets, and $y_i \in M = \{m_1, \ldots, m_{20}\}$, the set of 20 emojis. Let $X_{m_j} = \{x_i \mid y_i = m_j\}$ be the set of tweets that have m_j as the emoji label. Let $e_1, \ldots, e_K$ be the set of emotions, where K is the number of emotion categories, and let $p_{e_k}(x_i)$ be the probability of the emotion e_k assigned by

---

[2]http://www.nltk.org/api/nltk.tokenize.html#nltk.tokenize.casual.casual_tokenize

[3]Note that we cannot simply use emotion-labeled data as our dataset, since we also require the tweets to contain exactly one emoji.

[4]The emotion classifier seems to be biased towards the joy emotion, predicting on average 0.46 probability scores.

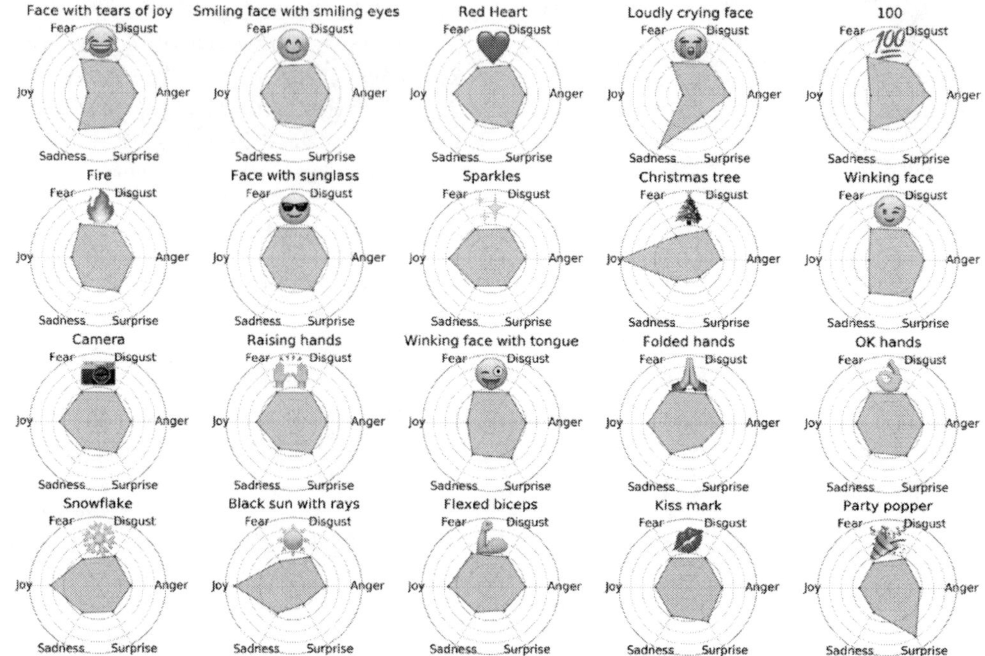

Figure 2: Emotion radar, showing the association of the 20 emojis in our UNION dataset with the six basic emotions defined by Ekman et al. (1969). These associations were calculated automatically by running emotion prediction model on tweets with emojis. Notice how 😭 has less joy and more sadness, and 🎉 has much more surprise. Ambiguous emojis, like 😂, which can appear both in positive (jokes) and negative (self-deprecation) context, have multi-peak distribution.

the emotion classifier to tweet x_i. Now, the **emotion score of an emoji** $S_{e_k}(m_j)$ as defined above is then:

$$S_{e_k}(m_j) = \frac{\sum_{x_i \in X_{m_j}} p_{e_k}(x_i)}{|X_{m_j}|} - \frac{\sum_{i=1}^{N} p_{e_k}(x_i)}{N}$$

We plot this deviation of probabilities in a radar chart, shown in Figure 2. In this chart, each emotion category is shown as separate polar axis from the center of the radar, with being closer to the center representing more negative value, and being closer to the perimeter representing more positive value over the baseline probabilities.

Some emojis are correlated with the emotions we anticipated, for example the 😭 emoji, which has very high sadness and very low joy although most emojis seem to be close to the average distribution. This might mean that the emotion classifier could not pick up the correct emotions in which those emojis are used, or simply that the emojis themselves are not particularly strongly associated with any of the six emotions. Nevertheless, we do see some intuitive trends in the emotion distribution, such as the high joy in 🎄 and the surprise in 🎉.

5 Models

To test the hypothesis that emotion information helps emoji prediction, we conduct experiments using Support Vector Machine (SVM) as the model of our choice.

As a baseline feature set for SVM, we use TF-IDF scores based on unigram bag-of-words features. This baseline model obtains 34.28% weighted F_1-score on BARBIERI dataset, which is comparable to the results in Barbieri et al. (2017) which uses bi-directional LSTM, which shows that this is a reasonable baseline model. This is also in line with the conclusion of Çöltekin and Rama (2018) that says SVM is a strong model for this task.

Inspired by our observation from the emotion radar, we consider two different ways to incorporate the emotion information produced by the emotion classifier, which we dub **basic** and **combi**. In **basic**, we use the probabilities of each emotion as features directly, resulting in 6 additional dense features on top of the unigram features. Since a single emotion might not capture the distribution of an emoji directly, in **combi** we also combine

Dataset	Emotion	P	R	F_1
BARBIERI	none	38.68	39.31	‡34.28
	basic	38.80	39.45	‡34.49
	combi	**39.25**	**39.73**	**34.86**
UNION	none	38.77	39.65	‡37.13
	basic	38.76	39.76	†37.22
	combi	**38.96**	**39.83**	**37.29**

Table 4: SVM performance with **weighted** F_1. Marked results are significantly different from the best in the respective dataset ($^\dagger p < 0.05$, $^\ddagger p < 0.01$) with bootstrap resampling ($n = 10,000$ for BARBIERI and $n = 1,000$ for UNION).

[emoji]		[emoji]		[emoji]		[emoji]	
[emoji]	-0.29	[emoji]	-0.04	[emoji]	0.18	[emoji]	0.30
[emoji]	-0.11	[emoji]	0.00	[emoji]	0.20	[emoji]	0.35
[emoji]	-0.10	[emoji]	0.14	[emoji]	0.20	[emoji]	0.50
[emoji]	-0.05	[emoji]	0.16	[emoji]	0.20	[emoji]	0.51
[emoji]	-0.05	[emoji]	0.16	[emoji]	0.23	[emoji]	**0.92**

Table 5: Change in F_1-score in UNION dataset from baseline SVM model to the model incorporating emotion combination features.

Emoji	Top Emotion Features
[emoji]	Sad (0.3737), Dis (0.1162), Ang (0.0596)
[emoji]	Sur (0.0981), Joy (0.0400), +Ang+Dis+Fea+Joy-Sad-Sur (0.0112)
[emoji]	Fea (0.0867), Joy (0.0691), Sur (0.059)
[emoji]	Dis (0.2752), +Ang+Dis+Joy+Sad+Sur (0.0133), +Ang+Dis-Fea+Joy+Sad+Sur (0.0133)
[emoji]	Joy (0.0822), Sur (0.0421), +Ang-Dis+Joy+Sad+Sur (0.0181)

Table 6: The top features associated with the emojis. The emotions are truncated to their first three letters, so 'Ang' refers to 'Anger', 'Dis' refers to 'Disgust', and so on.

the emotion features by considering binary indicator features for all possible combination of emotion polarities. A tweet is considered to have positive polarity of an emotion if the probability of that emotion is higher than the average probability of that emotion in the training set, similarly for negative polarity. For example, a tweet might have a feature `-joy+sadness` describing the lack of joy and the abundance of sadness. This results in 722 sparse binary features.

6 Experiment Results and Analysis

To test the efficacy of the emotion features, we ran the models with the various feature combinations on BARBIERI and UNION datasets.[5] Our baseline for SVM uses only bag-of-word features. The results are shown in Table 4.

We can see that the emotion features consistently improve emoji prediction in the SVM model, with statistically significant results. The emotion combination features also consistently perform slightly better compared to the one using only the 6 basic emotions.

Based on our results, which show significant improvement coming from emotion features, we focus our analysis on the role of emotions in predicting emojis.

From the emotion radar in Figure 2, we expect that the model incorporating emotion features would get much improvement in recognizing the [emoji] emoji, which has very distinct emotion distribution compared to other emojis, and we found that it is indeed the case. Table 5 shows the score

changes for each emoji in the UNION dataset from the baseline SVM model to the one with emotion combination features. We see that the [emoji] has the highest positive change compared to other emojis. This shows the usefulness in distinguishing certain emojis through the emotion semantic space.

Some top features in the model show that the emotion *sadness* is the emotion feature given highest weight by the model to predict [emoji] emoji. Some of which we display at Table 6. It is encouraging to see that the emojis with distinct emotion distribution, such as [emoji], [emoji], and [emoji] have the corresponding emotion feature ranked the highest by the classifier.

7 Human Evaluation

In Barbieri et al. (2018b), they observe that many emojis are semantically close, and propose to use coverage error (Tsoumakas et al., 2009) to measure "how far we would need to go through the predicted emojis to recover the true label." While this is effective in measuring how the system rank the emoji in the original tweet, it does not measure the quality of the top-ranked emoji by the system. Given the possible application of an emoji predic-

---

[5]For historical reasons we do not do in-depth analysis of SEMEVAL and subsequently do not report the results on SEMEVAL here. In general, we observe that the average weighted F_1-score is lower compared to BARBIERI.

tion system to recommend emojis to users, it is also important to see how well received are the top emojis predicted by the system.

To that end, we conduct human evaluation on the top-ranked emoji by each system (including the original emoji) to see which system is preferred by users. Note that this evaluation is different from the human evaluation performed in Barbieri et al. (2017). In that work, they ask human annotators to choose the best emoji from a list of 5 emojis, and compare the F_1-score with the system's predictions. In contrast, in this work we ask human raters to rate the predictions of several systems, enabling us to measure preferability of the emojis.

7.1 Methodology

We conducted human evaluation on the output of our baseline SVM model, our emotion-infused model, and also the original emoji in the tweets. We define emoji triple

$$< \text{emoji}_{\text{orig}}, \text{emoji}_{\text{bow}}, \text{emoji}_{\text{combi}} >$$

where $\text{emoji}_{\text{orig}}$ is original emoji, $\text{emoji}_{\text{bow}}$ is emoji predicted from baseline, and $\text{emoji}_{\text{combi}}$ prediction from our model infused with combination emotion features. From each dataset, we selected 1,000 pairs of (tweet, emoji triples); each pair has at least one different emoji in the emoji triple. Each pair is then given to *three raters* to be annotated. To ensure we will get sufficient data for distinguishing the preferability of different systems and of different emojis, we use the following criteria in sampling the (tweet, emoji triples):

1. The number of occurrences of all emojis in the original tweets should be approximately equal.
2. There should be at least one distinct emoji in the emoji triples.
3. There should be enough samples that have different emojis for all pairs of systems

Criterion 1 ensures that we can use the annotated data to gather baseline rating of each emoji in the original tweet. Criterion 2 ensures that we do not waste raters' time in annotating tweets that do not have distinguishing power. Criterion 3 ensures that for any two systems (e.g., BoW vs. Ours) we have enough samples to distinguish the presence or absence of preferability between them.

In the annotation interface, emojis in the triple are randomized so that the raters do not know if an emoji is the true label or a prediction from baseline or our model. Each emoji is rated in a 3-point Likert scale where 0 means that it does not makes sense to pair the emoji with the tweet, 1 means it is reasonable (there are some contexts where this would be applicable), 2 means it fits perfectly (something that they themselves would use). For this annotation task, we recruit English-speaking (not necessarily native speakers) university students and young professionals as our raters.

7.2 Result

We calculated inter-rater agreement using Fleiss's Kappa coefficient (Fleiss and Cohen, 1973), resulting in an agreement of 0.12 and 0.20 for Barbieri and Union, respectively. This rather low agreement shows that emoji use has quite a large variance between raters. Nevertheless, it is encouraging to see positive agreement between raters on this arguably very subjective task.

The average rating for each system is shown in Table 7. It is interesting to see that the output of our emotion-incorporated system is consistently more preferred compared to that of the baseline system, showing the benefit of emotions.

Another thing worth mentioning is the lower average rating of the original emoji compared to the system predictions. We believe this is due to the systems predicting more stereotypical emojis, thus have higher chance of being preferred by the raters given the tweets. This suggests that in a emoji prediction system, it would be better preferred by the users if the emojis are closer to the more stereotypical interpretation of the tweets, instead of second guessing the actual intent of the users.

We also note that even though the F_1-score of the systems are higher in Union compared to Barbieri (see Table 4), the average ratings for Union is lower. This shows that in evaluating the quality of emoji prediction system, using F_1-score alone is not enough, as it might not give rise to a more preferred emojis.

Looking at the detailed ratings per emoji, shown in Table 8 and Table 9, we see that the emoji 🌲, 💯, and 🍃 consistently get the lowest scores,. It is interesting to note that in Table 8, the four emojis ❤, 😊, 💕, and 😘 which have similar meaning also have similar ratings, and all of them are in the top-5 emojis.

Emoji	BARBIERI	UNION
Original Tweet	1.43	1.02
Baseline Model	1.48	1.03
Our Model	**1.50**	**1.05**

Table 7: Average rating of emojis in 0-2 scale from original tweets, baseline, and our emotion-incorporated model. The difference in rating is statistically significant for BARBIERI with Wilcoxon signed rank test ($p < 0.005$ between original tweet and the two models, and $p < 0.025$ between the two models), while in UNION they are not ($p > 0.2$).

🌲	**0.87**	😆	1.35	🙌	1.45	💜	1.57
💯	1.03	🙏	1.39	✨	1.48	😄	1.57
💋	1.31	❄	1.39	😎	1.48	💕	1.67
👌	1.35	🔥	1.41	💪	1.54	😻	1.69
🏠	1.35	💙	1.41	😊	1.56	🎉	**1.78**

Table 8: Average rating per emoji for BARBIERI

💯	**0.53**	🏠	0.80	🎿	1.03	🙌	1.32
💋	0.62	❄	0.83	✈	1.13	💜	1.33
🌲	0.77	😆	1.00	😄	1.13	😎	1.38
👌	0.80	💪	1.02	🙏	1.16	😍	1.40
🔥	0.80	📷	1.02	☀	1.20	😊	**1.41**

Table 9: Average rating per emoji for UNION

Tweet	Orig	BoW	Ours
sold out show at benedum center	😎 **1.33**	😆 **1.33**	🏠 **1.33**
miss you but glad you are enjoying the strong olympics !	💪 **2.00**	💯 1.00	💜 **2.00**
can't wait to use it too	😊 1.33	😭 0.33	😊 **1.67**
i'm always cute, wherever i'm going	😊 1.00	💯 0.67	💜 **1.67**
i saw a gif of mrs smith on twitter	😊 0.00	😆 **1.67**	🏠 0.67

Table 10: Sample tweets (lightly edited) with the original emoji (Orig), prediction from the bag-of-words baseline (BoW), and prediction from our emotion-infused combination model (Ours). Below the emojis are their average ratings from 3 raters. Pink highlight refers to phrase related to our system's prediction while blue highlight refers to original emoji.

7.3 Discussion

To dig deeper into the ratings provided by the raters, we analyze some example tweets, shown in Table 10. We see that in some cases indeed there could be multiple emojis that fit in certain tweets. In the first example, the three emojis look reasonable according to the raters. 😎 may be used to explain if a user happily can go to the sold-out show. Meanwhile, if the user is unable to go to the sold-out show, depending on how the user feels, 😆 and 🏠 may be used. The second example also shows that a tweet may have two different focuses. The more emotional phrase *"miss you"* can be described with 💜 while 💪 may explain *"strong olympics"*.

In the third example, the raters favor our model's prediction 😊 as the best emoji to describe the tweet. Even though the tweet contains a negative word *"can't"*, the overall tone of the tweet is positive, and therefore 😊 or 😊 fits the tweet better than 😭.

It is interesting to see the fourth example which is considered as flirtatious by the tweet user through the use of 😊, but the raters consider 💜 as a more suitable emoji since 💜 is more versatile to be used in different contexts. Most raters do not prefer 💯 for the tweet as we see in Table 9 and Table 9 where 💯 average rate is lower than 😊.

The last example demonstrates the highest-rated emoji 😆 is the one output by the baseline. The raters also like our model's predicted emoji 🏠 better than the original emoji 😊, suggesting that our model may be helpful to be used as emoji recommendation system since the model's emoji is more favorably stereotypical.

8 Conclusion and Future Work

In summary, we first show the correlation between emojis and the emotion content of tweets from a large corpus of tweets. Then we make use of this correlation to improve the prediction of an emoji prediction model. Although we found that most of the emojis do not have much emotional content, for those emojis with strong emotional content, such as 🏠, our experiments show significant improvements over the baseline models in terms of F_1-score.

We then further scrutinize the difference between the models through human evaluation. We confirm previous work that generally there could be more than one emojis that fit a given tweet, and conduct human rating experiments to see the preferability of the systems' recommendation. We found that the output of the model with emotion features is generally more preferable over the baseline models and also the original tweet. This suggests that a more stereotypical emoji might be rated higher by users.

Our findings further emphasis the need for a better measure in emoji prediction task. That is, one that is more geared towards users' preferability instead of based on a single gold standard. In this work, we use a slightly labor-intensive method of collecting human ratings as a way to handle this multiple suitable emojis. A future direction would be to explore more automatic methods as proxies to users' preferability.

Another interesting venue for future work is to analyze the context of each emoji to determine how versatile an emoji is (e.g., it can appear in many different context). An emoji recommendation system should be aware of this versatility, so that it does not fall into the trap of always predicting versatile emojis due to relatively high suitability with any tweet.

Acknowledgements

The authors would like to thank Adeline Anugrah Raphani, Naoki Otani, Aditi Chaudhary, Emily Ahn, Jeffrey Wong, Mark Lauda Lauw, Christopher Bryant, Stephen Haniel Yuwono, Karinska Eunike Muis, Mercia Wijaya, Peter Phandi, Raymond Hendy Susanto, Stefanus Setiadi, Victoria Anugrah Lestari, and Raissa Eka Fedora for rating the emoji-tweet pairs.

The authors are also grateful for useful feedback from Eduard Hovy, Geoff Kaufman, Teruko Mitamura, people in Carnegie Mellon University Social Computing reading group, and the anonymous reviewers.

The first author was sponsored by US DOT FAST Act - Mobility National (2016 - 2022) - CMU 2017 Mobility21 UTC #31.

The second author was sponsored by the Defense Advanced Research Projects Agency (DARPA) Information Innovation Office (I2O), program: Low Resource Languages for Emergent Incidents (LORELEI), issued by DARPA/I2O under Contract No. HR0011-15-C-0114.

References

Francesco Barbieri, Miguel Ballesteros, and Horacio Saggion. 2017. Are Emojis Predictable? In *Proceedings of the 15th Conference of the European Chapter of the Association for Computational Linguistics: Volume 2, Short Papers*, volume 2, pages 105–111, Valencia, Spain. Association for Computational Linguistics.

Francesco Barbieri, Jose Camacho-Collados, Francesco Ronzano, Luis Espinosa-Anke, Miguel Ballesteros, Valerio Basile, Viviana Patti, and Horacio Saggion. 2018a. SemEval-2018 Task 2: Multilingual Emoji Prediction. In *Proceedings of the 12th International Workshop on Semantic Evaluation (SemEval-2018)*, New Orleans, LA, United States. Association for Computational Linguistics.

Francesco Barbieri, Luis Espinosa-anke Jose, Steven Schockaert, and Horacio Saggion. 2018b. Interpretable Emoji Prediction via Label-Wise Attention LSTMs. In *EMNLP*, pages 4766–4771.

Hrvoje Bušić, Ante Spajić, and Nika Šućurović. 2018. How Much Context is Useful in Emoji Prediction? Technical report.

Spencer Cappallo, Stacey Svetlichnaya, Pierre Garrigues, Thomas Mensink, and Cees G. M. Snoek. 2018. The New Modality: Emoji Challenges in Prediction, Anticipation, and Retrieval. pages 1–13.

N. Colneriê and J. Demsar. 2018. Emotion recognition on twitter: Comparative study and training a unison model. *IEEE Transactions on Affective Computing*, pages 1–1.

Çağrı Çöltekin and Taraka Rama. 2018. Tübingen-Oslo at SemEval-2018 Task 2 : SVMs perform better than RNNs at Emoji Prediction. pages 34–38.

Paul Ekman, E. Richard Sorenson, and Wallace V. Friesen. 1969. Pan-Cultural Elements in Facial Displays of Emotion. *Science*, 164(3875):86–88.

Bjarke Felbo, Alan Mislove, Anders Søgaard, Iyad Rahwan, and Sune Lehmann. 2017. Using millions of emoji occurrences to learn any-domain representations for detecting sentiment, emotion and sarcasm. In *Conference on Empirical Methods in Natural Language Processing (EMNLP)*.

Joseph L Fleiss and Jacob Cohen. 1973. The equivalence of weighted kappa and the intraclass correlation coefficient as measures of reliability. *Educational and psychological measurement*, 33(3):613–619.

Saif M. Mohammad. 2012. #Emotional Tweets. In *First Joint Conference on Lexical and Computational Semantics (*SEM)*, pages 246–255.

Petra Kralj Novak, Jasmina Smailović, Borut Sluban, and Igor Mozetič. 2015. Sentiment of emojis. *PLoS ONE*, 10(12):1–22.

Grigorios Tsoumakas, Ioannis Katakis, and Ioannis Vlahavas. 2009. Mining Multi-label Data. In *Data Mining and Knowledge Discovery Handbook*, pages 667–685. Springer.

Wiesław Wolny. 2016. Emotion Analysis of Twitter Data That Use Emoticons and Emoji Ideograms. In *International Conference on Information Systems Development (ISD)*, pages 476–483.

Chuhan Wu, Fangzhao Wu, Sixing Wu, and Zhigang Yuan. 2018. THU NGN at SemEval-2018 Task 2 : Residual CNN-LSTM Network with Attention for English Emoji Prediction. pages 410–414.

Author Index

Association for Computational Linguistics
209 N. Eighth Street
Stroudsburg, Pennsylvania 18360